18.95

D1195521

Peter, the Odyssey of a Merchant Mariner

By
Captain Peter Chelemedos

With best wishes

Peter Chelemedos

Peanut Butter Publishing
Seattle, Washington

Page 18, "Far Side" cartoon by Gary Larson. Reprinted by permission of Chronicle Features, San Francisco, CA
Page 26, illustration by Amelia Craigen
Pages 64, 78 and 93, excerpts from "A Careless Word, A Needless Sinking" by Arthur Moore. Used by permission of author.

Cover Design: Heather Hitson
Typesetting: Grafisk

Copyright © 1992 by Peter Chelemedos
All rights reserved. Printed in the United States of America
ISBN 0-89716-406-7

For ordering information, write to:
Peter Chelemedos
P.O. Box 15617
Seattle, WA 98115-0617

Published by Peanut Butter Publishing
200 Second Ave. W.
Seattle, WA 98119
(206) 281-5965

CONTENTS

PART III
SETTLING DOWN

APPENDICES

Acknowledgments

My thanks to the many people I met in my travels who helped me realize this attainment. In particular:

Captain Martin of the SOUTHERN LADY, who consented to sign me on his ship as Deck Boy, thus giving me my start at sea. The Engholm family at Silvis, Illinois, who took me in for Christmas dinner and became my "second family." The late Rev. David McDonald of the Seamen's Church Institute in New York City, whose efforts along with "Mother Ropeyarns" got me into the navigation school. My pen pal, the late Beverly Jeanne Fulwider of Davenport, Iowa, whose sisterly encouragement inspired me to head for the top of my capabilities. John Marshall of Cheshire, England, whose address given me that day on the docks of Montreal gave me entry into the British Apprentices Club where I met Kay. Captain Earl S. Stevens of the SS WEST JAFFREY, who encouraged me to learn ship's business as well as navigation and started me toward the Officer's Candidate School.

And to Kay Hamilton, who saw enough potential in me to become my wife for more than forty-eight years.

Future sailors Peter and Fred, 1925

Prologue

The crying she heard coming from the house next door was punctuated by the swish-slap of a whip of some sort. Then a series of thumps that she couldn't quite identify echoed in the caverns of her memory. She heard loud voices and caught a few phrases such as: "— fighting with your brother," "You should do what he tells you, he's older," and "Never mind trying to explain, I don't believe you anyway." Then more thumps and slaps.

When the boy next door came over to bring her a magazine, she saw traces of tears still on his face. Under the edge of his sweater, she could see the edge of a scarlet welt. His hair was standing up as though it had been forcibly pulled and his hand seemed to be tracing bumps on the back of his head.

She couldn't ask him what the matter was, but the next day when she went next door to have a cup of coffee with his mother, she noticed a series of umbrella-shaped cracks in the plaster wall by the kitchen stove.

Over the years, she thought about that afternoon, wondering what had become of the boy after he disappeared one day.

Then, one day, she saw him again. He was wearing a "Lundberg Stetson," a cap usually worn by longshoremen and Merchant Marine sailors. He came to her door to visit an hour or so with her. As she sipped the coffee she poured, he told of his travels since he had left for school that day, so long ago, and just kept going.

He had hitchhiked down the coast and eastward, trying to find somebody to take him in, someone who would not beat him with a doubled-up cord from the flatiron or grip his hair and bang his head into the wall for punishment, as his mother had done when she was in a bad mood.

He had been fortunate in finding a ship's crew who took pity on him and asked their officers to sign the boy on as a "workaway" to give him a chance to get regular meals and a place to sleep while learning about the work on ships. Later on, a Seamen's Mission chaplain had helped him get a scholarship to a navigation school.

Over the years, he had made ships and the sea into a career, and was now sitting for his Mate's license. It was hard for her to believe this self-assured young man sitting across the table from her was the boy she had once known.

This is his story.

Part I

ADVENTURE BOUND

Chapter 1

The Long Road to Adventure

June 1937 - February 1938

The boy who had stood on the beach at Cephalonia Island, watching the ship carrying Odysseus from the neighboring island of Ithaca on his journey into the unknown waters of the Mediterranean Sea, had made a wish to travel, planting a seed into his spirit that was passed from generation to generation over thousands of years, finally coming to abide in the spirit of a distant descendant born in the year 1922 A.D. at Berkeley, California.

Restlessness first seemed to dominate my life about the time I was nine. I have faint recollections of spending nights in various places along the highways of California; of early morning walks through Wildcat Canyon in the Berkeley hills above Albany; and of the many times someone would send for my folks to come to take me home.

Such wanderings occurred often. About every three months I would be on the road again, each time going a little farther from home. Why? I don't know. I was curious and the wide world was more interesting than dull schoolbooks. Maybe it was because of the fights I had with my older brother, who was always trying to outshine me. Maybe it was because of the beatings I got for fighting with my brother. Anyway, I went.

Each time I went, I became better acquainted with the highways of California and the ways of the people using them. This included the Highway Patrol, who often were the ones who sent me home again.

On my fourteenth birthday, instead of the bicycle I so wanted, I was given a mandolin and told I would be taking lessons at the Greek Church in Oakland. To this day, I cannot read music and am told I need a wheelbarrow to carry a tune, so this was not a welcome birthday present. I did go for a while, and learned the "Persian Market Song" to play at the Greek Independence Day festivities at the Oakland Auditorium. When the great night came, however, the teacher gave me his baton to lead the group, so even then I didn't get to flaunt my talents. If only he hadn't added, "It will sound better that way."

During high school, one period was spent with the "advisor." My class had Mona E. Ross, a tall lady and a memorably nice person. She enjoyed reading to us to fill in time during the period, and started on a set of books by Howard Pease, *The Tattooed Man* and a sequel, both of which told the continuing adventures of Tod Moran, a young man who walked to the docks of San Francisco and found a job on a tramp freighter. I was enthralled by the stories.

When school was out in June that year, my dad took me over to San Francisco to the Matson Line offices to see about getting me a job of some sort on one of their ships. I guess the news items in the papers of the day hadn't registered with either of us. It was during the 1936 waterfront strike. A friendly picket near the docks told us what was going on and suggested we return after things were settled.

The following summer, when I "hit the road," I hitchhiked as far as El Paso, Texas. The next day I walked about seventeen miles down the highway to Fabens without even one ride. Talk about hungry! While walking down that highway on a hot afternoon, I reached across the barbed wire fence to pluck cotton bolls to chew on for what nourishment was in the cottonseed oil. When I went over to the water tank by the railroad to wash up a bit, one of the hoboes there told me the next freight train would be coming through in about an hour and would stop for water. I figured if I was going to travel in Texas, I might as well ride. So after sharing some "mulligan," I waited with him in the scrub bushes and hopped on a reefer (refrigerated) car when the train started up. He showed me how to find a "dry" reefer by looking at the drain under the end of each car. We climbed down into the empty ice compartment of a carload of dry groceries.

As the train bounced along toward San Antonio, I found that sitting on the steel gratings in the bottom of that compartment was not the most comfortable ride, but it was a ride. I still have dents in my hide from the gratings in that car. Later, this experience inspired me to write a poem called "The Jungle," which appears here on page 19.

I got off when the train slowed down on

The author at 14, contemplating the road to adventure

the approach to the railroad yards at San Antonio. I felt it would be smarter to walk around the freight yards rather than through since the "bulls" (as railroad police were known) were not kind to the free riders of their trains.

I stayed close to the yards, sighting the water tower near the other end as a landmark, and looked over the area. One of the hoboes told me that if I waited near the water tank, I would be able to catch the train "on the fly" as it started to pick up speed on its way out of the yard.

12

When I saw there were about seventy or eighty others waiting for this train, I had a feeling this would not be a good idea. Instead, while waiting for the train, I hid in a tree with nice leafy branches I had seen up in the center of the yard. When the train came, I noticed a big "bull" riding on the side of the engine looking over the yard. He got off by the water tower and stood with arms folded as if daring anyone to ride on his train. I managed to get on the train from my hiding place in the tree, and was the only one who rode out of San Antonio on that train.

The next water stop was at a place called Seguin. I made the mistake of walking uptown looking for something to eat. I stopped to stare into the window of a haberdasher's shop which featured ten-gallon Stetson hats. A teen-age dream of the life of a cowboy held me there. A local policeman picked me up and held me in the city jail while he arranged with my folks to send me back home on a train as a paying passenger.

On the train, I met Harry Ruser, an elderly gentleman on his way for a winter vacation in Tucson from his home in the east. He was friendly and, after hearing my tale, encouraged me in my seeking independence. Mr. Ruser, pointing out the benefits of more education, talked me into going home for another try.

After some time back at home and school and a few more fights with my older brother, wanderlust again came over me, and the the open road called to me on a warm January day in 1938. I listened. After school one day, I went down to Oakland to my mandolin lesson at the Greek Church, but I didn't go in. Instead, I took the red train over to San Francisco and a streetcar to Daly City, and from there walked southward. All night, I remember.

Morning came. I was past San Mateo and started looking to passing motorists for a ride, without success. I cut up the mountain somewhere along the line to try Skyline Boulevard to Santa Cruz. Once in a while, a motorist would stop to ask me why I wasn't in school, but I'd point to my mandolin case and say I was on my way to visit an aunt down the line at Ben Lomond who was ill and had been excused from school. I was taking my instrument to keep in practice. This expanation apparently was convincing, for even south of Santa Cruz when the county probation officer was one of my benefactors in the ride south, I told him a similar story. Only a few months previously he had been the one to contact my mother to get me out of the local detention home where I had been held during one of my "trips." But at that previous date I had told him that my aunt lived in Watsonville, a town farther south than Ben Lomond.

I didn't waste much time looking for another ride out of Watsonville, and rode over the pass into Fresno and south toward Bakersfield. Then off the main road to Barstow to ride freight trains over the desert along the Santa Fe trail to Yuma and on to Tucson.

13

Chapter 2

Tucson

February - April 1938

I had twelve cents, a camera and a mandolin to my name when I landed in Tucson in early February 1938. Harry Ruser, the friend I had made on the train the previous year, was no longer there, having gone back north on business. On my birthday, I found a job at the Six-Four Messenger Service under the name of James Patrick Royal, having a good idea that the usual "three-state alarm" had been put out for me from home. I did have a few bad moments when Mrs. Stallings, my employer, sent me after a Social Security card. But I applied for the card with my right name, and only gave Mrs. Stallings the number.

I was Messenger Number Nine. The Mexican boys who worked there dubbed me "Numero Nuevo" and that is what I was called for the two months I worked there. They loaned me a bike that belonged to one of the night-shift messengers, so it wasn't long before I learned the town pretty well. But I couldn't do much on my income of three dollars or so per week, depending on how many errands I had run.

Sleep? Yes, once in a while, whenever I could find a corner to crawl into where I was sure the cop on the beat wouldn't find me — on the roof of the Kings Cafeteria under the air conditioning unit, or in a car at the back corner of a used car lot in which I found a blanket. Sometimes, when I had a quarter left over from my payday dinner, I rented a bed at the local YMCA dorm and made the most of the comfort it offered. Other nights I would go over to the Coney Island lunchroom and wash dishes until two in the morning for what I could get to eat there. At two, I went to the newspaper plant and took out ten papers to sell on the streets to what early morning customers I could find. Until the last day I was there, I never thought to take them out to the all-night roadhouses outside of town to sell to the motorists there. So I wasn't what one could call a success at that job. It did give me a dime for a glass of milk and a doughnut to breakfast on every other day, though.

Once in a while, I would splurge twenty cents and get a whole meal at a Chinese restaurant, usually frankfurters and rice, but with soup, tea and bread included. When I had the twenty cents, that is.

One night, I doubled-shifted because the other boys were participating in some school activity. I was given a call to deliver a package from the drugstore on the corner out to the fancy El Conquistador Hotel, which entailed a short cut across a patch of desert. The amount to collect for the package was nine dollars, ninety-seven cents and eight mills (tax tokens). The hotel clerk wouldn't allow me to deliver it personally, instead passing it to one of the bellboys. He gave me a ten-dollar bill and said, "Give me the two pennies. You can keep the two mills change." Talk about tips!?

Bathing? Well, there was an irrigation ditch out on the west side of town, and sometimes I could get a remnant of soap from the YMCA or from a gas station. But I couldn't wash my clothes, not even a change of socks, so no one knew the difference when I did bathe. Once in a while, I would use the showers and swimming pool at the YMCA, but without clean socks there always seemed to be a "something" in the air which neither I nor anyone else appreciated.

After a couple of months of this, I got to falling asleep occasionally while riding on the bike and had a couple of near accidents. One day, I had a call to deliver a rush package from one branch of a chain drugstore to another two blocks down Congress Street. I was riding down the middle of the street in the abandoned streetcar tracks alongside a string of cars. In the middle of the next block, a large truck turned out of the alley on my left and headed right at me head on. I dodged between the moving cars on my right and rode between them and the parked cars at the curb, and was alongside of one as it made a right turn at the next corner. The driver saw me just in time and stopped. I passed in front of him, turned to wave thanks, and nearly ran into the policeman directing traffic at the corner.

The policeman gave me a ticket for "Speeding, Reckless Riding, and No Brakes on a Bicycle," and ordered me to go to night court. I sat in the court room listening to the fifty-dollar fines or thirty days in jail being meted out to various wayward drivers, all

the while holding my breath in fear that the one dollar I had in my pocket would not be enough, and that someone would put me together with the "three-state alarm" that I was almost sure was out for me.

The judge called me up and read the ticket: "Speeding, reckless riding and no brakes. This is pretty serious, son. How do you plead, guilty or not guilty?"

I answered, "Judge, you didn't read the whole ticket."

"What? There's more?" He looked at the ticket more closely and read, "On a bicycle??"

"Yes, sir."

"Well, this really is serious, son, but since this is the first one like this I've seen in this court, I don't know just what to do with it. I'll tell you what. I'll just put it in my top drawer here and think about it and if you come in here with another one like it, I'll have something in mind."

I managed to save up five dollars and, taking advantage of an ad in the paper, bought my own bike. When I saw the bike I understood why it was only worth five bucks, if that much. But if balanced right and not pushed too hard on the pedals and chain, it would run and still stay together.

Now that I had my own bike, I started thinking of the open road again. The road from Tucson to Lordsburg, New Mexico, was across a flat desert according to the map I looked at. I figured that I could ride my bike during the full moon-lit nights and rest during the heat of the day, so I started out. About ten miles out into the desert, the chain broke a link. I hadn't thought to bring any spare links, as my main concern was the nearly threadbare tires. I started walking along, pushing the bike, when a pickup truck came along and gave me a ride the rest of the way to the New Mexico border.

The driver did not want to carry me

across the state line, as the Lindbergh Law was being used as a prosecuting device by the local law enforcement officers of the day. (The Lindbergh Law, passed after the kidnapping of the Lindbergh baby, made it illegal to transport a minor across a state line.) I understood, so I started walking again until I reached a restaurant where I got breakfast. I couldn't get any chain links there, and it was still many miles to Lordsburg. I walked east for a while in the early morning cool, looking for a spot to get out of the rapidly warming sun. There was little traffic on the road, but about eleven o'clock a driver headed west stopped to ask if I needed help. I told him my problem, so he tied the bike on the back of his car and drove me all the way back to Tucson.

When I found a part and got the bike fixed again, I got a job delivering Easter telegrams for Western Union to pick up a bit more change. I collected a whole dollar for the week's work, and sold the bike back to the pawnshop where I had purchased it. The man gave me four dollars for it.

I headed for the freight yards again.

Chapter 3

Farther Eastward

April - May 1938

After the Easter stint at Western Union, I went down to the railroad yards at Tucson to wait for the afternoon train eastward. While waiting, I got to talking with a hobo. This hobo made a production of showing me a new switchblade pocketknife and how it worked. Another hobo came along, and the first one had me bet the second that I could open the knife without touching the blade. I concealed the button of the knife, but try as I might I couldn't open it and the two of them walked off with my five dollars.

I rode out on the train that night, across Arizona and New Mexico, and got off as we approached the yards at El Paso, Texas. I walked around the freight yards, since the word was out that the "bulls" on the Southern Pacific would shoot at riders on their freights. Since the Texas Pacific used the same main line, I went over to ride the Texas Pacific freight out of town. I got off at Fabens and waited there for the Southern Pacific to ride on down to San Antonio toward New Orleans.

Since I was familiar with the yard at San Antonio, I again climbed the tree in the middle of the yard, and again was the only one to ride out on the evening freight. This time I didn't get off at Seguin, but stayed in

the dry reefer car and rode on out again. At Houston, I was joined in my car by another rider.

Our next switch yard was Lafayette, Louisiana. I hadn't eaten since leaving Tucson, and was getting pretty hungry and listless. My companion noticed it and asked me why I didn't "hit up" a house for something to eat. I told him I couldn't do that as I was supposed to be independent (I couldn't admit I didn't have the nerve). He told me I shouldn't let my independence interfere with my health, and walked me up the street from the yards.

Since it was about five in the afternoon, he told me to walk up the street on one side looking into the houses, and he would walk the other side. When I saw a family eating dinner, I was to call him. When I spotted a couple eating and called him, he told me to sit by the light pole and watch. When they finished, chances were that the man would take his newspaper to the front porch while the woman would clear the table. When she did, I was to knock at the back door and tell her I hadn't eaten in over a week and ask her if she had anything left over from their supper.

I did as he advised. When I told my story,

the woman looked me over, then told me to go around to the front porch. Her husband was settling in the rocker with the newspaper when I came up the steps. He asked me what I wanted, and I told him his wife was getting me something to eat. She brought out a washbowl-sized dish of rice and beef stew, a loaf of french bread and a dipper of water. To this day, I can remember watching the sun set over Lafayette as I ate my way through this banquet.

What I couldn't eat at the time was wrapped in newspaper and I rode on to Gretna, Louisiana, that night with the warmth of this package close to me. Around midnight, I started to unwrap it to eat more, but the grease from the stew had soaked into the newspaper. I tore off the dry paper and ate the rest, newspaper and all.

When the train was broken up at Gretna, I walked over the Huey Long bridge into New Orleans during the early morning hours, and down past the Louisville & Nashville station to catch a train eastward to Mobile, Alabama.

That train was a slow one, but I got a chance to rest from the twelve-mile walk of that morning while I watched the scenery of the Gulf Coast pass by. When the train went onto a siding at Mobile, I saw a Norwegian freighter, the FERNBANK, at a nearby pier. I went over to it and found the crew hospitable. They fed me boiled potatoes and boiled fish for a week or so while the ship was being loaded with pig iron for Japan.

I translated their broken English as best I could as they tried to make conversation with the barmaids. They tried to talk the mate into signing me on the crew, but since I couldn't speak enough Norwegian to understand orders, he wouldn't hire me.

When they sailed, I wrote down the name of one of the seamen, Dagfern Anderson,

THE FAR SIDE   By GARY LARSON

"And stay off."

and then went back to the freight yards and rode north again as far as Louisville, Kentucky.

I got to thinking about the hospitality of that ship's crew and thought it would be a good idea to return to Mobile to try to get a job on a ship from there.

On the return trip, I was in the reefer end of a potato car and fell asleep. When we arrived in Birmingham, I was wakened by the "bull" and chased off the train, which was still going about fifteen miles an hour. I hesitated before jumping off, so he threw my mandolin case at me to knock me off the ladder. I jumped off and, besides barking my shins, wasn't scuffed up too badly on the rocks and cinders alongside the tracks. The mandolin was broken, but I took it with me as I trudged along outside the fence and up the hill to where the trains had to proceed slowly, and caught the next train south.

In Mobile, I found a boxcar way off on a grass-grown siding and holed up in it for a few days while I waited for another ship to tie up to the state docks.

One day, I walked down to the pier at the foot of Government Street where a white ship, the SOUTHERN LADY from Halifax, Nova Scotia, was discharging bananas. Several of the crew were standing on the pier painting the hull, and I got to talking to them. At least they spoke English.

About ten o'clock it started to rain, and they picked up their paint pots and went aboard. One of them came out to the rail with a cup of coffee and called me to come aboard. I did and, after some conversation outlining my plight, they talked with the mate and the captain. As a result, I was signed on as a deck boy for twenty-five cents a month and meals. I was to keep the crew's messroom clean, and was allowed to sleep on a coil of hawser on the "fan-tail."

Before I left, I went back to the freight yard to get my mandolin and camera, but the boxcar I had them stashed in had been switched out.

And so, on May 18, 1938, I started my career at sea.

THE JUNGLE

The path through the underbrush
Led to an unexpected clearing
At the edge of the scrub woods.
The group of men, sitting
On fallen logs,
On rocks,
And on the ground
Leaning against their bindles,
Were watching,
Watching the large,
Dented,
Square
Five-gallon can boiling
Over the smokeless fire.

Peter said, as he approached
And had a look at the boiling can,
"Hi, guys, I've brought onions
And carrots for the mulligan."
A gaunt old man sitting close to the fire
Reached for them and,
Along with Peter, shaved the sand
From them and sliced the carrots and onions
Into thick slabs before dropping
Them into the boiling can.

Then he gave the fire a little poke.
Peter found a seat and rolled a smoke
From remnants of tobacco from a sack
That had "Bull Durham" in letters black.
The aroma of the stew drifted over the crew
Of men who were gathered there.

All of them listened and cocked an ear
Listening for the far-off sound.
The sound of the train
Whistling for the crossing in the nearby town.
A whistle that would tell them clear
The eastbound freight was coming near,
And would soon be coming right on down
To stop at the nearby water tower,
For water it needed for steam for power.
It would stop to fill its empty tanks
So they could ride amid the clanks
And comfort of an empty boxcar's floor.

Peter dug into his bindle and came up soon
With enameled plate and old tin spoon,
Then waited for any sign
(Still with an ear cocked down the line)
That the "mulligan" would be ready soon.

When the old man gave sign to the crew
To come for a share of the fresh-cooked brew,
Each of the men brought forward can or
    dish
Whatever he had that he knew would do
To hold a bit of his share of stew.

When carefully wiping out the bowl
With the scrap of bread from the day before,
Peter ate the last of his share,
Each scrap of meat and carrot there,
Then heard the far-off whistle's moan
Of the train coming through the distant town.

As he waited for the train to load,
He looked around at the faces of friends,
His "brotherhood of the road,"
Of the road that never ends.
They were several there that night:
Frisco Tom, with his old, white
"West-coast Stetson" on his head
A reminder of the waterfront
And the strikes in 'thirty-four and -six.
Where the "goons" and "scabs" and
    workers mix
And saw his buddies there shot dead.
He was tall, his cheeks unshaven . . .
His eyes as black as any raven
He looked a bit more tired
Than the last time Peter saw him
Before those shots were fired.

"Old Joe from Kokomo" who seemed quite
    pale.
Peter wondered if he had been in jail.
Thirty days out of the sun and wind will do
    that to a man.

Peter knew "Big" Barney had been going
Away from the Midwest's threatened
    drought
To find work where the rest were heading,
To the harvests in the deep South.

Now Barney's ankles were chaffed and blue.
A chain-gang's irons marks that hue
On the bodies of men who spend the day
In the sun on road-gangs; it's the Southern
    way.

A pair of strangers were there that day.
To Peter's eyes they looked like quite new.
Probably kids who had run away
To seek the world as some kids do.
Their actions showed a strangeness
To the formalities of such a crew.
He encouraged them to bring cup or can
Or something to share a bit of stew.

Then the click-click sound along the rail
Heralded the approaching train.
While the train passed by with a slowing
    rush,
Peter led the kids along in the evening rain.
And had them crouch low in the brush
Out of sight of the railroad bull
Who would probably be riding in full
View on the engine top
When the train puffed to a stop.

When he could hear the "slam-clank"
As the fireman opened the water-tank,
Then heard the rush of water
Pouring into the nearly empty car.
He figured the fireman would remain
Too awfully busy to watch the train.
As it had passed, his eyes searched along
The side of the cars whose locks were strong,
Looking for an unsealed door
That would indicate an empty car.

But his experienced eye noted only one
Of all the cars along the train,
A refrigerated car with dry drain.
He motioned to the kids to climb
On the ladder of the car and then to swing
In between cars and there to stay

Out of sight of the crew who watched that way.

When the train whistle blew its one short blast
Indicating the train would start at last,
They climbed to the top of the railroad car
And opened the cold steel latch
To the ice-filling hatch.
Before climbing down, Peter sniffed all around
To make sure it would pass
And not contain fumigation gas.

When he found it was okay, he said, "We'll stay."
As they climbed down into the hatch.
Peter flipped the latch from where it lay
Under the lid where it would catch
A breeze of evening air as they sat
On those hard steel bars
And bounced along their way.

An old steam engine, relic of a bygone era

Chapter 4

SOUTHERN LADY

May - August 1938

When the crew of the SOUTHERN LADY invited me to come in out of the rain, it was an answer to many unspoken prayers of the past few months. I was to clean up the crew's mess, fetch the meals from the galley, and generally make their lives a bit easier.

They seemed satisfied with my work and asked the captain if he would sign me on as workaway for the trip at least to give me a chance to get rested up and fed for a bit.

Besides the twenty-five cents a month I was signed on the articles for, each man would give me twenty-five cents apiece at the end of the week if they thought I had earned it. One of the men gave me a clean pair of dungarees and a shirt, since the clothes I had left home in were showing many signs of wear besides the accumulated grime of the road.

That week I was on top of the world — three meals a day and a coil of hawser to sleep on. I worked hard to wash the plates as fast as one man finished so the next man could get his meal, since there were only five plates for the fifteen men and a small assortment of silverware and cups to go with them.

As I watched the turmoil of the water streaming aft under the stern of the ship and listened to the thump of the propeller like the heartbeat of the ship beneath me, I thought I felt a release from the chains that had bound me to the shore. Ahead were days of learning a new life. The feel of rough manila lines in my hands, blisters from hours of monotonous chipping of paint, of painting and repainting the steel bulkheads, bulwarks and other strangely named items around me. The exhilaration of standing high up on a mast looking over the blue expanse of the sea. Learning the names of the stars, and learning the mathematics connected with finding my way across the ancient deeps of the world. And the fresh salt air — I could almost feel it cleansing the coal smoke and dust of the road from my lungs. I was at sea. . . .

Time went by, and the sores on my legs healed with the soap and water treatment and the regular diet. The trip to Tuxpan, Mexico, for a cargo of bananas to bring back to Mobile added bananas and canned cream to my diet — at least until I got sort of green at the thought of more bananas. On our return to Mobile, I was offered the job of officers' messman at the rate of twenty-five dollars per month. I accepted readily.

The succession of incidents that followed, I think, often managed to make the steward regret the offer. He told me at breakfast one Sunday morning that the day would be a "field day." Since I hadn't heard the expression before, I inferred that it was some sort of holiday. So after the breakfast dishes were done, I went down to my cabin below the old passenger quarters and started reading a magazine. He came down roaring, and pointed out that when he said "field day" he meant I was supposed to work all day. I apologized, of course, and asked him what he wanted me to do.

"Soogie the passageway by the engineer's quarters," he said.

"Soogie? What's that?" I asked.

"Don't you know what 'soogie' is?" he asked.

"It's a new expression for me," I answered. "Please tell me what you want done and I'll be happy to do it."

"Get a bucket of fresh water and put it under the steam line and get it boiling hot. Add some lye and some soap powder and mix it good, then take a brush and brush it over the painted bulkheads. Then take a bucket of fresh water and rinse it off."

I got the bucket of water under the steam line and, when it was boiling hot, I poured in about half a can of lye and about half a pound of Gold-Dust, a strong soap powder, and stirred it up well (I wouldn't put my hand in it for anything as it was scalding hot). I brushed it down the bulkheads (walls) with a long-handled brush, then got the fresh water and rinsed the paint down to bare red-lead.

There was a carpet on the deck, and a couple of days later the steward vacuumed the passageway, slurping up pieces of the carpet where some of my concoction had spilled. He was not happy.

When we were coming in to Tampico, Mexico, one morning, they told me, "There will a party of shore officials aboard for lunch, so be sure that everything in the place is spick and span."

After the breakfast dishes were done, since I didn't want to leave coal soot tracks on the white tile deck, I set up the tables for lunch before I mopped the deck. While I was in getting the rinse water to rinse the soap off the deck, the second mate came in for an early lunch, so he could relieve the chief mate in time for the party. I tried to hurry him out so I could finish mopping, but he was a slow, methodical eater. Before he finished, the members of the shore party came in and were seated at the long table I had set up for them. The captain, in his white uniform, sat at the head of the table.

The steward came down in a spanking clean uniform to officially serve them himself. He strutted into the saloon, carrying a tureen on a platter balanced on one hand, and skidded on the soapy deck. The tureen of soup sailed up the table, taking all the condiment bottles with it and dumping the lot in the captain's lap.

I went up and hid under a lifeboat.

An hour or so later, a hand reached over and dragged me up by the scruff of the neck. "What are you doing here?" were the gruff words I heard.

"Where would *you* be about now?" I asked.

The steward thought a moment and let me go. "Give me a half hour more to cool off," he said. "Then come down to my cabin and I'll pour you a drink."

As the ship was approaching Mobile, I got the makings for the dinner salad from the ship's walk-in icebox. I also picked up a couple of oranges on the way out. I dropped the key into the pocket of my shirt, shut the door with my elbow and, with arms loaded down with lettuce, tomatoes, oranges, etc., used the inside route through the engine-room rather than going out on the rainswept decks. When I reached down to pass the oranges to the oiler on watch who was standing on the grating below, the key fell out of my shirt pocket and dropped into the crank pit of the main engine.

I couldn't imagine calling the bridge to have them stop the ship so I could retrieve the key. I didn't mention it to the steward, but after dinner, I went down to the engine room. The first engineer fashioned a long brass rod into a hook and, timing his movements to the revolutions of the engine, managed to snag the key and retrieve it.

On our return to Mobile, while I was carrying stores aboard, I brought a box of light bulbs up the gangway. The box, though not heavy, was rather large. The steward added a box of glassware to the top of my load, making it difficult to see in addition to being top heavy. On reaching the deck, I asked him where I should put them down.

He answered "Anywhere!" then seemed rather perturbed when I set them down on the hatch which, for the first time in a long time, was open.

The next few minutes found me thirty feet below sweeping up broken glass.

When I got my first payoff, of course, I went into Jake Kamil's waterfront emporium and bought some new work clothes and shoes. I had a few dollars left over. The first time the clothes got wet, they shrank and the colors left their marks on me. The shoes disintegrated, so I was back to my old worn pair for the rest of the next trip.

I took a trip off and paid a week's room rent at the Commercial Hotel in Mobile. When the girl brought up my change, I realized what "commercial" transactions the place was named for. But, since I had paid the week's rent and couldn't get a refund, I stayed to do battle with the bedbugs until the week was up.

On the Fourth of July, I rode to the end of a streetcar line and bought a small watermelon and a loaf of bread and walked off into the country down by Mobile Bay to find a quiet spot to have a picnic by myself. Some other people had the same idea and joined me. Afterwards, I walked over to their place on Orange Street, and later went to a "church meetin' place" with them. That was my first experience with "Holy Rollers."

One evening there, after listening to the various people go up front to tell about their past sins and how they had been saved, one of my ex-shipmates, who was in the congregation after a few hours in a bar somewhere, got up and proclaimed in a loud voice, "I can sum it all up in just a few words. 'A woman's ass and a whiskey glass made a horse's ass out of me.' " There ensued a bit more commotion than I had seen in a church meeting anywhere.

When the week's rent was up, I had no more money to pay the next week's, so I left my suitcase with Jake Kamil and spent my nights out in the freight yards again, swimming off the docks in the daytime.

When the SOUTHERN LADY returned, I was re-hired as deck boy. The steward told me not to set foot in his passageways again; he would rather bring my food out to me.

And so to sea again. They gave me duties as lookout, from eight in the evening until four in the morning. The night watches on the bridge watching the stars and the quiet, black tropic sea, the faint throb of the steam engine the only sound above the hissing of the passing waves, were graven into my memory for their beauty and solitude.

The old Danish bo'sun who came aft and found me chucking chunks of rust at a passing sea gull said, "Ach, kid, you should not do that. Is old sailor's superstition, those birds are the souls of departed sailors."

A short time later, a large "splat" hit the rail near him. I said, "I'll bet that one was a bo'sun."

He walked off muttering something like "Damn smart kid."

Every Monday, Wednesday and Friday afternoon, I was to work on deck from one until three. Maybe I wasn't healthy enough for those long hours. Though I tried, I couldn't stay awake at all in the daytime long enough to eat, and one night I dozed off about 1:30 in the morning. The mate had sent me down as usual to bring up coffee and toast from the pantry. This was okay until I brought the tray up and set it on the flag box on the starboard wing of the bridge. I remember going back to my station on the port side and pacing back and forth trying to stay awake. And then — well, I heard a crash of cups and awakened to find that in my sleep I had wandered around to the starboard side again and tripped over the second mate's feet and landed in the coffee tray and splattered some all over the skipper and the mate.

When we made our next arrival, it was at Jacksonville, Florida. I paid off there, as I wanted to get back to San Pedro to meet the FERNBANK when she returned from Japan.

THE STRANGER
dedicated to the crew of the SOUTHERN LADY

We saw him on the docks one day
    With dusty face and hair like hay
Drying 'neath the summer sun.
    Hunger showed in his pallid face,
His walk was at a snail's pace.
    Had he forgotten how to run?

The clothes he wore were tattered,
    As if it really mattered.
We could see he was no tramp.
    His face looked mighty thin.
He had an air about him,
    He wasn't just a scamp.

We called to him to come aboard
    As a coffee cup we poured
And placed a sandwich in his hand.
    'Twas as if some fairy wand
Had touched this rusty ship of ours.
    His face so lighted up.

He told the tale of the open road
    From 'Frisco to Mobile,

Of how his shoe had lost a heel.
    Along the road he'd hopped a freight,
Of weeks since he last ate,
    Couldn't remember his last meal.

Our old banana boat was laying
    At the docks in old Mobile.
The rain was pouring down,
    He was wetter than a seal.
We asked the mate to sign him on
    As workaway at best.
We could give him food and rest.

We could never guess when he said, "Yes"
    What the end result would be.
The youngster was a natural
    To the ways of men at sea.

The years passed by.
    We're proud of this guy
He learned what we could teach.
    Of ships and stars and harbor bars
They're all within his reach.

The bridge of this ship we take to sea
    Has a new captain, don't you see.
This selfsame lad we called aboard
    That day in old Mobile
Has learned his lessons well.
    That's all of my tale
I can tell today; we're ready to set sail.

So when you meet a stranger
    And lend a helping hand,
You never know for years to come
    The end result, you see.
You may have made a lifelong friend
    Whoever he might be.

Chapter 5

On the Road Again

August - November 1938

When I left the SOUTHERN LADY at Jacksonville, Florida, it was well into August. I had received a letter from Dagfern Anderson, a crew member on the FERNBANK, telling me of its scheduled arrival in San Pedro in early November. I started hitchhiking back to California. The morning found me on the outskirts of town on the highway west, a suitcase of blankets and a change of clothes, towels and soap from the ship in my hand, and San Pedro on my mind.

While I was standing by the highway awaiting a ride, I was approached by a man who asked, "Where are you headed?"

"California," I replied.

After a bit more conversation about my ship and reason for heading west, the stranger said, "I have a brother who works for Railway Express. Maybe I can get him to get you a pass so you can ride the train instead of hitchhiking. I can probably get him to fix you up for about twenty dollars."

I thought a bit about this and, thinking of the hassle of hopping the freight trains, having a pass began to sound like a good idea. I gave the man twenty dollars, which was most of the cash I had saved up. I watched him go across the road to the Railway Express office. I waited, and I waited.

Finally, I walked over to the office. No one was there. Another door leading out the back of the building was open. I slowly walked back to the highway, a little wiser to be sure.

I slept a couple of nights by the side of the road with the mosquitoes and, by the end of the week, reached New Orleans. By the time I reached Houston, my hitchhiking luck gave out altogether. It was back to the freight yards again.

I put the suitcase in at Railway Express, collect, shipped to myself c/o San Francisco. That was the last I saw of it. Then I went on into the freight yard. I slept that night in a boxcar. Not all night, as a switch engine started shunting the car around, and presently hooked it onto a train. Then I slept, confident that we were bound west. But no, morning found me in Galveston, a bit out of my way.

I tried the docks again for a meal, and got some black bread and coffee from a German ship, the BORKUM, and also was given a suit of German sailor's clothing. This consisted of a large jumper and a very baggy pair of black trousers that ended snugly below the knee in sort of a knicker affair. Also a "matrosser" cap. I took the ship's name band off this flat cap and hied myself to the freight yards to don this outfit and pack my dungarees.

I grabbed a freight and was on my way again toward Houston. I slept at the Salvation Army in Houston that night, and was dismayed to find they had put my clothes through a sulphur fumigation during the night. The following day when I tried to hitch-hike, I was politely let out of a car after only a few minutes. So it was back to the freights.

From Houston this time, I rode the "Katy" to Fort Worth and hit the Texas Pacific to El Paso, then the Southern Pacific to California.

I had been telling the railroad men that I had missed my ship in Galveston and was on my way to San Pedro to re-join it. This was okay so far as they were concerned, so they let me ride. But the border patrol was an outfit that accepted only the truth, so I gave it to them with no elaborations except to claim my parents had been killed in an auto accident, and I was on my way home anyway so it would be only an expense for them to send me there. So I rode on.

By the time I reached Ontario, California, my shoes had given out. They fell apart above the soles, and nearly tripped me up when I tried to hop a freight out of Bakersfield. It took all my strength to pull myself up on the car when I missed my footing. Although shoes had been offered me along the way, the railroad men all seemed to wear sizes seven, eight or nine; none of these would fit my size elevens. I had no recourse but to ask for a pair from the Salvation Army. The woman at the Salvation Army office called up a number of people and finally after much banter gave me a pair to try on. I did, but the pair she gave me were old and sun-rotted and fell apart as I put them on. She refused to give me another pair since I had received my "allotment."

Oh well, I spent the night at the mission and got supper and breakfast and a bath. I then went back up the tracks a mile or so and camped under a railroad bridge in a dry creek bed. I scrounged some walnuts from the trees near the tracks and ate grapes from a nearby vineyard. Another hobo and myself gathered some black-eyed peas from the platform of a warehouse where they had been unloaded.

There was a fruit-picker's camp up the line a mile or so at Guasti, and by the end of the week I was up there looking around. The people there were migrant workers from Arkansas, Texas and Oklahoma working on the grape harvest for the Guasti winery. They were being paid in scrip redeemable at the winery's company store. If they wanted cash, the scrip was discounted thirty percent. I couldn't get on at the winery for being underage.

I went over to a nearby dump and salvaged enough cardboard to build a shack against a barbed wire fence in the camp area. I cut the end out of an automobile gas tank for a stove and got a blanket from one of the Mexican women in the camp. Then I went to work for a nearby independent picker for a few weeks. I was paid five cents for a thirty-pound box picked and carried through knee-deep sand down the long rows to the road. I made enough this way to buy food for my little "home" as long as the crop lasted. Most of this time I went barefoot.

One evening, I sat with my Mexican friends on the porch of the one house in the campsite listening to a radio commentator's report of Germany's takeover of Czechoslovakia. Britain's Neville Chamberlain had negotiated with Hitler and promised "Peace in our time." The news of this event seemed to cast a pall over those of us listening, some of whom were veterans of the first World War.

By the time I was ready to leave, I had

only one dollar saved up. I saw an advertisement that there were tennis shoes for sale at a drugstore in Ontario for a dollar a pair. I walked the three miles or so over, but there, too, ran into some trouble. I had no socks and they were two bits a pair. The clerk wouldn't let me try on the shoes without them. I explained my predicament, so he gave me a pair of socks and I proceeded to try on shoes. The largest size he had were size ten. I took them anyway and cut the toes off after I left the store.

My hitchhiking and walking finally got me to San Pedro, arriving in early November. I found that the FERNBANK was in, but she was anchored out in the harbor taking on fuel. I counted the few pennies in my pocket. It was not enough to eat on, let alone pay for a water-taxi ride out to the anchorage. I sat on a rocky cliff looking at her over the misty harbor. I felt really alone at that moment.

Chapter 6

Beachcombing

November - December 1938

When I found it impossible to get out to the FERNBANK, I walked dejectedly back toward Wilmington, where I had seen some stacks of lumber near the pier. I knew I could find a place to sleep under one of them, as lumber is generally stacked up about two feet off the ground, leaving a dry crawl space underneath. A man walking the other direction way stopped me and asked, "What are you doing that's so hard about it? You look as though you have just lost your last friend."

He was close to the truth, so I just answered, "Starving, I guess."

He walked back to Wilmington with me and pointed out the piers where the "steam schooners" (the small ships that brought lumber down the coast from the "dog-hole" ports along the Oregon and Northern California coasts) docked. As they came in, I made a point of boarding them with the longshoremen and helping the cook in his galley and messroom in exchange for meals. My guide introduced himself as Bob Parre. He was an former merchant sailor, about thirty years old. Best of all, he was renting a room at a nearby auto court and he let me bunk with him.

When there were no ships in, we would cook up whatever we could find. I ate more gravy sandwiches and bean sandwiches those two months than I ever knew existed.

Around the middle of December, our discussions brought us to the conclusion that I would probably have an easier time finding a job in New York City. Bob gave me his mailing address c/o the Seamen's Church Institute, 25 South Street, New York, New York. He told me that if I could stop by in Berkeley and pick up my birth certificate, he would meet me in New York and help me get my American Seaman's papers.

Now, Southern California in December is summertime compared to the rest of our nation, and I was dressed for it. I hitchhiked up to Berkeley and went to the city hall to get the certificate. When I gave my name, the woman started to reach into a basket on her desk and asked me to repeat it. The realization struck me that she was probably reaching for the "missing person" bulletin that undoubtedly had been issued last January when I left home. I gave her my older brother's name and birth date. She looked at the paper she dug out and said, "Oh."

When she looked up the certificate, she said, "That will cost fifty cents."

My heart sank. I had only ten cents, and I wanted that for streetcar fare. I said, "I'll have to go out to get it from my dad. He's waiting out in the car."

I got out of there and boarded a streetcar bound for Oakland. It happened to be one that passed my uncle Spiro's place and, of course, he got on. I scrunched down in the corner next to the motorman, hoping he wouldn't recognize me. He looked at me a bit. I held my breath. I guess he didn't recognize me, for he went on back in the car. I got off at the next stop, transferred to another line and rode west to the freight yards by the bay.

I was wearing only jeans and a light shirt, having been acclimated to the weather in Southern California. I rode out that night on the Western Pacific freight, which was routed up the Feather River canyon in the Sierra Nevada mountains. It had been snowing, and I was riding on the walkway outside a rail-tank car. There was no place to get out of the wind. When the train finally stopped at a water tower, I got off and walked around a bit to try to warm up. I didn't realize the snow was clinging to the bottoms of my shoes. Later that night while riding, my feet became extremely cold. When I jumped off the car the next time, I could barely feel the ground under my feet.

Somewhere along the line, one of the railroad men gave me a sleeveless sweater, which helped somewhat since I had no jacket. I made a point of finding boxcars where I could sit out of the wind for the long trip over the Rockies and across the prairie states. I was still cold.

On Christmas Eve 1938, the freight train I was riding from California to New York stopped in the Burlington yards at Silvis, Illinois, for its usual maintenance and switching. I was sitting in a boxcar, shivering, when I heard the footsteps of a "car-knocker," railroad parlance for the man who checks the wheel bearings of the cars for hot wheel bearings, making his way along the snowy right of way. When he passed the car I was in, I asked him what time the train was leaving for Chicago.

He looked at me, a shivering boy without coat or jacket, and told me it would be a couple of hours yet. He told me to go down to the head end of the train to the switchmen's shanty there and warm up by the potbellied stove. "If anyone says anything, tell him John sent you to wait there."

Later on, John came into the shanty and shared his lunch with me. He suggested, "Since it is such a cold night coming up and there is a blizzard in Chicago tonight, you would be wise to stay overnight at Silvis." Since I had no money, he sent me over to the police station to have the desk man let me sleep in the jail overnight. A hard bed, but softer than the boxcar floor, with a blanket and warmth was pure luxury.

The next morning, after a big bowl of oatmeal, I was walking back to the freight yards again. I saw some children sledding down the hill. Because I grew up where it doesn't snow, this was my first time actually watching this sport. I watched for a while, until a mother called her children in for lunch. I turned to go, but one of them came back and said her mother wanted me to come in, too.

Chapter 7

New York

January - May 1939

While I was eating my way through a bowl of hot chicken soup, the children's father came downstairs to join us. He was John Engholm, the man I had met at the railroad yard the day before. The family invited me to stay with them for Christmas dinner.

I left the next day on the freight for Chicago. I got off at Blue Island, Illinois, and walked through eight-inch-deep snow along the railroad tracks to Hammond, Indiana. I caught a Nickle Plate freight train for Buffalo and New York City. I remember that ride, basking in the warm glow that was in my heart from knowing that family. The warm jacket they had given me helped, too.

Across the snow-covered landscape of Indiana, I rode on the back of the top of the locomotive tender, trying to find a warm spot. There was a dry spot sheltered from the wind behind the coal chute — until the train took water. Then, to find another dry spot, I climbed into the coal bunker itself. The car was fitted with an automatic stoker, a turning screw at the bottom that carried the coal automatically into the firebox. I had to keep climbing up the sliding coal pile to keep from getting my foot caught in this device.

In time, the fireman came back to adjust the plates in the floor to allow more coal

down and, finding me there, invited me up into cab of the locomotive to get warm. This I welcomed, along with the sandwiches and coffee they shared.

At Buffalo, I went over to the washroom of the roundhouse to get rid of some of the coal dust and soot covering me, and tried to get some circulation in my feet, which were numb and very cold. When the shift changed, one of the workers offered me the hospitality of the house for the night. The next morning, one of the men took me over to the police station and arranged to have me sent to the hospital to have my frostbitten feet tended.

To get authorization to put me in the hospital, the desk sergeant booked me for vagrancy, and I was taken to the Buffalo City Hospital. Since I was a police case, they had to put me in a lock-up ward, and the only lock-up ward they had was the Alcoholic ward. So for the month of January 1939, I stayed there getting an eye- and mindful of various patients getting over the DTs. The days were not too long, and I made up for the sleep and food I had missed in the past months.

I entered the hospital on December 31. On February 4, I was discharged into the custody of a policeman and taken before the judge. The judge asked, "What are you doing in Buffalo?"

"I'm trying to get to New York to find a ship to take me to Norway to find some of my kinfolk," I told him, nervously hoping the three-state alarm of California hadn't been posted nationwide.

"Where are your parents?" he asked.

Not wanting to admit I was on the road voluntarily, I answered, "My parents were killed in an auto accident."

"What about this hospital bill, one hundred nineteen dollars and thirty-seven cents?" he asked.

"Well, if you can get me a place to stay and a job, I'll stay here until I can pay it back," I answered.

The judge thanked me for the offer, but decided against the necessity of my doing so. I was very grateful when he discharged me, and the five dollars he gave me came in very handy on the road to New York City.

I asked him, "How do I find my way out of town, since I want to hitchhike on to New York City?" He sent me to the office in the back of the courtroom where a group of reporters told me which streetcar to take and where to get off.

I followed their directions and, at the end of the streetcar line, I stood by the traffic light and stuck out my thumb. Soon, a big black sedan pulled up and one of the four large men asked me where I was going. "New York City," I replied.

"How long have you been in Buffalo?" he asked.

"Thirty-four days. I've been out in the City Hospital."

"Do you want to tell that to the judge?" he asked.

"The judge just told me to get out here," I responded.

"Okay," he said, "but you'll have a better chance for a ride if you stand across the street."

After a few rides and much standing around in the cold, I again took to the freight trains.

On February 7, 1939, the fair city of New York greeted me, first of all by an Irish cop who suggested that I wash my face, and next by the security cops at the entrance to the Seamen's Church Institute on South Street, who debated about letting me in as I was so young and so covered with soot and coal dust. They finally relented on the strength of the discharges from the SOUTHERN LADY. I went up to the post office on the second floor looking for word from Bob Parre, since that was where we were to meet.

There was no message for me. I washed up as best I could, then took the subway over to Brooklyn and slept on some coffee sacks near the customs office on one of the piers there for a week or so. As I listened to the speech of the people I met, I tried to get my West Coast-oriented ears tuned to the accents of New York and Brooklyn. This I found interesting.

One day, as I walked along Warren Street, I joined a game of stickball with some local kids. One of them was wearing a new pair of black high-top shoes. I asked him, "Does your momma let you play in your good shoes?"

I've tried to quote what he said:

So on the subway we rode. All the way from Boro Hall to Delancey Street. To the shoe store Ma took me. The smells of glue and polish and the rubber and the leather. The stacks of shoes on the shelves — standing there like waiting for feet to fill them. The noise of machine and the hammer on

33

the sole of a shoe by the man in blue apron in back I'm hearing.

"Keds," I wanted. I could picture them running, racing with Moshe and Richie to the bases in the stick-ball game.

But "No," Ma says. "You should have some practicals."

I don't know this practicals.

Maybe she meant the black shoes with the high tops and the hooks on the side which old men from the park would wear.

What's thinking her? Those I wouldn't want.

Mr. George, the shoe-man wiped his hands on his blue apron and reached for them. I yelled the "No" which came from my heart.

Momma said, "Yes."

I said, "No" and crossed my feet so Mr. George couldn't take my shoes off to try them on.

So Momma says, "Enough already! You're knowing better than your momma? Take, honey, the practicals. We got to go to Goldie's wedding. Those monstrosities won't go with the blue suit from your cousin Joey. I got it from Aunt Hannah for you to wear. You got to take the practicals."

All the time on the subway back to Brooklyn I hoped she'd lose the package. But no. She carried them in the string-shopping bag with her purse tied to her arm. So for this I got black shoes.

This was my introduction to the language of Brooklyn.

About a week later, I went back to check for mail. Again there was none.

"Now, where do I turn?" I thought. "Should I go down to the Army recruiting office and join up? At least they'll feed me, even if it is only beans." I didn't have a birth certificate, so the recruiting sergeant sent me away.

I returned to the Seamen's Institute for a cup of coffee and a last-minute check before returning to Brooklyn. As I came out, heading for the subway, I met the chaplain of the building. He introduced himself as Rev. David McDonald. He asked me about myself over lunch in the cafeteria. Then he took me up to the housemother's office on the fourth floor and introduced me to Mrs. Janet Roper. Between the two of them, they arranged a scholarship for me in Captain Huntington's Navigation School on the top floor, and room and board in the building while I attended. Rev. McDonald then took me up to Hearn's Department Store on Fourteenth Street and bought me some new clothes.

I later learned that the housemother of the Institute was known as "Mother Ropeyarns" by seamen up and down the East Coast. It was an affectionate name for a wonderful person.

In order to repay some of the hospitality offered, I accompanied and assisted Rev. McDonald at the services he held at the marine hospitals at Staten Island and Ellis Island.

One weekend, he took me up to Mount Kisco and taught me to drive his new 1939 Plymouth coupe. He talked me into writing home for my birth certificate (which I hadn't gone back for that day in Berkeley). One day in May, he asked me to drive him to his home in Pepperell, Massachusetts. On the way back, we came by way of Boston, and he signed for me before the Steamboat Inspectors to get my Ordinary Seaman's documents.

Rev. McDonald of the Seamen's Church Institute, New York, 1939

Author on the roof of SCI looking over New York Harbor, March 1939

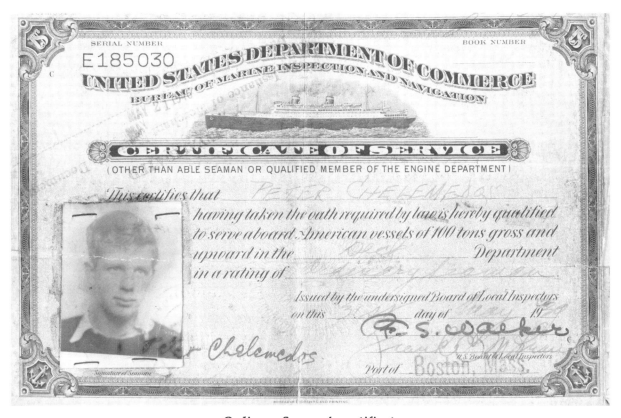

Ordinary Seaman's certificate

Chapter 8

CAROLITA

June 1939 - September 1939

The months at Captain Huntington's navigation school got me back into the habit of studying. I applied myself to all the courses and, on occasion, accompanied the instructor on a charter fishing boat outside the harbor to practice celestial navigation.

After several months at the school and after receiving my Ordinary Seaman's documents, I was sent by the employment office at the Institute to Bridgeport, Connecticut, to join the yacht CAROLITA, which was being fitted out to go to the Great Lakes.

I had a job at last. I joined the ship at Bridgeport and met Captain Freeman and the other eight men in the crew.

The CAROLITA, a 133-foot, steel-hull, German-built (1923) yacht, powered by twin Krupp submarine engines, was once owned by F. Donald Coster, who had been president of McKesson Robbins, the drug company. The story I heard was: Mr. Coster would never allow a photograph taken of himself. An enterprising newsman, however, talked Mrs. Coster out of a picture with the story that her husband was getting some sort of achievement award. When the picture was published in the Sunday paper, Coster was recognized by some of his old friends as Philip Musica, an ex-gangster from

Chicago in the '20s, who had disappeared. He was also being sought by the FBI, as auditors had uncovered some inventory fraud relating to his drug company, such as shifting audited warehouse contents during the night to the location where the next day's audit was to take place. When the Feds came to arrest him, he committed suicide. The yacht was one of the seized assets auctioned off by the government. It was purchased by the new owners, the Goldblatt Brothers of Chicago, for the sum of $15,000.

We sailed up Long Island Sound, through the Cape Cod Canal, and up through the Gut of Canso to the St. Lawrence River. This route gave me plenty of practice in the chart navigation I had been studying.

When we were tied up to the dock at Montreal awaiting the next day's transit of the Lachine Canal around Niagara Falls and into the Great Lakes, I got talking to an apprentice from the British ship MANCHESTER PROGRESS, John Marshall. We were approximately the same age and had a mutual interest in a career at sea. We exchanged addresses and promised to write from time to time. John was the first of the pen pals I was to make in my travels.

The following night, we tied up along-

CAROLITA, Chicago, 1939

side the canal. While I was walking ashore enjoying the warm June night, I was able to listen to the radio broadcast of the Max Baer-Joe Louis fight. The broadcast was coming from a series of radios in the houses I was passing, so I don't think I missed much of the bout. Everyone along the road I walked had their radios turned up full blast.

The CAROLITA proceeded across Lake Ontario to spend the night tied up to the locks at the Welland Canal around Niagara Falls. It was a clear, calm day as we crossed Lake Erie. The large lake freighters passing us seemed like monsters compared to the small ocean freighters I had seen on the coast. The wind came up as we traversed the St. Clair River past Detroit and stayed ahead of us up Lake Huron. As we passed through the Straits of Mackinac, the wind died to nothing. It was a clear night as we steered down the calm lake heading for the light of

the Palmolive Beacon atop one of Chicago's tall buildings, which was reflected with the stars off the surface of the water.

After seeing the beauty of that night, I am not surprised that many people find this area an ideal vacation land. I understand that wintertime is another story, though.

The CAROLITA spent the summer, when not laying at anchor off the Chicago Navy Pier, making various trips around the area behind the islands in Georgian Bay. These trips gave me an excellent opportunity to practice chart navigation, and Captain Freeman was patiently teaching me other facets of the operation of the vessel, showing me how to watch for drift in the wind and ease the behavior of a vessel when in rough seas, as the Great Lakes did get ornery at times.

One memorable night, the CAROLITA had anchored at the little port of Sturgeon Bay, Wisconsin. The townspeople were celebrat-

At wheel, Yacht CAROLITA, summer 1939

Heading home from Yacht CAROLITA, fall 1939

Starboard launch, Yacht CAROLITA, summer 1939

ing their Cherry Festival, and I sampled quite a bit of cherry wine. The storm in the lake when we sailed didn't help the aftereffects of the wine at all. I was never attracted to cherry wine after that.

The war in Europe broke out the first week in September. I tried to follow the events in the North Atlantic as they unfolded, as I still wanted to make the sea my career.

News items told of the sinking of the passenger ship SS ATHENIA *by a U-boat, then HMS* COURAGEOUS *on September 17 by another U-boat. Also of the torpedoing of several ships at Scapa Flow, including the carrier* ROYAL OAK *by a U-boat that had sneaked into this British naval anchorage in early October. Merchant ships weren't faring any better.*

Since I had renewed contact with my parents in Albany, California, when I asked for my birth certificate, I thought I should try again to go home and return to school. When I left the CAROLITA at the end of September, I headed for California.

I stopped for three days to visit the Engholms at Silvis, Illinois. The warmth of their hospitality was welcome, and I parted from them with much reluctance. Mrs. Engholm and her daughters, Clarisse and Dorothy, drove me down to Moline to put me on the bus and see me off. Maybe I cried a little then; there are too few people like them.

The bus went across the bridge to Davenport, Iowa, for a meal stop. I hadn't taken much interest in my fellow passengers, but a crowd of kids was seeing someone off on the bus as we left Davenport. The young lady in question was sitting in front of me, crying softly. When I moved up to sit with her, I took the step that brought a new friend and pen pal, Beverly, into my life. Beverly was on her way to San Diego so, in Denver, I changed my ticket to route myself via Los Angeles in order to ride that much farther with her.

As I saw her to her bus at Los Angeles and, before I reluctantly turned away, we exchanged addresses. Thus began an exchange of pen pal letters, words that, during my subsequent lonely years of travel, helped to tie me to the world ashore.

After I left her, I proceeded to Albany.

Part II

THE WATCH
BELOW

Chapter 9

Coal Passer to New York Again
Spring 1940

The war news told of the entry of the German pocket battleships SCHARNHORST *and* GNEISE-NAU *into the North Atlantic to raid the Britain-bound convoys of war materiels and food. One item told of the encounter with the British Armed Merchant ship* RAWALPINDI, *and of her being sunk in the encounter.*

At Albany, I re-entered high school and, at the end of the semester in December, sat through the commencement exercises of my class. I also attended evening classes at the Navigation School in the Ferry Building at San Francisco.

As time went on, though, I realized that nothing had changed in my relations with my brother and mother. To get out of this no-win situation, I headed again for the open road.

I hitchhiked south a way, then from Salinas "rode the blinds" on the Southern Pacific's night train south. That was a cold ride, behind the engine and in the mouth of the baggage car. The ground was frosty when I jumped off at San Luis Obispo. The next day I hitchhiked to San Pedro. I spent a couple of weeks at San Pedro and at Wilmington, beachcombing again.

As a way to get from San Pedro to New York, I had an opportunity to go as a work-away on a Swedish ship, SS O.A. BRODIN.

This meant I could be assigned to any work needing to be done in exchange for a place to sleep and my meals. I was assigned to the engine department and put to work assisting the lampere. When I heard this, I assumed it meant I would help take care of the ship's running lights and other lamps and lanterns around the ship. In those days, electric lights were not very dependable and all ships carried a reserve of kerosene lanterns for all emergency replacements. Such is innocence.

The job title, I found out, was the Swedish name for a coal-passer. I found myself in the 'tween decks coal bunkers shoveling coal into a chute down to the boiler room where the fireman kept a steady flow into the voracious fire boxes under the ship's boilers.

When we first sailed out of the harbor, the bunkers were, of course, full. I saw a pretty easy time of it. As we sailed south toward the Panama Canal, however, the combination of the heat from the fireroom and the sun on the steel deck over me combined to raise the temperature in that black hole higher and higher in direct relation to the increasing distance from the coal pile to the mouth of that ever-hungry chute.

In any event, the temperature remained

about 120 degrees. Even the pipe handles of the wheelbarrow picked up the heat. Occasionally, I would be able to stand under the big cowl vent that brought air down from its opening on deck near the smoke stack. Sometimes, a gust of wind would hit the vent straight on and, while it was welcome for breathing, it also stirred up a cloud of coal dust in the already stuffy atmosphere of the bunker. When it was time to go off watch, it took nearly an hour of scrubbing with salt-water soap and sea water to get most of the black dust out of my hair, eyes, ears and skin. Considering I would again enter that cavern of blackness in six hours, it was a pretty futile exercise.

About all I can remember of that trip is the spaces of blackness between meals and sleep in the fo'c's'le under the bows. When I got off that ship, I vowed I would never again knowingly sail in the "black-gang," but would learn all I could about the deck department.

As I heard rumors that the ship had received orders to Montevideo, Uruguay, for bunkers en route to India, I signed off in Panama and got a job as a crew member on a motor yacht that was being delivered back to San Pedro. I later learned that the BRODIN had gone directly to New York.

In San Pedro, I shipped on the yacht K'THANGA to deliver her to San Francisco. At San Francisco, I was transferred at the boat yard on Hunter's Point to work on the yacht PEZ ESPADA for a couple of weeks. I stayed in a hotel in San Francisco rather than going back to Albany.

In March, I wrote Rev. McDonald that I was on my way east. I paid twenty dollars to a "wildcat" transportation outfit and rode to Chicago by way of Los Angeles in a private car that was being returned east. I stopped in Chicago long enough to get a meal on the

CAROLITA, and in Buffalo overnight to give my regards to the railroad men at the round-house who had treated me so well the last time I was there.

The following Monday I was in New York, reporting to the Seamen's Institute for a haircut and a bath. I made the rounds of the union halls trying to get on their books for a trip-card. I was issued one by the National Maritime Union; this meant that if they couldn't fill jobs with their regular men, I could be called upon.

The war news in April was the invasion of Norway by the Germans. The German battle-ships LUTZOW and KARLSRUHE were torpedoed and damaged by British submarines, the HMS GURKHA was sunk and the HMS DEVONSHIRE was damaged in air attacks in the Norway area.

During my stay at the Seamen's Institute, I spent a few evenings in the apprentices room and there met Tommy Finn, an apprentice from the British ship WESTERN PRINCE. I accepted his invitation to visit the British Apprentices Club at the Hotel Chelsea on Twenty-Third Street.

My first visit to the BAC, a club set up like the living room and game room of an English manor house, introduced me to Mrs. George, Miss Alice Hayden and Mrs. Spaulding, hostesses at the club. Since this was a club for British Merchant Marine apprentices, I felt a bit out of place. But the room was so homey and restful for my travel-weary eyes, I couldn't help inventing a story of sorts that, if accepted, would allow me to visit the club occasionally. I signed in, using the home address of my pen pal, John Marshall, in England, and gave a made-up story telling how I had lost my ship and all my papers in the Far East and was making my way back to Britain on my own. Because of the war and the American Neutrality act, I couldn't get a ship to England unless I could prove I was a British subject. Being hardheaded, I would sail American ships until I was in a position to get a ship for England. My story was accepted, I believe, though with reservations.

A week or so later, I shipped out on a coal-burning steam tug, the NOTTINGHAM, as Ordinary Seaman, to relieve the skipper's son for a twelve-day trip hauling barges from New York to Baltimore, back to New York, on up to Rockport, Maine, and back again to New York.

March and April are not the months to be bounding around in that area of the Northeast coast fighting a twelve-inch wooden hawser that had to be let out and pulled in as we neared each terminal. Of course, I was on the winch detail, pulling the barges in and letting them out with ice cold seas sloshing around my feet and strong winds whipping me about the slippery deck. I was happy to see the skipper's son come back to reclaim his job.

The war in Europe had been taking an ominous tone. The fall of Belgium, the invasion of Holland, and the possibility of an evacuation of the British and French armies was paramount in the newspapers of the day.

I returned to the Seamen's Institute and, thinking I might be able to ship out in Canada, I scraped twelve dollars together from a dishwashing job at an Automat — eight dollars for the ticket to Montreal and four more to pay my way back across the border if I couldn't find a situation there. I even toyed with the idea of trying to volunteer for the Canadian army if I couldn't find a ship job.

The immigration official on the train was skeptical about letting me into Canada with so little money, but I told him I wanted to visit a brother whom I expected in on a ship sometime this week. I showed him, besides my seaman's papers, the discharges from the Canadian ship SOUTHERN LADY. After he had fixed up the papers necessary to send me back across the border, he held them and gave me a ten-day permit to stay.

I immediately booked a room at the YMCA and set about making the rounds of Montreal's waterfront in search of a job on any ship there. I even thought of sailing as a workaway on a ship bound for England, just for the meals and a place to sleep. Maybe it is a good thing I didn't, as the British troops were being driven back to the beaches of France. So when the ten days were up, I headed back to New York.

Chapter 10

SS NORTHERN SWORD

June - July 1940

Upon my return to New York, I resumed my studies at the navigation school at the Seamen's Church Institute. One night at about eleven o'clock, as I was busy studying for a test the next day, I was called down to the employment office on the second floor. Wondering what was in store for me as I rode the slow elevator down, I was surprised to be offered the opportunity to join a ship whose entire crew had quit just before sailing and a new crew was being recruited for a "pier-head jump" (where you go directly to the ship without stopping even to pick up your clothes).

Now, when the entire crew quits a ship just before sailing, the suspicion would run through one's mind of something amiss. But, desperate for a paying job, I accepted.

As I walked along South Street toward the pier, many thoughts went through my mind as to the possible reasons this job was available. In the glow of the lights from the pier warehouse, I caught my first glimpse of the ship. As I identified myself at the gangway and climbed aboard, I met the patrolman from the National Maritime Union, who was at the gangway checking aboard the replacement crew, all recruited at the Seamen's Church Institute hiring hall since

the National Maritime Union hall was closed this time of night.

I got the NMU patrolman to endorse the permit card I had obtained in my rounds, and was signed on as Ordinary Seaman on the SS NORTHERN SWORD.

As I looked around the ship that night, smelling the smells and looking over the painted-over rust spots on the deck and the old steam winches under the masts, I thought of the many sea stories I had read of foundering ships, sunk for their insurance. I wondered if this would be one.

The NORTHERN SWORD was a coal-burning ship with two hatches forward and two hatches aft, built in 1918 at Wilmington, Delaware. The crew's quarters were forward under the fo'c's'le head. Fresh water was carried in a small gravity tank on the bridge, and would run out from time to time when all four men coming off watch would take showers.

The ship sailed at midnight from South Street bound for Marcus Hook, Pennsylvania to load coal for Martinique. I checked over the mattress of my bunk for bedbugs, etc., and took my pillow up to the steward to exchange it, as it had the heavy odor of old sweat from a previous occupant. The steward was reluctant to exchange it until I showed it to the captain.

Captain Olsen threw it overboard and told the steward, "Issue a new one, and check all the others in the crew's quarters. I want to keep a crew for once."

Later, as I lay in my bunk in the forward fo'c's'le, I listened to the anchor chains as they clanked in the hawse pipes running alongside my bunk as the ship rose and fell in the ocean waves. The steel bulkheads were rusted through to the shower room of the old ship, so steam and odors wafted through the fo'c's'le.

After leaving Marcus Hook with a full load of coal, the ship sailed south, staying away from the coast to keep out of the Gulf Stream's strong northerly set. Captain Olsen and Mr. During, the chief mate, upon learning of my interest in learning navigation, gave me copies of their sun and star sights so I could practice my navigation lessons from school. On night watches, I tried to identify the main navigation stars as they rose in the east or appeared in the southern sky as the ship headed south.

The ship sailed past the Sombrero Island light into the quiet waters of the Caribbean, and on to Martinique. When the ship sailed past Saba Island, I recalled the agile crew members on the SOUTHERN LADY. It had always astounded me to watch them climb up the forestay to the masthead hand over hand. I thought, "There must be a developing strength when a child is raised with the only entertainment climbing coconut trees."

When the ship docked at Martinique, the stevedores rigged four long gangplanks straight out from the side of the ship to the pier, two forward and two aft. About 200 women and four men then descended on the ship, opened the hatches and proceeded to discharge our cargo of 3,000 tons of coal.

The men ran the winches to haul the coal from the hold to the deck, and the women filled their baskets; while two picked up the full basket placing it on one's head, each one carried off her own basket, picking up a tally stick at the gangway. At the end of the day, their pay depended on the number of tally sticks turned in.

This went on for four days. One day, one of the women took time out in the shelterdeck to have a baby, and an hour later was back carrying coal. I dedicate this poem to these women:

COAL AND THE WOMAN

She picked up in strong arms a basket
  And placed it on her head,
    Then stood erect to carry it
      Down the long plank to shore.

The white flower pattern
  On her bright red dress
    Smudged by the dust of coal.
      The traces of sweat streaked
        Down the determined brown face.

This day of heavy toil,
  Another in a long life of toil.
    The few francs earned this way
      To buy food for another day.

At the tolling of the nones
  She steps proudly ashore—
    Head erect.
      A slight tremble in her walk
        Echoes the weariness in her bones.

She has made her offering
  To the altar
    Of the Gods
      Of Commerce.

The war news from Europe was that France had been taken over by the Germans. In the harbor at that time was the French naval ship JEAN JADOT. There was much conjecture as to whether the officers would remain true to France, or turn the ship over to the Vichy France control of the Nazis. If this happened it would give the Germans a base in the Caribbean for their U-boats.

Docked in a nearby berth was a Greek ship, the POSEIDON. I went aboard and introduced myself to the captain. Inasmuch as I had some Greek ancestry, I was welcomed, and the captain searched his crew list for anyone who came from Cephalonia, the island from which my father's family had originated. There were none, but Greek hospitality is the same the world over.

The POSEIDON was loading a cargo of cognac, rum and champagne destined for Marseilles. Since the Germans had just taken over France, the captain was reluctant to take his ship into that area. I suggested that after he sailed he could divert at sea to New York, as he could surely sell his cargo there.

One of my shipmates on the NORTHERN SWORD, one of the firemen, was an old Bowery reprobate named Gus. Gus would stand his watch in the coal-burning fire room. When he got off watch, he would go to the gin mill at the end of the pier and drink until it was time to go back on watch.

Captain Olsen was on the wing of the bridge when the ship sailed on the fourth night. I was on wheel watch when we heard a commotion on the foredeck. Someone one on the foredeck was hollering up to the bridge for the captain.

"Hey, are you the captain of this ship?"

"Yes, I am. What is the problem?"

"I was taking a shower and ran out of water."

"Is that you, Gus?"

"Yes, it is, and I want some water to

Sweeping bauxite from the deck, SS NORTHERN SWORD, Surinam River jungle, July 1940

rinse the soap off of me."

"I'll call down right away, Gus. If anyone on this ship deserves a bath, it's you."

The ship sailed from Martinique to Surinam, Dutch Guiana, and up the Surinam River to the bauxite mines. The river is quite narrow and the ship brushed branches of the trees on both sides of the river. The monkeys in the trees were chattering and throwing at us twigs, nuts and anything they could find. People in dugout canoes called out for "chapeaux" as the ship passed and the calls echoed and re-echoed farther up the river so there was always another canoe to meet the ship as it rounded each bend. Hats were a valuable commodity in that hot climate.

The ship could only take half a load because of the depth of the river. This cargo was carried to Port of Spain, Trinidad, and discharged onto a barge. A return trip to Surinam for the other half of the cargo. Then back to Port of Spain to reload what we had left behind. During these two stops at Port of Spain, I was able to go ashore to sample life in a tropic setting. The girls at the water-front bar I stopped in all seemed extremely friendly. I thought it too bad I couldn't stay long enough to get acquainted.

When we sailed, we carried the cargo to Mobile, Alabama, for discharge.

When I left the ship in Mobile, I was recognized by the immigration officer from my trips in on the SOUTHERN LADY two years previously. The immigration officer looked over my recently issued Seaman's papers and congratulated me for getting them.

When I paid off, I took the train to Silvis and Davenport to visit the Engholms and my pen pal, Beverly, and to meet her mother and sister, Ruth, before I returned to New York.

SS Northern Sword

Company: Sword Steamship Co. New York, NY
Master: Not known
Built: 1918 @ Wilmington, DE
Dimensions: 300' x 45' x 23'

Home Port: New York, NY

Gross Tons: 2648
Former Name: (a) NORMA

The Freighter, SS NORTHERN SWORD, was sunk in a collision with the Liberty Ship SS FISHER AMES on February 8, 1943 about 50 miles off Cristobal, CZ (10-28 North/79-32 West) while en route in Convoy GZ-21 from New York to Brisbane, Australia via Charleston, South Carolina and Key West, Florida.
Photo courtesy of Mariners Museum, Newport News, VA.

Chapter 11

RICHARD J. BARNES
August - November 1940

At New York, I went back to the National Maritime Union hall, turned in the endorsed permit card, and was issued a probationary book, which meant I could throw in for ship jobs along with the regular members.

From the NMU Inland Boatmen's division came a call for an Ordinary Seaman for the MS RICHARD J. BARNES, which was loading sugar from one of the South Street piers to carry up the Erie Canal to Cleveland. The RICHARD J. BARNES was a canal freighter of 1,500 tons, long and narrow and, when loaded, low enough to pass under the bridges of the Erie Canal.

The trip up the Hudson River to Albany and Troy and then along the Erie Canal through the beautiful Mohawk Valley was different from the rolling waves of the ocean. After ridding my bunk of bedbugs, I settled down for a couple months of quiet cruising. The skipper had been a lighthouse keeper down east in Maine during the '20s, until he was discovered running rum in the government launch. He then went to work as cook on an Standard Oil canal tanker, made enough trips to qualify for sitting for a Pilot's license for the canal and eventually got one.

We sailed into Port Hope, Ontario, for a couple days to await our berth at Cleveland.

Robert Bennett, the messman, and I borrowed the local Sea Scouts sailboat one calm afternoon, and rowed it out of the breakwater onto Lake Erie before we put up the mast and rigged the sails. When we were about 500 yards outside the breakwater, a sudden squall blew up and we spent a few anxious moments roaring down the lake before we could lower the sail. At least I had sense enough to steer it toward shore so we did wind up in the lee of the breakwater.

We rowed over close enough so I could put Bob ashore to tow us on a "sea-painter" along the breakwater to the harbor entrance. By the time we reached it, the wind had died down so it was no trouble coming around into the harbor, but we had to row the entire length of the harbor to reach the dock. We were met by quite a delegation — Sea Scout skipper, a constable from the Royal Canadian Mounted Police, and various people who were preparing to rescue us if necessary. None of them expressed joy at that prospect, but were thankful we had returned safely. Confidentially, I was too.

After discharging the sugar cargo at Cleveland, we proceeded to Sault Ste. Marie, Michigan, for a load of calcium carbide to take back to Carteret, New Jersey, on our

On deck, MS RICHARD J. BARNES, Lake Erie, summer 1940

southbound trip.

The news of September 17 told of the SS CITY OF BENARES having been sunk by a U-boat. She was carrying about 191 children and their escorts to Canada, evacuees from the bombed-out cities of Britain. October 24, the SS EMPRESS OF BRITAIN was also sunk by a U-boat.

The third trip south was getting along into late October. All the trees in the Mohawk Valley were changing color and the beauty of the resulting scene was breathtaking.

Each trip, as we passed through the locks and I was ashore tending the mooring lines, I used my time memorizing bits of poetry. To this day, whenever I hear the lines of Kipling's "Gunga Din" or Paramore's "The Ballad of Yukon Jake," my mind is back again walking lines along the Erie Canal on a beautiful fall afternoon.

The last day in the canal I was painting the top of the wheelhouse, a five-gallon paint bucket beside me. When I saw we were approaching a low bridge, I scrambled off, but lacked the time to get the paint bucket off. The skipper walked out of the wheelhouse door to see what the noise was just as the paint bucket was knocked over the edge.

You guessed it. The red paint didn't go too well with his other clothes. I didn't get to make the last trip of the year.

I liked the canal experience, but the paint episode cut short my plans to continue on that ship and, since the winter shutdown was approaching, there were no other jobs available inland. So I put my card in for another deep sea ship.

While awaiting a new berth, I paid a visit to Silvis and Davenport, sharing Thanksgiving dinner with Beverly and her mother and sister. Over the year since I had met her, Beverly had become a pen pal whose letters, written in that round hand of hers, were a welcome addition to my life. As we talked, that afternoon, she asked me, "What are you going to do with your life? You have the potential to go far. Are you just going to sail about the tramp freighters of the world?"

Thinking fast, I said, "No. I figure that if I can keep up my studies and get the sea time necessary, I should be able to get my Captain's license by the time I'm twenty-four." Talk about confidence!

I returned to New York and registered at the NMU hall. Then I paid a return visit to the British Apprentices Club. It was still run by Mrs. Spaulding, a remarkable motherly woman who made the boys feel at home around the fireplace with conversation and tea. A select group of young ladies served as hostesses and gave a sisterly feeling to the youngsters (the apprentices ranged in age from fourteen to eighteen) far from home.

Since it was a club for Britishers, I had signed in the guest book using John Marshall's Wallesey, England, address. So long as I didn't overstay my welcome, I was invited back from time to time.

One evening I was standing with a group of chaps from the JERVIS BAY and the GOVERNOR, one of the Lamport and Holts rust buck-

Kay Hamilton

*Kay Hamilton, Fall River, Massachusetts,
January 1942*

ets which was in port, when a few of the young ladies arrived. In the group was a dark-eyed beauty who was coming for the first time as a guest of one of the other girls. My comment to the boys at the sight of her was, "She's for me." And I was introduced to Kay Hamilton.

After a few dances and chatter, I looked forward to seeing her again. I was happy to learn she had been invited to be one of the regular hostesses. When the evening was over, I walked her home to Preston House, a residence hall at Eighteenth Street and Lexington Avenue. Some evenings we walked by way of Times Square, where we spent hours at the Automat drinking cocoa and chattering away as teen-agers will do. Her personality was much like that of Beverly, and she was in New York where I could see her more often.

I had joined a new ship meanwhile, which was loading over in Brooklyn. So after I

walked her home, I would take the subway over to my ship to be there before breakfast. Then I would stand my day watch looking forward to evening again. Since we wouldn't break off conversation until about 5:00 a.m., I got little sleep for a week or so, until we sailed for West Africa on the SS CATHLAMET for Barber West Africa Line.

Just before we sailed, the newspapers carried the story of the sacrifice of the JERVIS BAY, an armed merchantman guarding a convoy across the North Atlantic toward England. The German pocket-battleship ADMIRAL SCHEER approached the convoy. JERVIS BAY, instead of scattering with the rest of the ships, faced the SCHEER and delayed her long enough for the other ships to escape. JERVIS BAY was sunk in the ensuing battle. There were, I understand, 65 survivors, but whether any of the apprentices I had met at BAC were among them, I never learned.

Chapter 12

SS CATHLAMET

December 1940 - March 1941

After walking Kay home from our last long talk over hot chocolate at the Times Square Automat, I returned to my ship at 5:00 a.m. and sailed for a three-month trip along the coast of West Africa.

The SS CATHLAMET was a "West" type vessel built for the Shipping Board in 1918. Deck officers and passengers were quartered in the bridge housing forward of the smokestack. The galley and the engineer's quarters were just aft of a small "bunker" hatch also amidships. Crew quarters were aft over the propeller and rudder instead of up in the bow. This was a step up from the old days, as we also had separate rooms for each three-man watch instead of all being in one large fo'c's'le.

It was pleasant to be at sea again; salt air is so invigorating. The ship was so loaded down that an occasional wave would wash across the deck load of wooden kegs of formic acid. Since we had to pass these kegs on the way to and from our quarters, we all hoped none would break; the odor was bad enough from what little did seep out.

I continued with my navigation practices, getting copies of the sights from the mates and computing our distances and courses run from the propeller revolutions and compass courses steered.

We carried twelve passengers on this ship, mostly missionaries on their way to posts in Africa. The captain always made a great show with his sextant when he took his morning sights, I guess to impress these ladies.

One day when he was going through his act, the chief engineer came on deck and said, "You don't need that fancy instrument to tell us where we are." He proceeded to place a monkey wrench upright on the deck, laid a length of pipe angled over it, and cranked the monkey wrench open until the sun shone through the pipe onto the deck. Then with a folding carpenter's rule he drew from his coveralls pocket, he measured the opening in the jaws of the wrench. He looked at his dollar watch, scribbled some notes on a scrap of paper, and went into his office. A few minutes later, he sent up the ship's position to the captain. It was right on. I think if the captain ever found out it was his ordinary seaman who had fed the position to the chief, he would have thrown him to the sharks.

We made Freetown first, to unload the barrels of formic acid to the little motor ships run by Firestone Rubber Company to its plantations up the river. Then we went

SS CATHLAMET, *Brooklyn,*
December 1940

around to Monrovia to pick up 200 "crew boys" to handle cargo up and down the coast.

At Accra, we anchored off the beach. One of my watch partners decided to build a raft of empty oil drums, which he planned to launch and drift ashore. He worked all night lashing drums and dunnage together, and finally tipped it over the stern rail, forgetting to put a line on it. This was fortunate, because he was able to stand on deck and watch it drift out into the South Atlantic instead of toward the beach.

A few days later we were docked at Lagos, Nigeria, behind the Polish ship BATORY. The raft builder, one of the able-bodied seamen on my watch, was a Brooklyn Pole. As we drank warm beer with the Polish crew at the canteen on the dock all evening, he had a great time conversing in Polish.

The next morning he was missing. We had the BATORY check to make sure he wasn't aboard before it sailed at daybreak. A couple days later, we received a radiogram from the port authorities that a body had been found in the harbor.

At Lagos, I also met the apprentices from the British ship CALUMET, an Elder Dempster

ship, whom I had previously met at the British Apprentices Club in New York. We shared some beer and brought each other up to date on the news of the day.

News of the combined U-boat and air attacks on a Gibraltar-to-Britain convoy (HG-53) in which five ships including the SS BRITANNIC were sunk in one day (February 9) and several others damaged. This was the first combined attack by air and U-boats together. A portent of things to come.

The CATHLAMET steamed up the river to Port Harcourt in the early morning. Wisps of fog over the river gave the quiet jungle growth along the river bank an eerie glow in the rising dawn. Birds came awake and the flowers in the trees blossomed out; I tried to drink in all of the peaceful scene.

On the way up the Congo River, I was called to take the wheel for the first time to replace the missing AB. I really got my exercise as I cranked the recalcitrant wheel to port and starboard as we came around the bends of the river on our way to the port of Matadi, about eighty miles upriver.

At Matadi, Belgian Congo, I watched the little wood-burning locomotives on a seem-

Narrow gauge wood-burning locomotive, Matadi, Belgian Congo, February 1940

ingly miniature railway in the dock area. I walked up the steep road to look over the town. I learned there would be a movie and a dance at the Hotel Metropole that evening. One requirement for admission was a coat and tie. I passed this information along to the second and third mates when I returned to the ship.

This was my eighteenth birthday, and here I was on the other side of the world, feeling a bit forlorn. That evening, I put on the required coat and tie. Since no one else on the ship wanted to go to this much trouble, I went by myself to the movie. It was held in a nightclub on the top floor of the hotel. After the movie, they served beer and played music on a Victrola. One of the songs I remember besides "There'll be bluebirds over the White Cliffs of Dover" was "We'll hang out our washing on the Siegfried Line if the Siegfried Line's still there." (The Siegfried Line was the string of German fortifications along the Franco-German border facing the French Maginot line.) Also, the romantic songs of the day — "Alone" and "Stars Fell on Alabama."

The conversation all around me was in French or Belgian, neither of which was familiar to me. I was the only member of the ship's crew there, so I had absolutely no one to talk to. By the time the dance was over, I was feeling pretty low.

I started down the lonely moonlit road to the docks when somewhere out of the night came a feminine voice: "Hi, Yank, where are you going?" In English! I found myself walking on down the road while the rest of the town was asleep with a dark damsel on my arm, and a lighter heart than before. She was from one of the British colonies up the coast.

The problem at hand was: Where could we go to sit and talk and not be disturbed? I couldn't take her to the ship or to the hotel, and I didn't think I should go over to the native village at the edge of town. As if in answer to our wishes, we passed a house with tall weeds in the yard instead of the cultivated gardens of its neighbors. We assumed it was a vacant house and went around back to sit on the back patio to talk.

As an evening like this goes, so it went. After a half hour or so, we decided to spend the night. But not knowing Africa and not wanting to sleep on the ground because of possible insects or whatever, we decided to try the upstairs back verandah. This was reached by a climbing the embankment and crossing a little bridge. She went up to check that we were not intruding on anyone and assured me it was empty. I picked up my clothes and her skirt and came up onto the balcony. The full moon was on our side of the house and put us in full silhouette from the house. When I hung my clothes over the railing, a couple of francs dropped to the concrete below in a ringing bounce. The girl went down under the porch to look for them, and I spotted a flashlight coming through the house toward the window I stood beside.

The flashlight was stuck through the bars over the window and shone over me as I stood against the wall about seven feet away.

Whoever it was couldn't get a good look at me, for the bars prevented him from sticking his head out. He gave what I took to be a short laugh at my shirt-tailed figure and pulled the flashlight back in.

I spent the next few seconds thinking up an excuse for my presence there, but found I didn't need one. I heard footsteps in the room, and waited for him to come to the verandah door to ask my explanation. Instead he went through the house to the front and started yelling, *"Gendarmes! Gendarmes! Complain! Complain!"*

I, of course, didn't wait for him to complain too much, but picked up our clothes and made fast time over the bridge and up the hill. I stopped a block or so away and dressed, and the girl caught up with me and did likewise. We separated. A blown promise of a romantic evening.

As I walked on down the hill to the ship, I passed a man on the corner who was yelling, *"Gendarmes! Gendarmes! Complain! Complain!"*

As I passed him, I said, *"Bon soir, monsieur."*

He replied, *"Bon soir."*

So I stopped worrying and went aboard. When I went up the gangway, the second and third mates were there and asked about the movie. I told them about it and about what a fine dance it was. Then I turned in.

The next day at coffee time, the chief mate came aft and told us that the chief of police was aboard with a complaint that two men from this ship, a tall one and a short one, were wanted for trying to break into a white man's house uptown about eleven-thirty the night before. Of course, no one knew a thing about it and I certainly didn't, for such a thing had been furthest from my mind. We sailed in a few days, and the mystery was never cleared up until, just before we arrived at New York, I told the captain about the evening at Matadi. He said, "Those people were so aroused that they were ready to put anyone in prison for twenty years."

A week later I was spending the night in a tree house in the jungles up the river from Douala, French Cameroons. I spent the days wandering along the jungle trails and swimming and fishing from a dugout canoe with various members of a family I met when walking ashore while waiting for the cargo of mahogany logs to be loaded aboard the ship. By the time loading was finished, I was ready to go.

I never have returned to West Africa.

Chapter 13

SS WEST JAFFREY
April - November 1941

News items — April 18, 1941: Twenty-seven survivors from the SS BRITANNIA landed in Brazil 23 days after their ship was sunk by a German raider in the South Atlantic.

May 19: The Egyptian passenger ship ZAM ZAM has been reported missing for more than a month in the South Atlantic. She was carrying 340 passengers, including 138 Americans being sent on assignments to the Middle East.

May 21: American ship SS ROBIN MOOR torpedoed by U-boat in South Atlantic.

May 24: British HMS HOOD sunk by German battleship BISMARCK.

May 21: German invasion of Crete. The German air attacks on the British fleet the next few days were unrelenting. The Cruisers HMS GLOUCESTER, CALCUTTA and FIJI and the destroyers HMS JUNO, KASHMIR, KELLY and GREYHOUND were sunk. HMS WARSPITE and HMS CARLISLE were badly damaged among others during this first major air-sea battle. The British withdrew from this area to Alexandria, Egypt, leaving the southern coasts of Europe controlled by the Germans except for the island of Malta.

May 28: German battleship BISMARCK sunk in battle with British naval forces in North Atlantic.

I found that Kay had left New York and returned home. I didn't know where her home was, so after paying off from the CATHLAMET at New York in late March, I took a quick trip out to Silvis and Davenport for a visit while waiting for my dispatch card to "age." (The dispatch system was such that the oldest card thrown in for a job posted had the first choice).

After blowing nearly all my money on the trip to Davenport, it was time for another trip to sea. At the National Maritime Union hiring hall, I threw my card in for a Red Sea trip on the SS WEST JAFFREY. I phoned Beverly to ask if there was anything I could bring back from Egypt for her. "Well," she said, "I've never seen a mummy."

I said, "I'll see what I can do."

WEST JAFFREY was a ship built during the first World War and had been laid up in New Orleans since early '20s. She was brought up to New York, given a new coat of paint and a cursory overhaul, and loaded with the first Lend-Lease cargo to the British and their army in Egypt.

There were rumors of submarines and sea-raiders operating in the South Atlantic along our route around Cape of Good Hope. We had a large American flag painted on each side of the ship, lit up at night by flood-

SS West Jaffrey, New York,
May 1941

lights to make any lurking submarine aware that we were a "neutral" ship. This cargo consisted of sacks of flour, canned goods, and tanks for the army fighting Rommel in the North African desert.

Having been laid up for so long, the ship's machinery was not in the best of shape. Consequently, most of the voyage was spent drifting around the ocean while making repairs to different parts of her engine and other auxiliary equipment. Our steaming time averaged about eighteen hours a day plus the drifting, all the time maintaining radio silence and a sharp fear of the unknown attitudes of the German raider fleet.

We had in mind the reports of the disappearance of the Egyptian ship ZAM ZAM, which had been transporting refugees, including 138 Americans, back from the Middle East to the West. Also, the sinking of the American ship SS ROBIN MOOR, which had been ahead of us on our route around Cape of Good Hope.

Since our evaporators were not working our ship ran short of fresh water. We put into St. Helena Island and spent five days at anchor while replenishing our supply from a barge that could only bring out five tons at

a time. On Sunday, the British army invited us ashore and conducted us on a tour of the island to Napoleon's quarters and tomb, and back to the ship again.

While waiting on the beach for the trucks to take us on the trip, I got to talking with Doreen Cranfield, a native of the island, and from her learned more about the people of the island. She told me, "About the only excitement the children can make for themselves is sliding down on the pipe railing along the seven hundred steps down the cliffside into the town of Jamestown."

When I looked at that staircase climbing into the clouds along the cliffside, I said, "I hope they use parachutes."

On the trip from St. Helena to Capetown, the ship's generators went on the fritz. We entered Capetown burning kerosene running lights and using kerosene lanterns in our quarters, and even to light the compass card in the wheelhouse. One of my tasks was to clean this small lantern each morning. As I performed this task, I remembered the lampere job I had signed on for with the O.A. BRODIN. War fears and all, I was happy to be where I was.

The ship lay in Capetown Harbor over

Jacob's Ladder (699 steps), St. Helena Island, in the South Atlantic

Off watch, SS West Jaffrey, en route to Egypt, summer 1941

the Fourth of July. The five American ships in port, of course, dressed ship (hung out all the flags we could find) for the holiday.

On the night of the sixth, we were at the repair dock, and I again met the boys from the CALUMET whom I had met in New York and in Lagos earlier in the year. In return for the time we spent together in New York, I accompanied them on a tour of Capetown's night life.

At the Del Monica club bar, a British navy sailor very sarcastically asked an American there, "Say, Yank, wot're all you Yank ships dressed for the other day? Celebrating something?"

Well, as all such questions must be answered come what may, the answer was,

"Yeah, celebratin' the last time we got away from the British Empire."

When we sailed the next morning, I noted several of my shipmates sported black eyes and various abrasions, and assumed they had been in last night's encounter.

The ship's course took us up the east coast of Africa through the Mozambique Channel, then around Cape Guardafui into the Gulf of Aden where the heat of the desert dropped down over us. We ran short of fresh water again before we reached Aden, Arabia. There was no water obtainable there, so we proceeded on up the Red Sea, running the boilers on sea water and drinking easy on the fresh.

The generators were run slow to conserve

steam, so the fans in the quarters were not operating most of the time. The sea water temperature was close to 98 degrees, and the sand in the air pervaded everything.

We were glad to get to Port Tewfiq (the harbor off the south end of Suez Canal). But we were dismayed to find that the cafes, bars and restaurants in Egypt did not make a practice of serving ice with their drinks. Ice was available, but only in ten-pound blocks. This meant that when I asked for ice for the drink, I was given a large block of ice and a hammer and chipped my own as needed. Since it was not served in a pot or bowl but placed directly on the table, the melting ice made it necessary to recall the waiter often to mop up the mess.

I took a weekend off with my watch partner, Al Rosse, to take the train trip to Cairo on the Egyptian State Railway system. The only system I found connected with that railroad was its system of stopping occasionally in the apparent middle of nowhere while the engineer and conductors got out and held a conference. Stops lasted fifteen to forty-five minutes depending on whether a water fountain was handy. The stay was shorter if there was one, which added to the confusion as all the passengers rushed off for a drink and back aboard again just as the train was starting up, which always happened when everyone was least ready for it.

I had purchased a third-class, half-fare (military rate) ticket for the ride, using our Seamen's papers, an official-looking document, for a pass. None of the train people could read it anyway as it was in English, so we rode in the first-class car. Of course, the conductor protested, but only until he got a drink of the whiskey we had had the forethought to carry. Then neither he nor we cared.

The train was scheduled to leave Port

Said around 4:30 p.m., though it didn't seem to mean at 4:30. Some days I watched it pull in and out at 5:00 and some days as late as 6:30. Well, the man did say "around" 4:30. It seemed that the ticket office didn't open until five minutes before train time, and only two agents were on duty. No lines formed, so the five hundred or so would-be travelers rushed the window at the same time, then had to elbow and push their way out again when they had purchased their ticket. The train rushed madly into the depot from the make-up yards three miles away whenever it seemed convenient and, two minutes after stopping, rushed out again into the desert to stop again as I mentioned before.

All this was to comply with the wartime speed-up of everything, though I hear that before the war it took an hour and fifty minutes to make the Suez-Cairo run, though I clocked it at a bit over four hours both times I made the run.

Anyway, we reached Cairo in time to look for a "bed and breakfast" (five piastres or twenty-one cents) then went out to look over the night life. We spent an hour or so looking in on the establishments down a street whose entrance was posted "Out of bounds to other ranks." Then we went to a couple of nightclubs to drink "John Collins" (without ice unless asked for).

The next morning we were wakened at daybreak to moans. It turned out to be a muezzin on a minaret across the street calling the faithful to prayer.

I found a button beside the bed that rang the thing they called a bell. It could have been a fire alarm for the noise it made down the hall. The attendant got up from his bed in the hall and broke out a frying pan and cooked up some eggs, some strong tea and some gin. And so, breakfast.

Breakfast over, Al and I hopped a streetcar to see where it would take us, since the destination board in Egyptian was impossible to read. The conductor came along and took the equivalent of a fourth of a cent from us and handed us a piece of paper with pictures of the pyramids on it. Later the "inspector" got on and asked for the paper. He tore it in half and handed both pieces back to us, and we rode on without interruption for a while.

As we rode along that early morning, we watched the scenes along the Nile as the day unfolded. The sailing barges on the placid river made a picture of their own. Along the shore, the camels, donkeys, burros and the biblical-looking wells complete with oxen pulling Archimedes wheels around to pump irrigation water made another memorable scene.

We finally reached the end of the line, which was at the edge of the Nile Valley and the start of the desert, at Giza, the place of the pyramids. We left the streetcar and were immediately besieged by dragomen and donkey and camel tenders offering the use of their animals and themselves as guides on our tour of the tombs of their ancients. Each man was fighting his competitors verbally and physically to get our business. But we waived their services and walked up to the tombs in the fresh early morning air.

As the day wore on and the sands became hot in the sunshine, we saw the worth of an animal to ride. Since we had seen most of the area by that time, we only borrowed a camel and a donkey to pose with for pictures. We then made our way back to town.

That afternoon, Al and I spent in the Mosque Market section, riding in a one-horse shay to the place, accompanied by four boys carrying drinks for us from the hotel. We reached the bazaars and dismissed our boys with their "backsheesh," and went our way

through the shops of rugs and silks and perfumes and amber, and the usual "Ramses" jewelry. Bargaining and haggling for this trinket or that, wallets and purses of camel hide, and souvenir junk they had to offer. I did get a small jade replica of a mummy case for Beverly.

One of the shopkeepers offered us chairs and, as we say, made us feel at home. He sent out for drinks for us, then proceeded to offer his line of goods. Three hours and five drinks later we started to bid him good day. But before we left, he asked me to send him the address of several American novelty manufacturers so he could lay in a stock of souvenirs to sell to the troops coming in on leave and the tourists after the war.

We then inquired about train service to Suez and were told, "The train will leave in an hour or so." We added a couple bottles of Johnny Walker to our souvenirs and boarded the train with a basket of ice and a basket of souvenirs.

We were tired and slept most of the way. We awoke as the train pulled into Suez at two in the morning. No taxis were available, so we "borrowed" a camel and donkey from the janitor at the station, and Al and I started down the dock road in the moonlight. It was a beautiful night, a light breeze rustling the palm trees along the road. The sky was filled with moonlight, searchlights, tracer bullets, ack-ack, planes burning, bombs whistling down over the port area, and the pair of us sang "Jingle Bells" as we rode our steeds toward the dockyard gates.

Maybe that is why the MPs at the gate sent us back to town. We returned the camel and donkey and gave their owner, who was hollering loudly, a couple of piastres apiece to quiet him down. He took the money and his animals and went his way.

No space was available at the Grand

Hotel Misr, so our bed that night was the concrete apron of an air raid shelter. Since the air raid was over the port area and not over the town, the shelters were locked so we couldn't go inside. A three-corner Haig & Haig bottle for a pillow left a lasting impression on my skull. My blanket was the sky scene described before.

Morning found us thus. Some guy on the second floor of the apartment building across the street saw us while opening his shutters and invited us up for breakfast. Our host was a young Scotsman, Archibald Jock, engineer on a small tanker operating up and down the Red Sea. His wife had been evacuated to Cairo the day before, so he had the run of the house and was taking advantage of it. It turned out that he didn't have quite enough coffee for all, nor enough tea, so we mixed the leaves and grounds and brewed a beverage that none of us could drink. We had whiskey with our eggs and bacon.

We spent the morning with our new acquaintance. Later that afternoon, we opened up the cafe next door to the Hotel Grand Misr and emptied the ice chest with our drinks. This time the waiter brought a pan to the table to keep the ice in.

That night as we headed back to the ship, we found that she was over in Attica Bay, at anchor. In order to get there, we hitchhiked around the bay on army vehicles, but had to walk the last mile to the small boat jetty. It was midnight by this time, and another air raid was on. We watched a ship blown up at the anchorage area, but it went too high to have been ours since we had no ammo aboard.

We found a large motor launch at the pier, her Egyptian crew asleep all over her. None of the launch crews would take us out during the raid for any amount of money. Quite a few men were on the pier waiting for transportation to their various ships, so

we got together and got the ancient engines started and cast off the lines. We were well on our way to the anchorage when the crew decided we meant it and took over. They delivered us all to our respective ships, so all was well.

During the long evenings in port, our crew sat around the fantail swapping yarns. Al told about the army major who had been arrested by the MPs who caught him nude, chasing a girl down the corridor of the hotel. They charged him with "being out of uniform." At his hearing the next day, he beat the rap by proving he had been dressed in the uniform for the sport in which he was engaged.

One of the evening bull sessions brought up the story of the ordinary seaman who had been killed on a ship similar to ours as the ship was covering hatches at a port in India. The captain didn't want to delay the departure to fill out all the forms, so he had the kid's body stowed in the ship's refrigerator and carried it back to the States. One night, the oiler was oiling in the shaft alley and saw the kid's ghost asking for a cup of coffee. On several occasions on the way homeward, various other members of the crew also saw the ghost, who apparently rode with the body and left the ship with it.

We finally discharged the balance of our cargo and sailed for Durban, South Africa.

Two days after we sailed, while I was at the wheel one morning, I heard a commotion on deck. The third mate came in and took the wheel, saying, "Peter, it's your friend Morales. Go down and find out what the trouble is."

I went down to find Morales, our Puerto Rican oiler, on his knees at the rail praying over and over, "Mother Maria, they no send me there no more. I no go there no more!"

When I asked him what the problem was, he threw his arms around me and repeated his plea, adding, "Oh, Pedro, I am so frightened. I was back oiling the shaft alley and I was thinking of the story of the kid's ghost when I hear something . . . 'Psst, Joe. You got a cigarette?' I look around. Is nothing there. I oil some more. I hear again: 'Psst . . . Joe. You got a cigarette?' Then I see two heads by the deck plates . . . covered with oil but eyes open and looking at me . . . I come out very fast. I no go there no more."

Investigating, we found two stowaways, deserters from the British desert army hiding there. Unfortunately for them, they had picked poor Morales for their opening. Their happiness at being bound for Durban was short-lived, though, as a fireman had gotten sick and we had to stop a British troopship to put him under a doctor's care. The MAURITANIA was northbound for Suez.

After turning over the stowaways to the crew of the MAURITANIA, we proceeded on down the Red Sea, turning into the Gulf of Aden about ten that night. When I had gone on watch, the air temperature was about ninety-five degrees, but when we made the turn the temperature dropped to about seventy degrees. So we all bundled up for our next few watches until we got acclimated to the comparatively cool Indian Ocean breezes.

When we rounded Cape Guardafui and headed down Indian Ocean toward the Mozambique Channel, we again heard rumors of U-boats in the area and resumed our attentiveness during the hours we drifted repairing breakdowns.

When we arrived at Durban, the boilers had to be overhauled, so we lay ten days between that and getting our cargo of manganese ore.

Al was put on the twelve-to-four watch, so Don Stoker, the messman, and I teamed up for town touring. We spent our day off riding in rickshaws, lying on the beach, etc. The place seemed to be a nice resort community, and we relaxed in the sunshine.

When we sailed from Durban with a full load of manganese ore, the ship was down to her marks (fully loaded).

While rounding Cape of Good Hope, we ran into a storm with following winds. The large seas coming over the stern washed away the gratings on which we coiled our mooring lines. In doing so, the loose gratings cut off the tops of the air vents around the poopdeck. A door on the midship house was also torn off and managed to sever the hydraulic lines from the bridge to the steering engine. For the rest of the trip into Capetown, we steered with the steam valves in the steering engine room, standing in seaboots and oilskins in the hot steamy room, occasionally sidestepping the columns of sea water pouring down the vents.

All along the trip, I had been getting copies of the sights from the mates and working out the ship's navigation for myself on a pilot chart for practice. At the ship's union meetings, I had been typing the minutes and sending typed letters to my pen pals.

After repairs in Capetown, as we were headed north to Trinidad for bunkers, the captain asked me, "Where did you learn to type?"

I said, "In high school."

He said, "Call your watch partner to take over the wheel." Then he took me down to his cabin and set me to typing up manifests, letters of protests and other items of ship's business.

When we arrived in Trinidad, we started meeting outbound freighters with anti-sub guns mounted on their sterns. The ominous feeling of impending entry into the war in Europe was heavy.

Captain Stevens told me he was going to approach the company, American Export Lines, about signing me up as a cadet. However, since the Maritime Commission was setting up training schools, the private company cadet programs were discontinued.

The day before we rounded Cape Hatteras, about 11:00 a.m., the usual engine breakdown was signaled on the engine room telegraph. The third mate started out to the wing of the bridge to answer it, and damned near jumped over the wheelhouse when he spotted a submarine surfacing about 200 yards off our port beam. The date was November 5, 1941. No armament was on these ships then, and a submarine surfacing so near! Needless to say, the mate lost no time in sending me aft to raise a new American flag, just in case. By the time I got it up, the sub had hoisted an American flag too and steamed off on the surface. We got the engines going a few hours later and were relieved as we sailed into Baltimore.

News events for the months of 1941 we had been at sea included the landing of the passengers of the ZAM ZAM who had been prisoners on the German Raider ATLANTIS from the time of their capture on the way to Capetown.

Germany attacked her Axis partner, Russia, on June 22. This event alone changed the face of the war as far as the Isolationists and also the Communist front organizations in the United States, whose propaganda up until that event had been to keep the United States out of the war in Europe.

September 18: Several Italian transports were sunk by the Malta-based British submarine UP-HOLDER while they were en route to Benghazi. This delayed reinforcements to Rommel in North Africa.

September 23: The sinking of Russian naval units MARAT and KIROV at Leningrad by German air raids.

November 14: The HMS ARK ROYAL, pride of British Navy, was sunk in the Mediterranean by U-81.

SS West Jaffrey

Home Port: Portland, OR

Company: American Export Lines, Inc. New York, NY
Master: Earle S. Stevens
Gross Tons: 5663

Built: 1919 @ Portland, OR
Dimensions: 410' x 54' x 28'

The Freighter, SS WEST JAFFREY, was stranded and wrecked on Harriet Ledge off Halfbald Island, Nova Scotia (43-36 North/66-02 West) at 2350 EWT on February 8, 1942 while en route from Boston, Massachusetts to Halifax, Nova Scotia. She carried a crew of 38 men plus an Armed Guard of fourteen. There were no casualties. The ship was declared a total loss on February 13th. Photo courtesy of Mariners Museum, Newport News, VA.

Chapter 14

JOHN ERICSSON
November 1941 - April 1942

After leaving the WEST JAFFREY at Baltimore in early November, I made a trip out to San Francisco to visit my parents for Thanksgiving, hoping things would have changed at home.

As my bus traveled toward Denver, two girls, one with pepper-colored hair and the other with red, got on at Fort Collins, Colorado, to ride into Denver. I was seated with a young fellow in Marine Corps uniform, but we split up and joined these newcomers in the large rear seat and made efforts to become acquainted. The girls were on a weekend pass from their National Youth Administration program at Fort Collins.

Since the Marine was under travel orders, he had to proceed west. But I was in no hurry, so I changed my ticket and laid over to enjoy dinner with Fern Canham and Esther Palmer at Denver. I enrolled them in my growing list of pen pals before they saw me off on my bus to San Francisco.

After spending Thanksgiving at my parents' home, I felt our relationship hadn't improved. I painted the outside of their house, but even that didn't ease the tension.

On my way back to New York, I stopped at Davenport, Iowa, and was having lunch with my pen pal, Beverly, when we heard the radio report of the bombing of Pearl Harbor.

I returned to New York and sat for my Able Seaman's and Lifeboat certificates. I visited the British Apprentices Club and got to thinking about Kay, the girl I had met the previous year. On a hunch, I called Preston House, the residence hall where she had been staying. Mrs. Garrison, the house supervisor, gave me Kay's forwarding address at Fall River, Massachusetts. I sent Kay a Christmas card and was overjoyed to receive one in return.

On January 2, I met Al Rosse again, and together we threw in our cards for jobs as able seamen on the Swedish ship KUNGSHOLM, which had been taken over by the War Shipping Administration and renamed the JOHN ERICSSON. She was being converted to carry troops; as part of our duties, we stood on a staging in a snowstorm, wiping snow off with one hand and painting her once-white hull gray with a brush in the other.

The Swedes, before they left, had locked all the doors to the passenger quarters and thrown the keys into a barrel. The key tags and door identifications were marked in Swedish. We spent a couple of days wheeling

MS John Ericsson

the barrel down the passageways trying keys one by one to unlock all the doors.

The weekend of January 17, I took a Friday night train up to Fall River and spent Saturday and Sunday morning with Kay at her home. I met her family and some of her friends up there. It was a pleasant weekend, brightened by the likely promise of adding Kay's name to my list of pen pals. I returned to the ship Monday morning and was logged for missing work Saturday morning.

We sailed from the Brooklyn Army Base with troops of the 132nd Infantry and the Illinois National Guard. They had been on maneuvers in Louisiana when Pearl Harbor was bombed. They were brought from the warmth of the South to the snows of New York by troop train, and now were heading for another part of the world. At least our small convoy was headed south.

At the Panama Canal, we were again over the side touching up the hull where the gray paint had washed off, so I didn't get to look around the area.

On the trip toward Melbourne, Australia, the troops lined up in the passageways outside our crew messrooms for their own

chow line. I made friends with several of the MPs and, on the long night watches, shared sandwiches with some of them.

We arrived at Melbourne on March 7, 1942. We lay at a dock there for a few days, during which time I did more painting on the hull. My watch partner, Al Rosse, and I would draw our paint from the storekeeper and head for the area under the pier to paint the lower part of the sides. When our paint was gone, we would head up the beach under the pier for a couple of hours. Return for lunch. Draw another pot of paint for the afternoon and repeat the process.

I met a young lady at Melbourne whose father was a member of Parliament. He gave me a copy of the minutes of the Australian Parliament from December 8, 1941, to January 1942. It contained copies of the speeches in Parliament summarizing the events leading up to the Japanese expansion in the Southwest Pacific and copies of the telegrams sent to and from the various governments announcing the declaration of hostilities between the various countries on the Allied side and the German-Japan-Italy Axis powers.

In Melbourne one day, Al and I sat on

the verandah of a hotel cafe and watched the American troops march by. The band as it passed was playing "Elmer's Tune" and the GIs were whistling it as they marched. It was quite impressive. Following them was a troop of Aussies; their band was playing "Waltzing Matilda" and their cadence was in stride with the music.

When we sailed from Melbourne, it was for "somewhere in the South Pacific."

We arrived at Noumea, New Caledonia, on March 17. As an able seaman, I was put in charge of a lifeboat used to ferry the first American troops ashore. When I got to the dock, I went up to a drugstore and bought some picture postcards, then to the post office to buy stamps and have the cards postmarked before the Army shut the civilian post office down.

Since I had to wait for another boat back to the ship's anchorage, I walked around the town to look it over. I heard singing coming from one of the houses, and the words were in English, not French, so I knocked on the door. An Australian schoolteacher was living there with a French family. I was invited in and was introduced to the family of Lucien Baumier. After a bowl of potato soup and some conversation, I headed back to the ship.

After disembarking the troops and discharging the small cargo of guns and ammunition from the baggage holds into lifeboats to ferry ashore, the ERICSSON sailed from Noumea direct to San Francisco.

By April 1942, the ERICSSON was in need of some voyage repairs and would be in 'Frisco for a while, so I paid off with the rest of the crew.

Chapter 15

The Search for a License

Spring and Summer 1942

When I reached San Francisco in early April, I placed a long-distance call to Kay in Massachusetts. When the operator asked me for the overtime charges of twenty-three dollars and some cents, I figured it would be cheaper to take a bus back to New York than to call her again.

On the Trailways bus heading east, I stopped off in Denver, hoping to look up either Esther or "Pepper." I located Esther's aunt, who told me that Esther had gotten married and was somewhere in Kansas. Since I was on my way through that part of the country, she suggested I stop by and congratulate the couple. I thought it a good idea, and waited in Denver a week until she received a postcard with Esther's new address.

I took the next bus to St. Joseph, Missouri, stopping off at Troy, Kansas, to meet the newlyweds. The reception I got was not the welcome I had anticipated; the farmer Esther had married was not sociable with "city slickers."

The German U-boats had been busy along the Atlantic coast during the first few months since the U.S. entered the war, sinking more than 150 ships ranging from the mouth of the Mississippi River to Cape Cod.

I returned to New York and was reading the morning paper over a cup of cocoa at an Automat, when I found a write-up of the new Merchant Marine Officers school at New London, Connecticut. I compared my sea time with the listed requirements, and promptly went down to enroll. I was just over the minimum age and had just over the minimum sea time. I was accepted, and spent four months of the summer at New London.

The navigation courses and practice I had had previously gave me an advantage at the school. I concentrated my efforts on courses in such things as signaling, first aid, ship construction, cargo stowage, and so forth. I also did some tutoring on the navigation portion with some of my classmates.

During the summer months, the war at sea was getting extremely hot, not only along the Atlantic coast but also with convoys from Iceland to Russia being set upon by U-boats and air attacks from Norway as they passed between North Cape and the polar ice. Convoy PQ-17 between June 24 and July 7 was particularly hard hit when the British fleet was called home from escorting the convoy because of rumor that the German battleships TIRPITZ, ADMIRAL HIPPER, ADMIRAL SCHEER and LUTZOW had left their bases in Norway and were probably on the prowl. The result is that, between U-boats and

Visiting with Kay at Fall River, Massachusetts, summer 1942

air attacks, twenty-four ships out of a total of thirty-five were sunk between July 3 and July 9 from that convoy.

August 7: The Americans landed at Guadalcanal in the Solomon Islands.

August 9: A British commando force launched a raid at Dieppe, France, that was not too successful.

After graduating with the September class and receiving my Third Mate's license September 18, I was offered a position teaching navigation at the new Kings Point Merchant Marine Academy. If I took this, I would not get sea time on my new license toward raise of grades, and I had promised Beverly in one of our conversations that I would have my Master's license by the time I was twenty-four.

During these months, I debated long and hard with myself over which of the two young ladies, Beverly and Kay, I should cultivate as a prospective bride. They had similar personalities and were equally attractive to me. I so enjoyed Beverly's letters, but she was a thousand miles away and Kay was nearby.

I was able to spend every other weekend at Fall River with Kay. During these visits, I more and more felt that this girl would be someone with whom I would like spend my life if I were ever to come ashore and settle down. Of course, I had to convince her of this. Since I was still under twenty-one, I would have to get parental consent, which was, of course, not possible.

The North Atlantic didn't appeal to me with all the submarine activity going on at the time. Every day's papers brought news of more ships being sunk off the coast by the "wolf packs" that were uncontested for the year or so it took to build up our defensive navy.

I headed for San Francisco to find a West Coast ship. Even though some Japanese submarine were reported to be active in the South Pacific and Indian oceans, they were not so plentiful as the German fleet.

Conversations at the British Apprentices Club and the news of North Atlantic sinkings inspired these words:

WHITECAPS

Whitecaps scudding before the wind
    covered the surface of the sea.
The lumbering ships plunged on.
On the bridge of each a small light
    glowed from the compass repeater
    to silhouette the dark form
    of the man at the wheel.

On the wing of the bridge another man
   peered into the wind and darkness
   at the ship in the next column.
While silently uttering a prayer
   that the watch would soon end
   so he could get into the warmth of his
     cabin.

The stars seemed to wink at him,
   playing hide and seek
   in the clouds that scudded past.

Suddenly, as the ship rolled to port,
   an explosion and a flash of fire

came from the edge of the convoy.
The serenity of the night was gone!
The war had come to his cold,
   stormy section of the ocean.

The thousand miles the ship had traveled
   were not even traced on the surface of
     the sea.
   And now it was gone!
The young mate wondered at the fate
   of the crew as he conned his own ship
     through the frantic maneuvers
     of his place in the convoy.

Chapter 16

CAPE DECISION

September 1942 - February 1943

News items of the day — November 1942: General Eisenhower and American troops land in Algiers and Morocco.

November 19: American 32nd Division attacks Japanese at Buna, New Guinea.

November 23 to December 5: Australians take over Kokoda, New Guinea.

In September, when I left the school at New London, I rode the train to New York. I stood on the platform at the end of the coach, watching the passing scenery — a proud new ensign in the U.S. Maritime Service posed to show off the new gold stripe on my sleeve. A young boy came up to me as I stood there and asked in a plaintive voice, "Where is your cart, mister? Don't you have any more ice cream?"

I stopped off in Silvis, Illinois, and Davenport, Iowa, on my way to San Francisco. Upon reaching San Francisco, I made the rounds, my new Third Mate's ticket in hand, of the San Francisco dispatch halls of the Master's Mates and Pilots Union as well as the Maritime Service dispatch office to seek a berth in the Pacific. I figured it would be warmer sailing there, and there wouldn't be so many submarines as the North Atlantic held. The War Shipping Administration (WSA) recruiting and manning office in San Francisco bil-

leted me at the Sir Francis Drake Hotel.

One evening I was in the nightclub on the top floor and heard a commotion at the door. It turned out an air force officer wearing the gold leaves of a major wanted to enter with two gorgeous blonds. The maitre d' wouldn't let him in because he couldn't prove he was over twenty-one. The major's bluster while trying to impress his friends and show his "authority" came to naught. Many of us were secretly pleased at the outcome as he left.

The WSA sent me to the New Orleans office for assignment.

The train trip to New Orleans was uneventful. I arrived in that fair city on a Tuesday morning about nine o'clock. I checked in at the WSA office and got a room at the St. Charles Hotel. Then I set out to see the town and meet its people. It looked a bit different from this view than it had in 1938 when I had ridden in on a freight train and walked across the Huey Long bridge and down to the Louisville & Nashville railroad yards to hop a freight on eastward.

The next morning I was up at the Master's Mates and Pilots Union hall to register and look for a ship. I was dispatched to Beaumont, Texas, to join the MS CAPE DECISION as Third Mate. I met the second mate, Mr.

Murray (also from San Francisco), on the train. We went to the Pennsylvania shipyard together to find the ship. The ship was one of the new C-1 types being mass produced for the war effort by this shipyard as well as other yards around the nation. It was a brand new ship and, compared to the World War I rust-buckets we had sailed on in the past, a floating palace.

We started aboard the ship and were met at the gangway by an official-looking personage wearing the uniform of a Merchant Marine Cadet. He introduced himself as Harry Shafter, who, with his partner "Tiny," would be with us this trip. Mr. Murray and I were in civilian clothes. We didn't introduce ourselves but, when he told us the captain was not aboard just yet, we asked him to show us, a couple of landlubbers from the WSA office, around the new ship. He did.

The age-old way of indoctrinating a newcomer to a profession calls for a bit of "hazing" or other form of trickery. Mr. Shafter seemed to be a perfect foil, so we let him take us from the crow's nest to the bilges, answering all our questions from a little notebook he had compiled and adding new things we asked him about. Anyway, he was pretty well acquainted with the ship by the time we finished our inspection tour. Then he showed us to the captain's cabin and we met Captain H.E. Sorensen for the first time.

Captain Sorensen, when I told him this would be my first trip as Third Mate, said, "I hope you're not like all third mates and get married first thing now that you have your license."

Mr. Murray and I came around the ship from day to day, looking over this and that, and in a roundabout way getting this cadet, Shafter, and his partner, Tiny, to work cataloging charts and ship's stores while we supervised as "shore representatives." Conse-

Third Mate, MS Cape Decision, Beaumont, Texas, November 1942

quently, most of the ship's paperwork was in shape for us by the time the stevedores finished loading our cargo of rice and beans to sail for Puerto Rico. We casually mentioned to Cadet Shafter that we had heard rumors up in the office that they were having trouble filling the Third Mate's berth and, if he did good work, we would be in a position to recommend him for a waiver to fill that berth himself.

He took us at our word, and made every effort to work diligently at the tasks we found for him to do. When it came time to sail, he stepped aside for us to go down the gangplank, but we then introduced ourselves as the new second and third mates. He was silent for a few days.

Captain H.E. Sorensen

We sailed on to Guantanamo and San Juan, Puerto Rico. We started to discharge our cargo there, but at daybreak the next day, we were ordered to proceed around the east end of the island to Ponce, on the south coast.

As the morning watch went on, we sailed into the reef-filled waters east of Puerto Rico. At one point, the course headed directly for the next island east. The channel ran very close to the coast at that point. Cadet Shafter was watching from the side of the wheel platform, getting more and more worried as we approached within a mile of the land at fourteen knots. Finally, he came over and informed me of his belief that the pilot was trying to run the ship aground and suggested that I order the course altered.

I had been checking our position on the chart and thanked him for calling it to my attention, saying, "This is the place we go over the land on the wheels with which this ship is equipped. Please pay my respects to the engineer on watch and inform him that we will be using the wheels and make sure

he has sufficient air in the tires."

Mr. Shafter looked rather skeptical. I assured him that this was one of the experimental ships fitted with wheels to counter the submarine menace by traversing land where feasible and that he had better hurry about the errand.

It so happened that the first assistant engineer was at work on the compressed air lines to the ship's whistle at the time. When Shafter paid my respects to the chief and informed him of my desires, the chief sent word back: "The first is at work on the air lines, and the wheels will be ready any time they're needed."

By the time Mr. Shafter returned to the bridge, he was just in time to watch us change course around the buoy and head on down the next leg of the channel. In the water. Then, for some reason, he stopped speaking to me altogether for a few days.

We reached Ponce, and proceeded to discharge the balance of our cargo, then shifted down the coast to Guanica for a cargo of rum and sugar. We sailed out of the tropic warmth of Puerto Rico to arrive in New York Harbor on Christmas Day. Captain Sorensen went ashore from the anchorage to get docking orders. Cadet Shafter, meanwhile, was on the bridge looking through binoculars at his family's home in Bay Ridge, Brooklyn. He was overjoyed at the prospect of spending the holidays at home. The captain returned to the ship with orders to sail to Charleston, South Carolina, to discharge our cargo.

News for January 1943 included — January 3: Entire Buna area of New Guinea in Allied hands.

January 7: Japanese landed at Lae, New Guinea.

In North Africa, Americans were advancing eastward in Algeria.

Kay's Christmas letter had given me her address in Washington, D.C. So on New Year's weekend, I took the train up from Charleston and arrived in Washington during the aftermath of a blizzard. The ground was frozen and after the tropical climate of our recent trip, I was *cold*. I found Kay's address, and visited with her and her roommate, Lillian, for the weekend. It was too cold for much sightseeing, so we just stayed inside and chatted. I managed to catch a terrific cold and laryngitis to go with it; by the time I returned to the ship, I could not talk.

The next weekend, I visited a beach playland, inspiring the following:

THE GIRL

As I walked one day by the side of the bay
   Watching the ships go by
The flash of the gown of a red-haired girl
   Was a sight that caught my eye.
She was alone and I was alone
   And I heard her softly sigh.
I couldn't leave her alone like that;
   I'm not that kind of guy.

I walked up to her and I spoke with her
   In what I thought a winsome way,
She smiled, you see, and answered me,
   " 'Twould make a lovely day
If you'd share a bit of time with me."
   I hardly knew what to say.
We walked a bit and we talked a bit
   That day by the side of the bay.

We listened to the music of a carousel,
   We rode the dodge-'em cars
We spent some time in the "House of Fun"
   And took the sky-ride to the stars.
It was a kind of day that should never end
   For a lonely couple of kids.

It was long ago, but still I know
   I always hope we'd meet again.

When I walked this young lady home that night to her old, side-porch house in Charleston, she said, "I want you to come in and meet my daddy. He's the sheriff."

The CAPE DECISION stayed in Charleston after discharging her cargo, shifting to the army dock to load her outbound cargo. Captain Sorensen ordered a pair of long masts and larger sails for our two lifeboats, and I worked with Cadet Shafter going through the supplies in the boats. The other cadet worked with the second mate cataloging the new charts and updating them from the Notices to Mariners.

All the time we had been aboard the ship, the second mate and I tried to recall just where the Cape Decision for which the ship was named was, and couldn't.

We sailed on January 23 for Dakar, West Africa, with a cargo of drums of gasoline and various military supplies. The eight-to-twelve watch through the blue waters of the Gulf Stream was peaceful. We were still quite aware of the submarine dangers, though increased air cover had driven the wolf packs farther out into the Atlantic and down along the coasts of South America near Trinidad.

We traveled alone at fourteen knots. When Mr. Murray, the second mate, relieved me at midnight January 29, we were just about halfway across the Atlantic. I wrote up my log and, as I was leaving the chart-room, my eye caught the name "Cape Decision" on the radio direction finder chart of the West Coast posted on the bulkhead. I went back up on the top bridge to tell him about my find, and we spent a few minutes wondering what mystery we should now turn our attention to.

Our ship was torpedoed at five that morning, and we went off in separate lifeboats. I did not see Mr. Murray again until the middle of May half a world away.

The submarine (U-105) came alongside the lifeboat, and their skipper asked for our captain. I pretended I didn't see Captain Sorensen sitting in his bathrobe over an oar, and said he must be in the other boat. I saw one of the men on the conning tower counting us before the submarine left to go over to the other lifeboat.

A little while later, the submarine came back and said that the men in the other boat had said the captain was with us. I said, "No, I was under the impression he had gone to the other boat. He sent me off while he checked around the ship for other possible casualties."

The skipper asked me how many men in my crew. I stretched my answer a bit and said eighty-two. His reply was: "I am sorry you lost ten men, but this is the war. Your job is to sail the ships and my job is to stop you. I saw you first and sank you." He asked if any of us needed medical attention.

I then asked where the nearest land was, as this was my first trip as Third Mate, and I was new to these waters. He sent down for a chart and pointed out that by sailing southwest, we should encounter either Barbados or Trinidad with the favorable northeast tradewinds and the prevailing currents.

We waited a bit until they had scouted around in the debris then left, before putting up the new masts and sails. We used the original lifeboat sail for a balloon jib and set out for Barbados, navigating with the sextant and pocket watch the captain had, set to Greenwich time. With the fair winds, we were covering about 100 to 110 miles a day, and sailed the 953 miles in just under ten days, picking up a light on the island around midnight.

THE SUN

The warm trade winds scudded
The lifeboat
At a good clip
Across the empty tropic sea.
There was no shade for the forty men
Sitting uncomfortably as they had to do
Except for those fortunate few
Who sat in the shadow of the sail
On the hard wooden benches along the rail
And thwarts of the open boat.

The men used anything,
Handkerchiefs,
Undershirts,
Even torn cuffs from their trousers
To make covering
For their heads from the merciless rays
Of the burning sun.
But when the cool night came,
A shiver
Would wrack the bodies
Of the forcibly chilled men.
They would once again
Be looking forward to morn
And the rising
Of the warming sun.

We sailed around the south end of the island after daybreak and through the submarine nets of Bridgetown Harbor before the police launch picked us up and towed us to the dock.

Our arrival in Bridgetown, Barbados, in a lifeboat after sailing nearly a thousand miles was a welcome event for us, to say the least. Getting our "land legs" after ten days rolling around in a small boat wasn't easy. One reporter inferred that we were probably drunk because we seemed so unsteady on our feet.

We were taken to the police station for

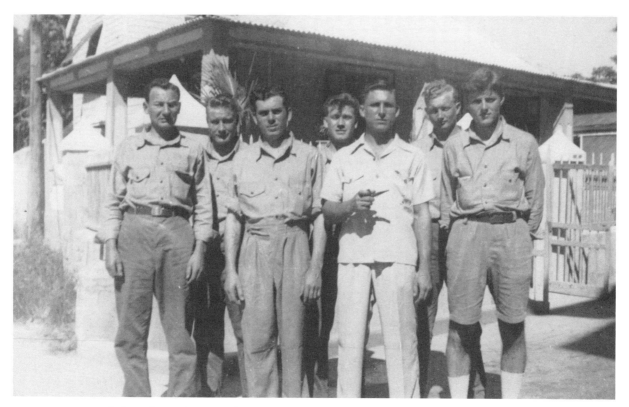

Armed Guard survivors, MS Cape Decision, Bridgetown, Barbados, February 1943

registering, each given a fifty-dollar draw so we could buy some clothes, then assigned to several of the resort hotels along the beach that lacked customers because of the war.

I was assigned to the Hotel Royal and given a room on the first floor on the ocean side. Trying to sleep with the roar of the breakers on the beach outside the door was interesting, as I dreamt I was still in the lifeboat. When I heard the waves approaching, I would automatically duck down to avoid getting wet. Then I would awaken to realize where I was, and go back to sleep to have the same dream.

The young lady at the desk, Madeline Bradshaw, seemed friendly enough and I got up my courage to ask her for a movie date. She wouldn't say yes unless her mother approved, so I borrowed a bicycle and biked home with her to meet her mother. Mrs. Bradshaw welcomed me and took me under

her wing, drove me around the island, and threw a party for me for my twenty-first birthday. Madeline and I never did make that movie.

I stayed in Bridgetown about ten days, while the forty members of the crew and gun crew were flown to Trinidad a few at a time for repatriation to the States. When it came time for me to leave, I did so reluctantly.

At Trinidad, I checked in at the War Shipping Administration office for a letter of identification and stayed there another three days awaiting transportation back to Miami. Flying the thousand miles to Miami in a few hours seemed to take away the feeling of accomplishment of the ten days in the lifeboat to cover the same distance.

Catching up on the news — January 28, 1943: The Japanese attacked the Australians from Lae, New Guinea, but were driven back on January 30.

CAPE DECISION lifeboat, 1943

Twelve U.S. flag ships had been sunk in the North Atlantic, including the CAPE DECISION, during January, and another nineteen in February, including the troopship HENRY R. MALLORY with heavy loss of life.

When I landed in Miami I read the headlines of the paper: "Admiral Raeder Has Ordered: No Survivors." The accompanying news item outlined his orders to the U-boat fleet to leave no survivors from the ships they sank. The thought passed through my mind of how the U-boat skipper who had sunk our ship would react to that order. I assumed from the few words I'd had with him that he would not appreciate it, as he had a seaman's feeling for his fellow seamen.

I took the train over to Mobile to Waterman Steamship Company's office to get paid off. Captain Sorensen told me that if I went back to San Francisco, I could join the CAPE SAN MARTIN, which was outfitting there for Waterman.

I didn't commit myself, but went over to

New Orleans to check in with War Shipping Administration to get copies of my license and seamen's papers.

A letter I received from Esther told me she had been abandoned by her husband and was in a Denver hospital to have a baby.

While at New Orleans, I had called up Kay, who was in Washington, D.C., working at the Pentagon. Apparently, she had read the same headlines and also an article about a ship (the HENRY R. MALLORY) having been sunk and fifty percent of the crew and troops lost because of the cold waters. She thought it might have been my ship. Anyway, she seemed happy to hear from me and, as soon as we got off the phone, she was on her way to Mobile to meet me.

I had been assigned by WSA to the liberty ship GEORGE CHAMBERLIN, which was being operated by Luckenbach Steamship Company. She was laying at the state docks at Mobile. I took the night train over to meet the ship. I must have gotten on a milk train, for it seemed we stopped at every farm along the way and didn't arrive at Mobile until nine in the morning. I reported to the ship and found it wasn't to sail for a couple of days, but I was so tired and nervous that I told the captain I couldn't sail with him. I really felt the need of a rest.

He understood and called for a replacement for me. Before going to the depot to meet Kay, I stopped by the Waterman Steamship Company office for some last-minute adjustments to the pay due me. I told Captain Sorensen that Kay was on her way down so we could be married. He said, "You're just like all the rest of the third mates. I warned you that license would change your life."

I went down to the depot and met Kay getting off the train. I had purchased tickets to New Orleans and took her right back aboard the same train. We arrived in New Orleans late that night and checked into the New Orleans Hotel.

The next day we set about to find out how to get married in a strange city. We went to the Officer's Service Bureau at the St. Charles Hotel.

The charming ladies there, Mrs. Aldige and Mrs. Scranton were helpful. The day being Mardi Gras, though there was no celebration during the war, all the city offices were closed. They sent us over to Gretna, across the Mississippi River, to get a license, and one of them recommended a Lutheran minister she had met at a party the previous week, a Dr. Kramer.

After we had gotten the license, I called Dr. Kramer and, after outlining our situation, was invited to his church at 7:30 that evening, with the added instruction to bring two witnesses. I asked Mrs. Scranton and Mrs. Aldige if they could recommend someone, or if they themselves would be witnesses for us. They were pleased to oblige, so we told them the name of the church and the time.

We went shopping for a new hat for Kay, and returned to the hotel to find a phone call from Mrs. Scranton awaiting us. When we returned it, she invited us to come to her home for the ceremony, and it was there we were wed.

MS Cape Decision

Home Port: Beaumont, TX

Company: Waterman Steamship Corp, Mobile, AL
Master: Holger Emile Sorenson
Gross Tons: 5635

Built: 1942 @ Beaumont, TX
Dimensions: 393' x 60' x 25'

The Freighter, MS CAPE DECISION, was torpedoed at 0447 EWT on January 27, 1943 by the German submarine U-105 (Nissen) in mid-Atlantic (23-00 North/47-29 West) while en route from Charleston, South Carolina to Freetown, Sierra Leone with a cargo of war supplies including a deck cargo of 2 planes and 2 landing barges. She was sailing independently. Her complement was 42 merchant crew and 22 Navy Gun Crew plus 3 U.S. Army passengers. There were no casualties. Photo courtesy of John Lockhead.

At 0516 EWT, the ship was struck by two torpedoes on the port side between #4 and #5 holds, opening a hole in #5 hold, and starting fires in the after magazine. About ten minutes later a third torpedo hit on the starboard side in the engine room. The ship took an immediate list to port and sank by the stern at 0601 EWT on January 27, 1943.

The crew abandoned ship on the Captain's orders after the first attack. Both lifeboats were safely launched and several rafts were cut loose. Two Navy men stationed at the after gun were the last to leave. They were forced to jump overboard and were in danger of being caught in the suction near the stern of the ship. The Master dived overboard from his lifeboat and brought the exhausted men safely to his lifeboat. Number 2 boat with the Master and 40 others (22 crew, 3 U.S. Army personnel, and 16 Navy Gun Crew) landed at Bridgetown, Barbados February 5, 1943 having

traveled 957 miles. The Captain hove to 2 miles off Ragged Pt. Lighthouse and about 0430 when daylight broke, sailed the boat to the mouth of the harbor. The other boat in charge of the Chief Mate with 35 survivors landed at St. Barthelmy on February 9, 1943. The men in this boat were very grateful to the natives on St. Barthelmy for the food and medicine they provided.

After the ship sank, the sub surfaced and the survivors were questioned. Two crew members (Third Assistant Engineer and an A.B.) were taken aboard the sub. The Third Assistant Engineer held an unlimited Chief Engineer's license and this was taken away from him. The A.B.'s papers were also taken, but were later returned to him. The two men were later allowed to return to the lifeboat.

U-105 (Nissen) was bombed and sunk June 2, 1943 off Dakar, French West Africa. There were no survivors.

Chapter 17

ISLAND MAIL
March 1943 - July 1944

News events — North Africa: The February battles at Kasserine Pass that pitted General Patton against Erwin Rommel's forces had been fierce. Getting through opened the way for an assault on Tunis in early May.

In the South Pacific, the Japanese landed at Salamau, New Guinea in March.

After our marriage, Kay and I visited her home in Fall River, Massachusetts, before taking the train out to San Francisco. On the westbound trip, we stopped at Silvis, Illinois, to introduce Kay to the Engholms, and at Denver where we became godparents to Esther's baby.

When I brought Kay over to Albany to introduce her to my parents, the reception we got was rather cool. We found a hotel room in 'Frisco to stay in until I shipped out.

In April 1943, I went to the Master's Mates and Pilots office in San Francisco to see about shipping out again. When I had left Captain Sorensen at Waterman Steamship Company's office in Mobile, he told me I could join the CAPE SAN MARTIN, which would be leaving from San Francisco in late April, if I wished. I had my doubts about wanting to make a career with Waterman, as they were based in Mobile.

I was sent over to War Shipping Admin-istrations office and was offered a Junior Third Mate's berth on the MS ISLAND MAIL with American Mail Lines, a West Coast company. I took it.

I went up to the offices of Williams, Dimond & Company and was introduced to my new captain, Dick Williamson, before heading down to the ship. The ISLAND MAIL was a diesel-powered Sun Shipyard C-2 type, sister ship to the CHINA MAIL and OCEAN MAIL, and was to be a nucleus of the North Pacific peacetime trade of American Mail Lines. The war had changed their plans somewhat. The OCEAN MAIL went to the British on a lend-lease deal, and the two remaining C-2s joined a fleet of C-1s and Liberty ships being operated under an agency agreement with the War Shipping Administration.

The ISLAND MAIL was converted to carry about 1,500 troops in the 'tween decks, and cargo in the lower holds and had refriger-ated spaces at Number Four hatch.

I had brought Kay to San Francisco, and she was left to find a house or apartment when I sailed. I was happy to get her letter that she had located a rental at San Mateo.

The ISLAND MAIL's first stop was Suva, Fiji Islands, to discharge some army cargo. Willie Maul, the second mate, and I went to

MS ISLAND MAIL after post-war reconversion, 1947

the local hotel for a swim in an outdoor pool during a rain squall. We figured we would be wet anyway before we got back to the ship, so we might as well do it in style.

From Suva, we went around the west coast of the island to Latoka to discharge more supplies for the army hospital there. I walked about two miles up to a hotel to find some magazines for the ship. As I was passing the bar in the hotel a voice called out, "Hey, Pete, what are you doing here?"

I didn't recognize either the soldier or the voice, until he said, "You were on the KUNGSHOLM a year or so ago. We were the MPs on the ship and you used to give us sandwiches from your messroom while we were on guard duty."

Then he turned to his compatriots and re-introduced me. They were in Fiji on R&R after the Guadalcanal campaigns. They each

had to buy me a drink and wouldn't let me get by with just a sip. I wound up with thirteen triple gins lined up on the bar. I did drink them. Then I walked across the road and climbed into the back of an MP jeep.

After a few minutes, an MP came out and asked me what I wanted. I said, "I have to get back to my ship, and I'll never make it under my own power. Can you please take me back to the pier?"

"Sure, Pete," was the welcome response, and he drove me back to the ship. Since we didn't have a gangway down, I had to climb up a rope "save-all" net to the deck at Number Three hatch. Fortunately, we had a spaghetti and tomato dinner being served to help me digest the gin. I will never forget that climb, nor those friendly soldiers. I know if I'd had to walk back to the ship that day I'd still be in a sugar cane field somewhere.

Second Mate, MS Island Mail, *spring 1944*

We then sailed to Noumea, New Caledonia, where I visited again with Lucien Baumier and his family, whom I had met while there on the John Ericsson. I also went aboard the Cape San Martin, which was at the ore dock to visit with Mr. Murray, who had been second mate with me on the Cape Decision. I hadn't seen him since that midnight in January on the bridge of the ship in the middle of the Atlantic.

Mr. Murray told me of his experiences with the chief mate, Cadet Shafter and the others who had sailed the other lifeboat west to Ile Saint-Barthelemy where they landed after fourteen days. There, they had lived in an abandoned schoolhouse and found the only other inhabitants to be a herd of wild goats. They were spotted and returned to the States after spending a week or so on the island eating wild goat meat along with their lifeboat rations.

The Island Mail returned to San Francisco in time for Kay's birthday in June. She had made a trip home to Massachusetts and hadn't returned yet. After I received her letter that she was en route, I met her train ferry the next day.

We had a few days to catch up with each other before I sailed for Port Hueneme with Captain John Smith, who had relieved Captain Williamson. On the way down, I got a bad toothache and, when Kay met me there, it was to take me to a dentist to get an abscessed tooth pulled. Then we went to the beach so Kay could get her first swim in the Pacific.

We sailed with a bunch of navy CASUs (Casual Replacements for men killed or wounded at sea) for the South Pacific. When we crossed the Equator, we had the usual ceremonies. An announcement over the public address system said, "We will be passing a mail buoy at eight p.m. Letters can be mailed from there." Six sacks of mail were collected and, of course, put into storage.

A day or two later, one of the CASUs asked me about that mail, since he couldn't remember us stopping. I reminded him of the destroyer we had sighted near the horizon the previous evening and told him that was the mail boat, and that we had signaled them the position of the mail buoy we had dropped, assuring him that his mail was safely on its way. He said he was happy to know so much was being done for them.

This was the same young fellow I told about burning sea water for fuel when he asked me why he never saw any smoke coming out of the ship's smokestack. I showed him the overboard discharge water coming out of the side of the ship and told him that we processed sea water and took out some of the chemicals, which were burned, and what he saw was what we couldn't use. A few days later, he told me his chief thought I was not giving him the straight dope.

On our approach to Noumea the night before arrival, we had passed a C-1 and her escort shortly before sunset. Our course indicated that about 7:30 we were to make a ninety-degree right turn to the north, which would have taken us across the path of the ship we had just passed. The night was pitch black by then, so I told the Armed Guard officer that I was going to sound the ship's whistle when I made the turn.

He told me that if I did, I'd have all 1,500 troops on deck in alarm. I told him to alert his lookouts astern to keep a very good eye out for the other ship for me as well as their usual submarine alert.

Shortly after I changed course, we saw two star shells in the area to our starboard. Then a glare of searchlight flashed on and off. The radio shack messenger brought up a message: "AM UNDERGOING ATTACK BY SURFACED SUBMARINE. LAT 22-57S, LONG 166-26E. SEA WITCH."

Of course, we sounded General Quarters and I had all the troops on deck anyway. We watched various tracer bullets and flashes of gunfire for about three hours. Then over the horizon the beam of a signal searchlight blinked out: "ALL OK. ALL OK."

When we had anchored and I was riding ashore in the water-taxi, we stopped alongside the SEA WITCH to pick up one of her mates to take ashore. I asked him, "What went on last night?"

What we put together was that the SEA WITCH had come to the South Pacific from San Francisco under army orders, and somebody had neglected to let the Navy know she was coming. The escort for the C-1 that I had

passed had challenged this strange ship but the recognition codes had not been updated. She had fired a star shell to illuminate the ship; at the same time, the SEA WITCH had fired a star shell to light up the low silhouetted vessel that was approaching. The result was they apparently blinded each other.

The escort fired a shot across the SEA WITCH's bow, which went over the heads of the forward gun crew. They in turn fired a round from their three-inch gun, which went between the stacks of the escort. When the escort turned on her searchlight, the gun crew on the SEA WITCH shot it out with their twenty millimeters. Fortunately, no one was hurt in all this, but when it was finally sorted out it gave everyone a sense of relief.

About two weeks later a Japanese submarine was sunk in the area.

We anchored in Noumea for a few days awaiting orders. While ashore, I learned that a group of navy nurses had come in on one of the other ships from Oak Knoll hospital in Oakland. I wondered if Bea Hankin, the nurse I had met in Oakland before I went to New Orleans last fall when she was on her way to get her graduation certificate as a nurse and later joined the Navy, would be among them. She wasn't. She had been assigned to the dispensary at Boulder, Colorado.

Her letter told of her disappointment, since she had joined the Navy to see other parts of the world, and I had painted such a beautiful word picture of the tropics in my short conversations with her.

Later in the day, I was walking up toward Lucien Baumier's house, my mind going over the events of the fourteen months since my last visit. The new Lieutenant's bars I was wearing, New Orleans, and my marriage to Kay, when I heard a voice bellow, "Hey, you!"

I turned to be confronted by a blustering army major. "Why didn't you salute me when you passed?"

"I didn't see you, sir," I responded.

"That's no excuse. Don't you know you are supposed to salute your superior officers?"

"Why yes, sir. Anytime I meet one I consider superior, I do salute him. How do you qualify?"

"I want your name, rank and serial number and what ship you are stationed on."

"James Patrick Royal, sir. Number 323235569, and I am stationed on the EDGAR ALLAN POE." (This was a Liberty ship with a great torpedo hole in her side that was being used as a supply ship at the pier.)

When I went aboard my ship, I mentioned the incident to the Navy Armed Guard officer. He showed me a directive from the Port Director's office that stated: "The Armed Guard officers on merchant ships may have shore leave, but not liberty unless they take two men from their crew as shore patrol with them and turn in to the Port Director's office the names of ten enlisted men who fail to salute him." He said he wouldn't even go ashore under those conditions. I hadn't known the Merchant Marine rated so highly.

When I visited with Lucien, he drove me up to visit the nickel mine where his office was as well as other places of interest on the Island. Later that afternoon when I returned to my ship, as I came up the gangway, a navy chief asked me, "Is your name Chelemedos?"

"Yes, Chief, it is," I answered.

"Do you have a brother in the navy named Fred?"

"Unfortunately, yes," I said.

"Well, he and I were on the COUGHLAN together and when the ship was being repaired, the new orders came up. Fred and I flipped for them, and Fred is now at Bremerton to take out a new baby flat-top. And I am herding this bunch of CASUs to the Russell Islands north of Guadalcanal."

By the flip of a coin, I missed the opportunity to know I had dropped off my brother on some faraway island in the South Pacific.

After we left off the navy people and their equipment at Russell Island, we sailed to Efate in the Hebrides for orders.

We anchored in Efate Harbor on Monday morning and promptly blinked a message to the Port Captain identifying our ship and the fact that we were in for orders.

Tuesday morning the Port Captain's message queried, "What ship? Why are you here?"

Our reply: "ISLAND MAIL, awaiting orders."

Wednesday morning: "What ship? Why are you here?"

Our reply: "ISLAND MAIL, awaiting orders, same as Monday and Tuesday."

That afternoon their message read: "Am sending fifty sacks of mail for your next destination. Can you spare any potatoes?"

Our reply: "Affirmative."

Soon an LCM (landing craft medium) came alongside with the fifty sacks of mail marked for San Francisco, but no orders. We gave them some potatoes and waited.

Thursday morning: "What ship? Why are you here?"

Our reply: "ISLAND MAIL, awaiting orders. We have received mail for next destination but no orders. Please follow up."

Later that afternoon, an LCM came alongside and we were handed orders that read: "Proceed to Pearl Harbor at your utmost speed." We hove anchor and pushed the ship up to seventeen knots to Pearl Harbor.

Arriving there, we were boarded by a pilot who took us to the dock. As I lowered the gangway, a navy lieutenant came aboard and asked, "How much cargo do you have and where is it stowed?"

I answered, "No cargo. We have fifty sacks of mail for San Francisco, but no cargo."

He raised his hand to his forehead and said, "Jesus Christ, who done that?" and went ashore again. Soon another pilot came aboard and we shifted ship out to the "X-ray" berths, buoys on the Pearl City side of the harbor. When we were tied up, the pilot asked, "Where's Pearl City from here?"

I pointed it out and asked why he as a pilot on the harbor didn't know where Pearl City was. He replied, "I just flew in from Halifax this morning. This is the first time I've been here."

We lay out there for thirty days awaiting orders. I used the time to sit before the Steamboat Inspectors to get my Second Mate's license.

The ISLAND MAIL was finally shifted to a berth and loaded equipment and troops for the Makin Island invasion (November 11-24).

News from the European theater was mostly about the landings at Anzio beachhead in Italy.

When we returned from Makin Island, we discharged our retrograde cargo in Honolulu and loaded 1,800 cases of pineapple for San Francisco arriving there on Thursday, December 16.

I went down to 643 Birch Street, San Mateo, to spend some time with a very expectant Kay. We sat up late that night talking about things in general and about her troubles with the landlady. The landlady had decided she could get around the rent control ceiling and raise the rent if Kay would move out and she could move in for a while. But Kay didn't want to move from such a quiet neighborhood, at least until I returned and the baby was born.

That Saturday night, I took Kay over to the hospital and went back to the ship in Oakland. I called the hospital later to find that we now had a son. When I went to meet the new captain, E. J. Stull, I was told that I was now Second Mate. When I told him of the baby, he sent me home for the day.

On Tuesday night, when the ISLAND MAIL sailed for Pearl Harbor, we carried a deck crew of Greek seamen whose ship was in the shipyard awaiting parts for her engine. Captain Stull was pacing back and forth on the top bridge, and I asked him why he was so nervous.

"This crew," he replied, "they're all Greeks."

"So what?" I said, "they're all seamen."

"Yes," he said, "but suppose something happens. How are you going to tell them what to do?"

Just then, the navy telephone talker came over and reported that the door to the radio shack was open and a light showing. Captain Stull said, "How are you going to shut that door?"

"That's easy," I said, turning to call to the lookout on the wing of the bridge. "Say, Alephoritis, epXomai etho." When he came over and saluted, I said, "Clise ta borta on casa rathio."

"Okay," he said and went off.

Captain Stull said, "Why, Mr. Chelemedos, I didn't know you could understand Greek."

I said, "I can't."

"But didn't you just speak to him in Greek?" he asked.

"Yes, sir, but he understands the stuff," I replied.

He said, "I'm not going to worry about you," and he walked off the bridge.

I didn't have the heart to tell him that the only Greek I knew was "come here" and "clise ta borta" and had made up the rest of the sentence in what Spanish I could remember.

When Alephoritis came back, I asked him to teach me to give course changes in Greek.

I learned later that Captain Stull's previous trip was on the Liberty ship SAMUEL PARKER, which, following air raids and strafing attacks in Tripoli and shuttle runs between Alexandria and the beachheads of Italy, was pretty well scarred up. While at the Sicily beachhead, the ship again came under attack and, by the time she sailed back to the States, she had so many shell holes in her that she was scrapped rather than repaired. No wonder he was nervous!

We participated in the invasion of Kwajalien Island (February 1-7). On board we carried a unit of Seabees who were to handle the cargo. Troop commander this trip was a naval reserve lieutenant, Paul V. Petty, who decided that he, as senior naval officer on board, he would take charge of the cargo operations.

Anyway, when the ship was approaching the entrance to the reefs, we were using untranslated Japanese charts and aerial photographs of the reefs to navigate by.

On entering the reefs we were to make a sharp turn to starboard. I heard the Lieutenant Petty tell his petty officer, "As soon as we entered the reefs, I want the 'M' boat [which was stowed 'thwart ships on Number Three hatch] hoisted up from its cradle and swung over the side so it will hit the water at the same time as the anchor is dropped."

I tried to point out, "Since the 'M' boat is to be picked up by the ship's jumbo boom and hang on a single hook with nothing to steady it, that's not a good idea. It should be left in its cradle until we are anchored."

Of course, the Merchant Marine isn't supposed to tell the United States Navy what to do, so as soon as we entered the reef he gave the signal to hoist. When the thirty-five-ton "M" boat was about three feet above its cradle, we made our course change and the ship took a roll to starboard in the cross wake. The boat on the end of the falls started to swing and knocked askew the troop head on one wing of the hatch and the troop shower on the other wing. I respectfully asked the lieutenant, "Is this procedure what the Navy refers to as a 'clean sweep'?"

After the troops were put off in the landing craft, we began discharging cargo from the lower holds. Petty's method of cargo handling was by use of the ship's public address system: "Now hear this, gang from Number Three hatch prepare to load 'M' boat alongside" etc. The P.A. system suddenly ceased to function. The lieutenant came up to Number One hatch and saw that his men were discharging ninety-pound sacks of cement on a cargo board to the landing craft alongside with the long slings that had been used to discharge the landing craft. He asked the petty officer, "How many sacks are you putting on each cargo board?"

"Twenty sacks, sir."

"There's lots of room in those slings and we must speed up this operation. Put forty sacks on the boards."

"Forty sacks??? But sir —"

"Forty sacks, that's what I said."

The petty officer called down to the holdmen, "The lieutenant wants forty sacks on the next board."

"Forty sacks???"

"That's what the lieutenant said."

The men put forty sacks on the next board, then all climbed out of the hatch. The lieutenant asked, "Here, where are these men going?"

"It's lunchtime, sir. Besides, that is all we will be doing here for a while."

85

When all the men were clear, he gave the signal to the winchman and the pallet was hoisted up out of the hold to just about deck level when the pallet broke and all forty sacks dropped the fifty feet or so to the lower hold and broke, sending a cloud of cement dust up through the troop quarters in the lower 'tween deck and the ship's hospital area in the upper 'tween deck. The petty officer turned to the lieutenant, saluted and said, "Forty sacks, sir."

When we sailed, I noticed fire hoses being led down the troop companionway into Number One hold. I called the engine room and told the engineer not to put water on deck until I called him. Sure enough, the lieutenant intended to have his men wash down the cement in the hold. When I explained that this would be a sure way to have us go into the shipyard when we returned to Pearl Harbor to get our bilge lines unplugged, he changed his mind.

While en route back to Pearl Harbor, we received the news of the sinking of the aircraft carrier USS Liscombe Bay *and the torpedoing of the USS* Lexington *and USS* Independence *in a sea battle west of the Marshall Islands, as well as the massive American raid on the Japanese Naval base at Truk.*

When we returned to Pearl Harbor in early February, I went up to Honolulu to find a valentine to send to Kay. I looked over the selection carefully before picking out a cartoon booklet type I figured would appeal to her, signed it and mailed it off.

When I returned to the ship and received my own mail from her, I found the valentine she had sent, which contained the same set of cartoon characters as mine and the same sentiments. Talk about two minds being on the same track.

Our return to Pearl Harbor also brought us another short run to San Francisco with a load of pineapple. While loading at Honolulu, I watched the longshoremen load pallets of canned pineapple onto a four-wheeled cart in the hold and pull it back into the "wings" to unload it and stack the cases. I asked the stevedore superintendent why he didn't put a forklift truck into the hatch to carry the pallets into the wings. He tried it, but they didn't have any lift trucks with a short enough mast to get under the "coaming" around the edge of the square of the hatch. In later years, they came out with shorter masts on the lift trucks and many were used for this purpose. I only regret I didn't know I could have gotten a patent on this idea.

While at San Francisco one day in early March, I thought to give Kay a day off on her own. I took the three-month-old baby, Peter Steven, down to the ship with me.

I had Steven on my bunk, blocked in with pillows and was sitting in the chief mate's office next door when one of the shore-gang sweepers walked through the passageway. His partner followed him and happened to glance through the open door into my room to see the baby peeking over the pillows taking in his surroundings. I heard him call out to his partner, "Hey, Joe. There's a baby on this here ship!"

"Nah, there ain't. You're trying to con me."

"But there is. I seen him myself."

"Nah. I ain't biting. You handing me a line."

After this went back and forth for a bit, the first one finally came back to see for himself.

Captain Stull heard this conversation and came back to see what was going on. I took the baby over to the captain's office. While the captain was holding the baby up, standing on his desk, he turned to me and said, "He's certainly built like the proverbial brick

Duplicate valentines, February 1944

outhouse, isn't he."

Just at that moment, the baby christened the captain's desk with a fountain that wouldn't shut off. I grabbed a towel and started to blot it up, apologizing, of course. Captain Stull said, "Don't worry about it. He's just like my grandchildren."

That evening, when I boarded the streetcar for home with the baby, a woman said, "I thought I saw you bringing that baby off the pier. What is he doing there?"

"Oh, he's our ship's mascot," I replied. "We're raising him aboard ship."

She seemed to have trouble believing this. I pointed out the suntan he had acquired on our recent trip to the West Pacific (Kay says he would kick his blankets off and enjoy the sun at their outings in Golden Gate Park), and added we were just going to see some of

the waterfront places of the port. When I got off to transfer to the McAllister Street line, she was still shaking her head and muttering: "I don't believe it. That little baby. . . ."

We returned to Pearl Harbor and reloaded for another invasion. I heard Lieutenant Petty had been promoted to lieutenant commander and was on one of the other vessels in our convoy.

While en route to a new destination, our attention focused on the radioed news reports of the Allied landings at Normandy, which everyone followed with much interest.

One morning I came on watch at four o'clock. I expected, at daybreak, to see only the six ships that were in our convoy group when we were the last ships to leave Pearl Harbor. Imagine my astonishment when I went out on the wing of the bridge to get my early morning star sights to look out at ships covering the sea from horizon to horizon. I counted more than 750 ships that I could see.

I asked our convoy commodore about them, for I hadn't seen that many ships at Pearl Harbor. He showed me a book, each page of which was the itinerary of a single ship for the past six months or so, tracing them from ports in Alaska, along the West Coast of the United States, down the coasts of South America and to islands of the South Pacific, each one spinning a strand of a giant spider web across the Pacific to center in on this morning's rendezvous for the assault on Saipan Island.

We arrived at anchorage south of the sugar mill that was the landmark on the west coast of Saipan. Our assigned anchorage was south of the MOUNT WHITNEY, the communication vessel for the invasion. Early the next morning, the guns on Tinian Island opened fire on the airfield near us, and the trajectory of the shells appeared to be coming right over our ship. After watching a few of these go over, we picked up the anchor and steamed around to the other side of the MOUNT WHITNEY and dropped the anchor.

Only this time we missed the bottom.

It seemed the shelf of the island dropped off sharply from less than 100 fathoms to possibly more than 1,000 fathoms. The result was that all of the eight shots of chain ran out before the anchor stopped dropping. Fortunately the chain was shackled in and the pad eye held. Anyway, it took the combined pulling of the Number One cargo winches to assist the anchor windlass in pulling up the chain. While we were working at this, we were drifting seaward, but finally managed to get to a more secure anchorage.

All the time we were there we were on alert for a foray threatened by the Japanese fleet. We did have some alerts for submarines in the area, and later learned that admirals Turner and Halsey had headed off the main Japanese fleet near Surigao Straits in what came to be known as the Battle of the Philippine Sea.

We returned to Pearl Harbor and then on to San Francisco, arriving in time for Kay's birthday in late June.

After I paid off the ISLAND MAIL, I attended the July class at the Maritime Service upgrading school in San Francisco, then sat for my Chief Mate's license.

Chapter 18

JOHN A. JOHNSON

July - October 1944

The news of summer 1944 included the landings in Southern France in August.

In the Pacific, the landing at Guam in July; the meetings of MacArthur, Nimitz and Roosevelt at Hawaii; and the American/ANZAC landing at Sansapoor, New Guinea.

The news gave much play to MacArthur's return to the Philippines. On September 12, MacArthur's troops landed on Mindanao and on September 13 on Leyte. The landings at Peleliu, Palau Islands, by the Marines were hardly mentioned.

The two months I spent with Kay while I sat for my Chief Mate's license went rapidly. When I was assigned to the Liberty ship SS JOHN A. JOHNSON, Kay went home to Massachusetts for a visit.

Since we had rented a flat out on Golden Gate Avenue and had had to buy the furniture from the previous tenant and were paying only $27.50 a month, I didn't want to let it go. But I couldn't think of what I could do with the foodstuffs we had.

When I joined the ship, Captain Beekin left for a visit to his home in Tacoma, Washington. I told him I would be around the ship most of the time, as I didn't know many people in the area.

One night I was walking up Market Street thinking about how I was to dispose of or use up the food at home when I overheard two WAVES walking ahead of me contemplating where they were to have dinner, as the food at the barracks wasn't worth the hike back, and the restaurants were too high-priced for them. I introduced myself and asked if they would like to cook their own dinner for a change. They looked me up and down and asked how come. I explained my problem and told them they would be welcome to come by and help me finish it up. They said, "That sounds swell. Can we bring our roommates along?"

I said, "Of course." They didn't tell me they lived in a dormitory. Thirty-two of them were with us on the streetcar as we all trooped to my apartment.

They came back each evening in groups of ten or so for the three weeks until I sailed.

I spent my time between the ship and the American Mail Lines Port Captain's office arranging to get new mooring lines and stores for the ship. Because of shortages, I could only get two mooring lines from the Maritime Commission. Because we were getting army cargo, I got two more from the Army. Because we were going to load at Port Chicago ammunition dock, I scrounged two from the Coast Guard. And because we were topping off our deck load at the naval supply depot, I got two more from the Navy. It was interesting and all that, but a lot of trouble. I think the Port Captain was happy to see us sail.

Among the new crew joining the ship was a young chap who was signing on as Ship's Carpenter. I looked at his toolbox and welcomed him to his first trip to sea. He asked me how I could tell by looking at his toolbox that it was his first trip. I asked him how he planned to use the spirit level he had in his toolbox.

When we were sailing from the naval supply depot in Oakland, I was standing by on the bow when the bo'sun called my attention to the pier. A contingent of WAVES was marching in formation toward the ship; when the women got abreast of the bow, they all turned toward me, waved and shouted "Good-bye, Peter." Then, saluting, they turned and marched as a unit back toward the office building.

Just then the phone from the bridge rang and the captain said, "Mr. Chelemedos, I thought you said you didn't know anyone around here."

I replied, "But that was three weeks ago, Captain."

I came down with a terrific cold after we left San Francisco. The fifth night out was our first night to run blacked-out as we were more than 1,000 miles from San Francisco, about halfway to Honolulu with a load of provisions and supplies heading for the Philippines. I was coughing and sputtering and feverish, so the captain called me into his office as soon as I had written up the log from my watch at 8:00 p.m.

The radio in the chartroom was broadcasting the eight o'clock news. This included a report: "Admiral Halsey has made a speech today in

Lieutenant Peter Chelemedos, U.S.M.S.,
October 1944

which he states, 'The United States Navy now controls the Pacific Ocean from the North Pole as far south as you want to go.' "

Captain Beekin gave me a water glass with about three fingers of whiskey and told me, "Go down to get some hot tea. Drink the whiskey with the hot tea, take a hot shower, and pile the blankets on and stay in bed. I'll stand your morning watch for you."

I did as he said.

Just as I reached up to turn off the bunk lamp, we were torpedoed. The torpedo hit in Number Three hold, and the ship broke in two, taking the bulkhead at the head of my bunk with the forward section so the water from the splash came down over me. I grabbed my lifejacket and went up to the top bridge to survey the damage. Captain Beekin told me, "Get the crew in the lifeboats over the side. I'll check through the ship for any possible casualties."

On my way to the lifeboat, I stopped by the chartroom to pick up a sextant and a chronometer in case we had to navigate our own way to Honolulu. I looked across the passageway and saw "Sparks," the radio operator, having trouble with his big radio set, which had come loose from the bulkhead. I took an emergency lantern over and helped him shove it back upright. I had put the sextant and chronometer down on the deck outside the chartroom and, when I went to pick them up, I watched the doorway squeeze shut as the forward section of the ship struck the aftersection in the seaway. I'm glad I went to help Sparks instead of going back into the chartroom for navigation books.

The night was black, the full moon hidden behind a cloud bank. The boats on the starboard side were damaged but the port side boats were okay. We got them off without any trouble. I started my boat's engine and cruised around the stern of the ship and up the starboard side picking up some men from the water, before moving off into a patch of floating debris to put out a sea anchor.

Soon we saw machine gun tracer bullets being fired toward a set of lifejacket lights a short way off. The submarine was, at the same time, firing its deck gun at the still-floating sections of the ship. The deck load of crated aircraft and machinery caught fire, which, of course, lighted up the area. When I saw the submarine heading toward us, I ordered my men to get out of the boat and hide among the flour sacks, boxes and other debris. When the submarine rammed the lifeboat, it was light and just drifted off in the bow wave without damage. We clambered back into the boat. Later, the sub returned for a repeat, this time hitting from a different angle, and cut the sea anchor line so the boat started to drift away from us.

Fortunately, the sub concentrated on shelling the ship and apparently did not see any of my men, and we all returned to the boat to watch the burning ship. Later, the fire reached the 1,000 tons of ammunition stowed in Number Two 'tween deck. The resulting blast sent a thin column of flame up about 20,000 feet, where it ballooned out to a huge orange flare. A Pan Am plane flying from 'Frisco to Honolulu came over to investigate, and the submarine left.

The navy weather ship, a converted yacht, the ARGUS, came over to pick us up the next afternoon to take us back into San Francisco. When we were all together on the ARGUS, we learned that ten of our crew including the young carpenter, Jim Brady, had been killed by the machine-gunning. Seven others had been wounded, all on the raft we had first seen under fire.

I also realized I didn't have a cold anymore, and it was at least five years before I caught another one. That cure for a cold is not one I recommend, however.

We were landed at Treasure Island and were debriefed by the Office of Naval Intelligence before being allowed a phone call. We were all wearing clothing donated by the sailors on the ARGUS, few of which were a good fit. No shoes, as we needed ration stamps for those. We were given paper slippers by the Red Cross and, after we were debriefed, we went up to the American Mail Lines office on Montgomery Street for a draw and some ration points to pick up shoes and clothing.

I placed the ship's sextant and chronometer on the Port Captain's desk and said, "Okay, Captain, shall we start over?"

Jap Raiders Rove Pacific

American Convoys Are Alerted After Ship Is Sunk, Crew Strafed.

SAN FRANCISCO, Jan. 20, (AP)—Tacit admission that convoys sailing out of Pacific Coast ports have been alerted against roving Japanese submarines came today after the Navy disclosed the loss of the Liberty Ship John A. Johnson and ten of its crew in a torpedoing and lifeboat strafing attack.

The sinking and machine-gun attack came last November between the mainland of Honolulu, about 400 miles west of Hawaii.

Of the 10 American seamen killed' most of them died under sprays of bullets fired, survivors said, by frenzied Japanese who danced on the submarine's deck,

shouting banzais and cursing the Americans.

The survivors told how they spent two terrifying hours submerging themselves and hiding behind wreckage to keep out of the range of the rampaging enemy craft.

They said the submarine in its surface hide and seek hunt strafed a lifeboat with machine gun bullets and rammed a life raft.

Lieutenant Peter Chelemedos, San Francisco, experiencing his eighth torpedoing, said all of the ten who perished died after abandoning the Johnson. One was crushed between a lifeboat and the sub; another was sucked into the sub's propellor.

Five men were seriously wounded in the machinegunning.

Seventy Americans survived the harrowing night. They watched the sub shell the sinking Johnson then circle the wreckage strewn water in attempts to ram rafts and boats.

Lieutenant Yates counted 18 Japanese on deck shouting gleefully and cursing survivors.

The submarine disappeared shortly before an American plane came overhead; the survivors were picked up by dawn.

The Johnson's skipper, Captain A. H. Beeken of Tacoma, Wash., was rescued after 15 hours in the water; he had escaped after his lifeboat was cut in two by the raider.

Tells How Japs Rammed Lifeboat

SAN FRANCISCO, Jan. 20 (INS).—Tales of a night of horror following the sinking of his ship, the SS John A. Johnson, between the West Coast and Hawaii, were related today by one of the survivors, First Mate Lt. Peter Chelemedos.

The torpedoing was the first in this area since January, 1942, when Jap submarines were harassing the West Coast of the United States,

One of the 60 crew members that managed to dodge Jap machine gun bullets as they hid in the bottom of lifeboats and rafts, Chelemedos told of treading water behind floating sacks of flour as the Jap sailors viciously strafed the swimming Americans.

Seven of the 10 men lost in the torpedoing were killed in this heartless fusillade, two were drowned attempting to escape the sub's ramming tactics, while the other was cut to pieces in the propeller of the undersea craft, which was believed sunk shortly after sinking the American merchantman.

Sinking of the ship by a Jap submarine was old stuff to Lt. Chelemedos, in fact it's getting to be boring.

This is the eighth time he has been ducked as a result of Jap or German action.

"I had just been relieved," he said, "and was catching a cold, so I took a dose of medicine and hit the sack. A few minutes later I was swimming in the ocean.

NO WARNING.

"The missile hit without warning. It blew me out of my bunk and I could instantly feel the ship breaking up. It was kind of a familar feeling to me, so I grabbed my lifeboat kit and my navigation instruments and rushed out to help Captain Beeken, our skipper.

"He sounded the general quarters alarm. Water was running into the hole and the ship was settling. We launched the lifeboats. No SOS was sent out because the shock of the explosion wrecked the radio.

"The captain searched the ship for dead and injured and found members of the gun crew standing by the gun. They were waiting for the submarine to appear so they could shoot.

"We told them there was no use waiting and ordered them all to jump into the ocean with us. They all swam to a swamped lifeboat and crawled into it. My boat was full—21 men—but we kept close to the others.

'SUBMARINE MOON.'

"A bright 'submarine moon' was shining and we lay off watching the ship settle and wondering if we dared go back aboard, when the sub surfaced not 100 yards away from us and about 5 yards from the captain's boat.

"I ordered the men in my boat to jump into the water and hide among the debris floating around.

"First they tried to ram our boat. We heard shouting and the big black shape bore down on our boat. Some of our men were still clinging to the sides. The waves from the sub pushed our boat to one side, and one man was crushed between the lifeboat and the sub. Another man was swept into the propeller of the sub and drowned.

"Then we heard the sound of firing, and saw tracer bullets hit one of the other lifeboats. They shot down some of our men. Not one man was lost during the abandoning of the ship, but the Japs killed 10 men out of our crew of 70 with machine gun fire.

"Well, the Japs kept cruising among our lifeboats, trying to ram them, spraying the occupants with all deck guns, and shouting 'Banzai' with each hit."

SS John A. Johnson

Company: American Mail Line. Seattle, WA
Master: Arnold H. Beeken
Gross Tons: 7176

Built: June 1943 @ Portland, OR
Dimensions: 441' x 57' x 37'

The Liberty Ship, SS JOHN A. JOHNSON, was torpedoed by the Japanese submarine I-12 (Kudo) at 0605 GCT on October 30, 1944 in the North Pacific (29-36 North/141-43 West) while en route alone from San Francisco, California to Honolulu, Hawaii with a cargo of provisions, explosives and a deck cargo of crated and uncrated trucks. Her complement was 41 merchant crew, 28 Naval Armed Guard and 1 Army Security Officer. Of this number, 4 merchant crew, 5 Navy gunners and the Army Security Officer were lost when the Japanese submarine rammed the lifeboats and rafts and then machine gunned survivors in the water.

At 0605 GCT, as the ship was taking a heavy roll to port, a torpedo struck just forward of the midship house at the turn of the bilge below #3 hold. There was slow flooding in this hold. A few minutes later, a second torpedo was seen passing astern of the ship. The main engines were secured 3 minutes after the attack. The ship began to split in two, forward of the midship house, and ten minutes later she broke apart. All hands were in the after section at the time of the attack because the lookout was stationed on the bridge. About half an hour after the ship was abandoned, the sub surfaced and shelled both sections of the ship which were about ¼ mile apart. The shells set both sections on fire, and at 1025 the forward section blew up with a violent explosion. The after section was still afloat and burning when last seen by the survivors around 1500 GCT the same day.

The Captain sounded abandon ship on the ship's whistle. All hands left without injury, getting away in #2 and #4 boats. Lifeboat #1 was damaged in the explosion and #3 boat swamped when it hit the water. Those in the water climbed aboard #2 and #4 boats. A raft got away safely. The sub surfaced and rammed #2 boat with 28 survivors in it, firing pistols and machine guns at the men swimming in the water. After the sub left, the men reboarded the boat but when the sub returned, those who were able jumped overboard again. No guns were fired this time, but the sub tried to catch the men in its screws. Five from this group were killed by gunfire. The sub then headed for the raft which held 17 men. When about 150' away, machine gunfire was directed at the occupants of the raft. The men jumped into the water and kept the raft between them and the sub until it had passed. The sub circled and again attempted to ram the raft, but a wave threw the raft clear. When the sub returned a third time, it sank the raft and directed its machine guns at the men in the water. Five more men were killed by this strafing.

At 1012 GCT, a Pan American Airways plane sighted the boats. At 2135 GCT October 30, the survivors were picked up by USS ARGUS (PY-14) and landed at San Francisco on November 3, 1944.

The I-12 (Kudo) was not heard from again after January 5, 1945. She was a probable marine casualty somewhere in Pacific waters.

After calling Kay and telling her my ship had engine trouble and I would be signing on another one, I called the WAVES barracks and also told the young ladies that my ship had had engine trouble and I was back for a few days before joining another ship. They came out to the house and helped me clean the fuel oil out of my hair and ears.

Chapter 19

GEORGE H. WILLIAMS, First Voyage
November 1944 - March 1945

Barbara Watson, port manager at the American Mail Lines office in San Francisco, sent me to join the Liberty ship SS GEORGE H. WILLIAMS. On November 13, 1944, I signed on the GEORGE H. WILLIAMS at San Pedro. This was a week after landing in San Francisco on the Navy weather ship ARGUS which had picked us up after the loss of the JOHN A. JOHNSON.

The rain was pouring down as I rode the "Red car" from the Los Angeles railroad station to San Pedro.

While in San Francisco, I had only taken time to pick up a new uniform, a set of khakis and three white shirts, which I had in a "loot bag" as I came into the office. When I introduced myself to the agent, he in turn introduced me to my new captain, Alvin C. "Smokey" Johnson. Captain Johnson said, "We're just heading out to the ship. Would you like a ride?"

Of course, I said, "Yes, sir."

He looked at the sextant and the loot bag I was carrying and asked, "Where is the rest of your gear?"

I said, "Do I need more than this? We're just going around the world."

Smokey slapped me on the back and said, "Just what I need, a West Coast man. Come

along." I rode out to the ship with him.

The ship had just returned from East Coast. She had earlier participated in the Normandy landings. The chief mate, whom I was relieving, was returning to Greece since that country, his homeland, had been liberated.

After looking over the ship and bringing myself up to date on the progress of the voyage repairs and storing, I set to work washing the three white shirts I had bought in 'Frisco but had used up by now. This was before the days of wash and wear. I hung them in the "fideley" (the inside of the smokestack above the fire room) to dry. That evening I was going to borrow a flatiron and finish the chore, but at supper time the third engineer said he had a car and would take us uptown to a movie.

I begged off as I hadn't a clean shirt to wear with my uniform, that I was intending to iron them. He said, "Just wear a wrinkled one and wear a scarf with your raincoat. No one will notice." Thinking that a good idea, and really wanting to go to a movie, I dressed accordingly.

The third squeezed about six of us in his large old DeSoto all right, but instead of stopping at the moviehouse he took us out to his sister's house in Long Beach. "Come in and

Chief Mate, SS George H. Williams, *New York, March 1945*

make yourself at home," was his invitation.

Of course, I had to take off my raincoat and scarf. After doing so, I went out to the kitchen and pulled the ironing board down from the wall and plugged in his sister's flatiron. By the time the third came out, I had my shirt off and was busy ironing it.

"What are you doing?" he asked.

"Ironing my shirt," I replied. "You said 'make yourself at home' and if I were home I would be ironing my shirt."

"Jesus, I said make yourself at home, I didn't say 'move in,' " he said. "I guess I better watch what I say around you.

Anyway, after tea and cake, we went on to the movie and the world was right again. I had called Kay in Massachusetts and asked her to send out my license so I could sign on another ship, since the John A. Johnson had had engine trouble. I couldn't tell her the reason the engines wouldn't run.

The shipyard people finished the voyage repairs, and stevedores loaded a full load of mustard gas bombs to transport to India — a full load except that Number Three 'tween deck held some PX stores, cigarettes and such items, for the Navy in Perth, Australia, topping off with a deckload of crated machinery for India.

Six men of the deck crew were from the same high school graduating class from Cape Girardeau, Missouri. There was also a young man from Boston. I did have one old-timer, the boatswain. The captain, bo'sun and I were the only ones in the deck department who had been to sea in a merchant ship before. The second and third mates had been yeomen in the Navy, and had just come out of a maritime school. When we sailed, we ran a school for the crew at the same time we were lowering the cargo gear, taking each man through the steps one at a time. Also at lifeboat drills, each man was taken through all the steps necessary to launch the boats safely, rather than having to depend on someone who might not be able to do a vital part in the operation. After the John A. Johnson experience, I didn't want any delays if it came to abandoning ship again.

I was still rather jumpy from that experience. One night, while standing on the wing of the top bridge, a bolt of lightning hit the water right alongside the ship, and the immediate *boom* of thunder in my ears made me jump at least three feet off the deck, believe me.

Outside of the Equator crossing ceremonies and the meeting of a Foss tugboat near the Ellice Islands, our trip via Bass Strait south of Australia was uneventful until Christmas. That night, when the third mate relieved me at eight, he told me I should report to the officers' messroom. I couldn't think of a reason for such an unusual request, since I generally stopped there for a cup of coffee anyway.

I found that Captain Johnson and the first engineer had set up a Christmas tree there. The first was a perfect size for the Santa Claus suit he wore as he distributed small gifts to each member of the crew. Now, the ship was running blacked-out, which meant all the portholes and doors to the outside were closed, and the messroom measured about twelve feet by twenty feet. When the seventy men of the crew all mustered in that non-air-conditioned space, it was, shall we say, rather warm. But it made for a memorable occasion as we sang carols in the midsummer heat of that Christmas Eve.

We arrived in Perth for New Year's weekend to find that the longshoremen were on holiday. The Navy sent down a crew of yeomen and storekeepers that night to work cargo because the men were anxious for their cigarettes. To get them, they had to unlash and unload the large crates of machinery on deck, uncover the hatch boards and beams, discharge their cargo, and then cover everything back up again.

Since none of them had handled ship's cargo gear before, I had to stay with them all night. It was 6:00 a.m. before they finished lashing the last crate and went ashore, and we shifted ship to anchorage.

The captain went ashore for orders and I went to bed.

At about eight o'clock, I was wakened by a Coast Guard ensign who told me, "I am to observe your crew in an abandon ship drill."

"Abandon ship, you say?" I said as I sleepily picked up my lifejacket and went up to the wheelhouse to ring the abandon ship alarm. I then went on down the other side of the ship to my boat station. As the crew assembled, each man took up the next chore in line as I had taught them — open-ing the covers, leading out the sea painter, cranking out the davits, putting in the plug, etc., so by the time the boat's crew was all there, the boat was in the water and they were climbing down the nets to it. By the time the ensign came out on deck to see what was going on, my boat was in the water standing off waiting for the third mate's boat to clear so I could come back alongside.

I climbed up the rope net to the boat deck, saluted the ensign and reported, "Abandon ship, sir."

He said, "I have never seen anything like it!" and was being complimentary. I told the bo'sun to get everything back aboard, and I went to bed.

From the newspapers the captain brought aboard, we learned of the Battle of the Bulge in Europe and, closer to us, the rumors of Japanese submarine activity in the eastern part of the Indian Ocean.

We sailed on up the Indian Ocean and up the Hooglie River to Calcutta. My station was at the bow standing by the anchors while we were going up the river, and it was a trip of several hours. I set up King Neptune's throne, left over from the Equator crossing, on top of the small hatch to the forepeak, sat on it, and leaned back against the gun-tub. I noticed that the natives in passing craft were pointing at me and jabbering away, but didn't understand until I looked around and found members of the gun crew holding a large purple umbrella over me.

We docked and cargo operations were started, taking about a week to discharge the crates and bombs. Then we shifted to another berth inside the locks to load a cargo of gunny cloth and tea for New York.

One day, while walking near the Hogg market, I ran across a USO club. I went in for a cup of coffee and a doughnut. While there, three girls were being introduced to the club.

This was done by the MC asking, "Is anyone was here from Texas?" and then sending the Texas girl over to talk with them. The girl from Kansas, likewise. I was the only one from California, so had a one-to-one conversation with the Californian, only to find out she was from Albany High School and had been in classes with me in the days before I left home for the sea.

Our return to New York was via the Red Sea. When we sailed into the Gulf of Aden from the Indian Ocean, I came on watch on a dark, overcast night. The sea was flat calm. The porpoises swimming alongside the ship were leaving phosphorescent trails through the water, and occasionally jumping and splashing. The splashes of phosphorus gave the scene the quality of diamonds on black velvet. I think this was one of the most beautiful scenes the sea can offer.

The second mate came down with something, and we sent him ashore to hospital at Aden. The third mate took over his watch, and the bo'sun took the eight-to-twelve.

Since U-boats were apparently not operating in the Red Sea, the ship ran with running lights in that area. For the first time in three years, I had a relaxing night's sleep at sea. It was such a relief; I could feel my whole body unwind.

We transited the Suez Canal and tied up to buoys at Alexandria to await orders.

We got word that the second mate had not survived an air crash at Khartoum, so we were without him for the voyage home. Having already upgraded the third mate to second, we went ahead and officially upgraded the bo'sun to third mate.

On a rather stormy night in the Mediterranean Sea, a freak wave hit us broadside and splashed down the engine room ventilators on the top bridge. I could hear the engineer below hollering about the "clumsy deck apes" when we took another sea. He told me later that as soon as he said it, he realized that the water was not turned on on deck, that the water had come down the ventilator above him as he stood by the log desk, and he had just backed away when the second shower came down.

We joined a convoy at Gibraltar and arrived in New York in time for me to celebrate with Kay our second wedding anniversary.

When we arrived at New York, we docked at a pier in Staten Island near a Maritime Training School. At coffee time, I went ashore with my deck gang to get a fresh cup of coffee and some shoreside baked goods after the four months of ship's cooking. I hadn't thought much about it, but while walking back to the ship, a group in Maritime School uniforms who had apparently just passed through a Saturday morning inspection came marching by. One of them pointed to me and said, "Look, he's a full commander."

It didn't dawn on me what he was so particularly impressed with until I got back aboard and took off my uniform jacket and hat. The cap had a big splotch of red lead on it and the jacket was splattered with spots of gray paint and one button was missing. I guess the four months' trip around the world "schooner rigged" had taken its toll. I got a new cap cover and replaced the missing button on the jacket before I went ashore again.

I contacted Rev. McDonald from the Seamen's Church Institute and had him come out to Kay's aunt's home on Long Island to officiate at baby Peter Steven's baptism during our short stay in New York.

Captain Johnson got off to return to Seattle for another ship. I decided to stay aboard for another trip rather than head across country to San Francisco.

Chapter 20

GEORGE H. WILLIAMS, Second Voyage
March - August 1945

The big news from Europe was the Allied advances across France and Germany. In the Pacific, the news was of the invasion of Iwo Jima in February and Okinawa in March. We kept getting updated reports of the Japanese kamikaze attacks on the ships off the beaches and the hard fighting ashore.

Captain Johnson was replaced by Captain H.R. Bieneman, a Lykes Brothers skipper. When I first met him, my impression was of a buzzard — his heavy black eyebrows and steely black eyes made me think to myself, "What have I let myself in for by staying?"

We shifted up to Newport, Rhode Island, to load Seabee equipment at the Portsmouth navy base, and sailed from there for Samar Island in the Philippines.

The first night after sailing from Portsmouth, Captain Bieneman came up on the bridge just after twilight and asked, "Did you get any star sights?"

I said I had, to which he responded, "I'll take over while you go down to the chartroom and work them out."

Since I had learned to use the Air Almanac and the HO 214 navigation books, and had developed a system where I looked up all the stars at the same time and worked

them out together, I was back up on the bridge in about ten minutes.

He asked me, "Didn't they work out?"

"Yes, sir," I answered. "They made a perfect fix and are plotted on the chart."

"Impossible," he said. "There's no way you could have worked them out so fast. Are your sights down there, too?"

"Yes, sir."

"Do you mind if I go over them?"

"No, sir."

When I came down to write up my log at eight o'clock, he called me into his office. He had worked my sights out by the old "time sight" method, a long, involved sequence of sines, cosines, haversines, etc., which the old-timers used before the new tables were calculated. He said, "I don't seem to come up with the same answer you have. Are you sure about your work? I can't believe you could be accurate if you did it so fast."

I looked over his work and pointed out that he had subtracted a correction that should have been added. When he added it, the position he arrived at was exactly on top of mine. He pushed all the papers into the waste basket and said, "Teach me how you navigate."

From then on, we got along fine.

We were saddened a few days later to learn of the death of President Roosevelt. We were sorry he didn't live at least another month to witness V.E. Day when Germany surrendered.

We proceeded on through the Panama Canal, where the authorities took our chief cook off because he was of Japanese ancestry. They would let him sail in the Atlantic, but not the Pacific. Since they couldn't provide us with a replacement, we upgraded the second cook. After the first day of his cooking, we asked him what his trade really was, since he was certainly no cook. He said he had been a blacksmith, and since they figured he could handle a coal fire, they put him in cook's school. We wondered many times in the next ten months why the Fates had blessed us with him.

It was also the chief steward's first trip as steward. He had been our bedroom steward the trip before. He was quite a comedown from the chief steward we had had last trip, whose peacetime position was head of the culinary department at the Bel-Aire Hotel in Beverly Hills, California.

We had left the States with stores for only three months. As the months stretched out to eleven, we felt the pinch.

The days passed slowly. I re-read a copy of the *Berkeley Daily Gazette*, which had written up the story of the sinking of the JOHN A. JOHNSON. It also carried another article about the sinking in the Indian Ocean of a different Liberty ship, JEAN NICOLET. George K. Hess of Berkeley told the story:

"When our ship sank, most of the crew managed to climb on life rafts. The Japanese submarine emerged to the surface. Armed with machine guns, they machine-gunned most of the rafts. Then they brought about 100 of us aboard the deck of their vessel.

"We watched them bayonet 60 of our men and hit others with lead pipes. They stripped us of most of our clothes and tied our hands behind us. Then, unexpectedly, the submarine crash dived, and we were left to the shark-infested water, our hands still tied.

"After swimming for about 10 hours, and managing to free ourselves from the bonds, we sighted a raft which supported us for two days when a British trawler picked us up."

With this running through my mind, and the fact that we were crossing the longitude of San Francisco, I was moved to write the following Morning Report:

And we sail on. The sea is flat and rolls up and down in an almost unnoticeable swell, restlessly surging. The stars this morning tell me I am a bit west of the longitude of San Francisco, latitude of the Equator. We are en route from Panama to New Guinea. The peacefulness of the scene this morning gives no indication of last night's horror.

The torpedo struck in Number Two hold about ten o'clock last night. The moon was almost full, and bright, for there were few scattered puffs of clouds in the sky. I was in bed at the time so was unable to see the first action, but I picked up my clothes and lifejacket and made fast time to the bridge.

The ship was a bit sluggish, but still making way through water, and under fair control. The sub was not in sight at the time, but since the torpedo had struck starboard, it was that side we watched.

The ship did not appear to be breaking up; the cargo of canned goods apparently absorbed the shock of the explosion and was dense enough to exclude too much water pouring in, so we seemed to be in little danger of sinking. We stayed aboard, running ahead at what few knots we could make. The sub did not show. We waited.

Remembering a previous experience of the war in which the Japs machine-gunned our lifeboats before shelling the ship, I figured that this would be what these were waiting for. I told the skipper and Armed Guard officer of my thoughts on the matter and an idea I had. We laid plans to put away the portside boats with an armed crew. Under cover of the ship's guns, we would go off and wait for the sub to surface, then attempt to board her. Sticking our necks out, true, but, under the circumstances worth a try. At least as long as we had the ship's guns to back us up.

Calling for volunteers looking for a fight, twenty of the merchant crew came forward, borrowing rifles and .45s from the Armed Guard officer. The cooks brought cleavers from the galley, and we had among us a dozen or so sheath knives and the skipper's and my own .38s. We then set about our task.

Putting Mr. Ralston, the second officer, in the Number Two lifeboat, and taking the motor lifeboat for myself, we set off.

We did not use the engines, but rowed and stayed about twenty yards away from the other boat until we were about a thousand yards away from the ship on the upwind side, since we wanted to keep clear of her drifting in the light wind.

Looking back at the ship, we saw that they had set off smoke bombs, and the smoke really gave the effect of a fire aboard. I hoped it would not interfere with their visibility. Soon, as expected, the sub surfaced about a hundred yards ahead of us. We boated our oars and watched. We could see men climbing out on deck and on the conning tower and man the guns immediately. A star shell from the ship burst over them and lighted up the entire scene. Then a shot from the ship's big gun hit the deck gun of the sub. 20mm shells raked the decks clear at the same time. The sub was moving slowly toward us at dead slow. I could see no one on deck at this time, so I fired a red flare as a signal the the ship to hold fire. I started the engine to proceed to the far side of the sub.

I could see Mr. Ralston getting his boat underway under oars and steering to move alongside the sub as she passed. The sub came closer . . . closer . . . slowly . . . closer . . . ready . . . now *jump*. We made the foredeck easily, though it was about four feet higher than the boat, and a bit slippery at that. We rushed aft. One man stayed to make the boat fast, then he, too, joined us. I wondered if the men below knew just what was going on on deck.

By that time, we met Mr. Ralston's men coming from aft. There was not a soul alive on deck but our own men. The firing had been very effective.

The shell from the ship's gun had hit the deck of the submarine at the base of its deck gun, cracking the hull and part of the front of the conning tower. We cleared the dead Japs from the deck.

Now at least we had the decks. I sent a man back to the boat for a flashlight and signaled the ship to that effect. Now what to do? None of us could speak Japanese and they had the controls below us, though we knew they could not submerge because of the holes in the hull.

On a hunch, I tried the remote control devices I found, which I hoped would be connected to transmit orders to the engines. Slow ahead. At least I moved it to the equivalent space on our ship's telegraph. We heard the engines increase a little in their tempo. They didn't suspect? I signaled stop. We stopped. Good. I had some of the men load up the big gun to fire at the horizon, but the blast from the ship's gun had been effective. No go.

I then sent Mr. Ralston with five men to take the motorboat back to the ship, and sent word to get ready to bring the ship alongside of the submarine.

The slight swell made the two vessels bang together a bit, and I was afraid the outer diving planes on the sub would split seams on the ship, since Liberties are notorious for their light construction. I sent instructions and presently received a number of tools, an engineer and a small rope ladder. We then let go and the ship cruised off a way. We set to work over the bow to unship the diving planes, just in case. Then the same procedure in the stern. It was easier than we expected, for the sub rode well up on the swell and there was not much interference by the waves. I had hung my hat over the periscope

early on, so visibility from below was cut off.

Ringing "half ahead" on the telegraph, we caught up with the ship and, in a half hour or so, were alongside again. I proceeded to take a set of navigation instruments, a tarpaulin, blankets and emergency rations. A chart of the San Francisco approaches, a general and pilot chart of the North Pacific, all of which were stowed in a waterproof bag on the conning tower platform.

Taking the bo'sun, two ABs, the second engineer, an oiler and the deck engineer and lots of sandwich makings, we bade good day and bon voyage to the ship and headed north on one of the most unusual escapades known of the war. An American deck gang controlling an enemy's sub with an enemy crew at the engine controls not knowing what was happening above.

Wireless contact had been made by the ship, and the Navy would know what to find if they came looking for us. We estimated speed at eighteen knots and set a course for San Francisco. We were on the way.

Daybreak and moonset were almost co-incidental. Sunrise found us alone steaming steadily northward on the surface of a quiet sea. The tarpaulin was spread on deck abaft the conning tower and all the gang except a man at the con and a man watching the escape hatches slept.

I took star sights and worked them out by "time sight" and plotted the position on the chart, checked the compass, and set the course for San Diego instead of San Francisco, since it was more of a naval port and there would be fewer problems.

I wondered at this time again what the thoughts of the men below were when trying to ascertain what was going on on deck. I found out soon enough.

About 6:30 apparent time, things began to happen. A messman came up the ladder with a tray of tea. When he saw us instead of his own officers, he nearly fell over himself going back in. A quick jump by the lookout aft prevented his doing so, and rescued the tray at the same time. A quick splash, followed by the bitter tea. And silence again.

About 6:45, the deck hatch forward opened and six men climbed out and shut the hatch behind them. They walked aft as far as the gun and looked around for the crew they were evidently to relieve. And kept the surprised look on their faces as we turned the machine gun at them and forced them over the side. (This, because some of my previous shipmates were lost with a crew that had this done to them).

Then all hell seemed to break loose. The forward hatch came open and men streamed out, yelling. I opened fire with the small machine gun and the helmsman left the control and started shooting at the men coming up from aft.

The men who had been sleeping were now awake and entered the fight on a hand-to-hand basis, so we had to stop shooting for a bit. The battle was a weird one, knives flashing, guns blazing, fists flying in true movie style. I heard a noise behind

me and saw that a man on deck was preparing to throw grenades up our way. Shot one, then another, then the gun jammed. My pistol . . . six shots . . . the bo'sun was trying to load the gun again . . . a grenade was coming, duck, "Bo'sun, throw it back quick." "BLAM!!!"

"Mate . . . Mate . . . are you awake? Hey, Mate . . . Three-thirty . . . weather clear, warm, smooth sea . . . Hey, Mate . . . Coffee in the messroom . . . Are you awake . . . ?"

Slowly I opened my eyes . . . a dark room. Where was I? . . . Who's talking? I reached around and found a light switch over my head. Turned it on . . . Where? What? The clock says 3:30 . . .

It must be morning . . . Faintly in the distance I heard seven bells striking. Yes . . . Where am I . . . ? The sub . . . ? This wasn't the sub. What happened . . . ?

Little by little came the realization that I was awakening in my own bunk on the GEORGE H. WILLIAMS. A dream . . . ? Egad . . . Ah me.

And so I climb my weary way out of bed, dress and go down for the coffee. I'll take it black, thank you. And so to the bridge again. I watch the early morning sea, the fading stars, the breaking day, the rising sun. (Rising sun . . . hmmm, I wonder how that fight came out . . .)

So it goes. The tropic sun, the vast emptiness of the sea, stories and tales heard, and experiences of the past all mixed together seem to tell on one's imagination. Maybe I'll stay out of the sun for a day or two. Maybe it is as Shakespeare's Jacques said about the theater of life: "Then the soldier, bearded like the bard, full of strange oaths, jealous in honor, sudden and quick in quarrel, seeking the bubble reputation even in the cannon's mouth . . ." Yes, I think I will stay out of the sun for a few days.

After that nightmare, the balance of the voyage to the Admiralty Island off New Guinea was relatively peaceful and routine. We arrived there for orders and were sent to Samar to discharge the Seabee equipment that had been loaded at Portsmouth.

When we had loaded the equipment, the navy stevedores made it plain that they were in charge of the loading. Period. When I protested that they were using cardboard cartons of bottled Coca-Cola for filler cargo and, instead of stowing it, were throwing it into the spaces between the pieces of heavy machinery, they re-affirmed that they were in charge *period*.

While discharging the cargo at Samar, the navy sent some enlisted personnel wearing Shore Patrol armbands aboard to "guard" the hatches. One of the petty officers came up to my office and asked me to sign for an accounting of damage to some 60,000 bottles of Coca-Cola in their cargo. I didn't sign for them. I pointed out the mandate the loading officer had given me that it was the Navy's responsibility. He left. Not very happy, but I heard no more about it.

From Samar, we were sent to Finschaven, New Guinea, to load some equipment to bring back to the Philippines. The guy who ran the army post office asked me to take his puppy back to the ship with me, in hopes that we would be returning to the United States soon. He also gave me ten cases of "C" rations for feeding him. The dog, Juno, was a Belgian shepherd, a pup of one of the "war" dogs stationed there. She was a beautiful and friendly dog. When she walked out on the boat deck the first day, the gunnery officer's black Scottie looked up at her and let loose a stream of water that wouldn't quit.

Instead of being sent back to the States, we proceeded on to Lae, Wewak, Milne Bay, and other ports along the New Guinea coast, picking up retrograde equipment and ferrying it to the Philippines.

Sailing along the coasts of New Guinea and the area southeast of the Philippines was mostly done with a sailing direction book compiled in the late 1860s by someone in a sailing ship. Instructions such as, "We sailed three days on the starboard tack and saw at a distance of three furlongs of the port bow discolored water" were rather difficult to translate to modern usage on a low-powered steamer without radar, especially as the mostly overcast sky did not lend itself to a reliable series of star fixes.

The currents of the area were not plotted sufficiently to be totally reliable, so a lot of our sailing was done by dead reckoning (RPMs of the engine and compass direction and whatever local knowledge the navigator could come up with.)

On the approach to the Surigao Straits on the east coast of the Philippines, the only lighthouse on the coast was on top of Suluan Island, listed in the light list as a "ten-mile light." It lay about sixty miles north of the entrance to the Surigao Straits.

According to our dead reckoning navigation, we were due at Surigao entrance about 8:00 a.m.. At 3:30 a.m. when I was called to go on watch, the man who wakened me told me there was a light ahead.

Since one of my standing instructions was to not turn lights on in my room (so as to not affect my night vision), I told him to send my coffee up with my helmsman and went immediately to the top bridge.

It was raining hard. The second mate pointed out the light nearly right over the foremast. He said, "There's Suluan Island Light. Just broke clear."

I went in the wheelhouse and told the helmsman to turn the ship around and put her on the reverse course until I could verify something, then went back out to the wing of the bridge, from where I could see breakers ahead through the binoculars.

The skipper was standing there and asked, "Here, Mr. Chelemedos. What are you doing?"

"I'm turning the ship around, sir. We aren't a mile off that beach."

"I can't see anything. They turned the lights on in my room when they called me," he said.

"I can see fairly well. Go down in the chartroom and check the fathometer and see how deep the water is, and plot a course to pass clear of Homohon Island," I said.

He went down and a few minutes was back with the news that we had six fathoms of water under us. We adjusted the course and at daybreak passed clear of Homohon. Plotting back, we found that we had been only a mile from running smack into the island with our load of ammunition.

I asked the second mate how he figured the light was ten miles off. He answered, "Well, it is listed in the light list as a ten-mile light, and it had just broken clear."

I said, "Mr. R., please go down and read the front cover of the light list and come back and tell me what it says."

"THE WORD 'VISIBLE' WHEN USED IN THIS BOOK SHALL MEAN VISIBLE ON A DARK NIGHT WITH A CLEAR ATMOSPHERE."

It was a lesson learned that could have been disastrous.

We discharged our cargo at Tacloban and, after a second-round trip to the same ports in New Guinea, we discharged more retrograde bombs and equipment cargo, then loaded about 5,000 tons of bombs to carry up to supply the proposed invasion of Japan.

While we were loading this in our five-hatch, 10,000-ton vessel, a small, two-hatch army FS ship was laying ahead of us at the berth. I noticed that for every truckload that came alongside of us, there was one alongside of the FS boat. I asked the cargo officer if that ship was loading empty cases, as her capacity was around 500 tons. He said, "No, and it is none of your concern. The Army knows what it is doing. We are loading her until she is down to her marks."

I said, "I think you have something wrong there, and you should check it out."

He repeated his previous statement.

I pointed out that that ship would have to sail before we could leave the berth because of the narrow channel. Anyway, when it came time to sail, they cast off their lines, but couldn't move. The Army brought over an LCI (landing craft infantry) to use as a tug, and towed her away from the pier. As she left the pier, she slid deeper into the water. When they finally stopped pulling on her and realized she was on the bottom, she was too far from the pier to use her gear to unload.

So we waited a couple more days until they brought over a barge and unloaded part of her cargo to get her afloat again.

While we had been loading these live bombs, I tried several times to stop the operation because I felt the army stevedore battalion was being very careless about the loading. Occasionally, a bomb would fall out of the rope net slings and drop to the deck. I chased the longshoremen off the ship and requested the lieutenant to get a safer crew. I had a strong suspicion these men had been drinking some of that powerful Philippine whiskey.

When we were covering up the hatches and all the trucks had left, we found a 1,000-pound bomb still lying on the main deck. I told the lieutenant that he would either have to re-open the hatch and stow it in the lower

A Liberty Ship, North Atlantic, circa 1943

hold with the rest of them or have it taken ashore back to the ammo dump. He wanted to just lash it on deck where it was.

Neither I nor the captain thought the ship would be seaworthy going to an invasion with a live bomb lashed on deck where it would be subject to strafing as well as the inherent danger of the cargo itself. I told him we couldn't sail until it was taken care of. The lieutenant went ashore and sent his Captain down to order us to sail. The Captain went ashore and sent his Major down to order us to sail. The Major went ashore and sent his Colonel down to order us to sail. The Colonel went ashore and sent a representative for War Shipping Administration down.

When he came aboard, he said to me, "I understand you refuse to sail your ship."

I said, "Yes. I don't consider it seaworthy with a live bomb lashed on deck."

He went up to see Captain Bieneman and was told the same thing. Captain Bieneman asked, "Sir, in all the years you have gone to sea would you take a ship to sea which you didn't consider seaworthy?"

"No."

"Would you order me to?"

"Of course not."

The lieutenant got a truck back and discharged the bomb.

We then loaded some machinery on deck before going out into the bay to anchor and lash it.

When we were ready to sail and the lieutenant was heading down the gangway to the landing craft alongside, the second mate called down to him: "Good-bye, I hope I never meet a p— like you again."

Captain Bieneman was standing on the boat deck and called down to the second mate, "Mr R., you shouldn't call that man a p—."

The lieutenant stood back with a smirk on his face to watch the second mate get a dressing down. The second mate said, "But sir . . ."

Captain Bieneman said, "I know, I've watched him. But you must always remember . . . a p— is something useful to a man."

It was a parting pleasure to watch the grins on the faces of the longshore troops in the boat as the lieutenant spluttered.

Chapter 21

War's End and Homeward

August 1945 - March 1946

We sailed from Tacloban and up to Batangas Bay, Luzon, where we dropped the anchor. When I returned to the bridge to write up my log and take anchor bearings, the radio reports that Japan had offered to surrender came over the air.

When we heard the report, we glued ourselves to the radio room to get the latest word. Yes, a new bomb had been dropped on Nagasaki and later another one on Hiroshima. What these bombs were we didn't know, but the results changed the future for us far more than we imagined. For one thing, the holds full of bombs we carried would not be needed for an invasion of Japan. But, if they were not needed, what would we do with them?

We lay at anchor there in Batangas Bay waiting for news on a day-to-day basis. August 14, August 21, August 31, and on into September, when we heard MacArthur had accepted the surrender in Tokio Bay. Then we waited another week. Then another. There was a ship anchored outside of us that had some heavy timbers for the Army Engineers to use for building a pier. They discharged them over the side on the incoming tide and let them drift in toward the beach where they were gathered and hauled ashore

for construction of the pier.

When they drifted by our ship, some members of the navy gun crew swam out and corraled them, bringing them alongside our ship and tying them with the end of the two-inch rope guys for the jumbo boom to use as a swimming platform.

The first of October brought the tail end of a passing typhoon over the anchorage. To prevent the ship dragging anchor, we started the engines and steamed at slow speed against the anchors. When I told the gun crew to release the timbers tied alongside, instead of untying them from the ropes, they cut the ropes at the rail level. This allowed the timbers to drift aft with about thirty feet of two-inch rope trailing and, of course, it fouled in our turning propeller.

I donned a lifejacket and climbed over the stern on a "jacob's ladder" and swam in the rough waves trying to cut the line loose from the propeller. My opinions of the actions of the gun crew would not add to this account, but I did have them.

While I was being tossed around by these waves around the propeller, I suddenly had a vision of my baby son calling out to me. A few days later, I received a letter from Kay that Peter Steven had been badly burned on the legs while standing in the bathtub and that the girls from the American Mail Lines office in San Francisco had volunteered to give him blood transfusions.

This didn't help my impatience at the enforced idleness while anchored so far from home awaiting orders.

Since we had left the States with only three months' stores, and were out five by this time, things were scarce around the ship — food, paint and any other thing you could think of.

I had taken Juno ashore and left her with the army postmaster at Batangas to care for until we were sailing again, and went ashore to visit whenever I could. One day, the postmaster put me in touch with the motor pool and I requisitioned a jeep to drive to Manila to try to get some paint to give my crew something to do to help pass the long days. The army gave me twenty gallons of apple green and twenty gallons of a chocolate "box-car" red. Since by themselves they would look out of place on a gray ship, I had the bo'sun mix them together in a fifty-five-gallon drum and we used the resulting olive green to paint the ship from water level up to the load water line.

One day while my crew was painting over the side and the gunnery officer was ashore, the gun crew broke out their rifles and entertained themselves by shooting at fish in the waters around the ship. My crew wouldn't work while this was going on for obvious reasons, so I took it upon myself to take the guns from the navy people and locked them in the "slop chest" (the ship's store). When the gunnery officer came aboard, he raised hell with me for taking away United States Navy property. He wouldn't listen to an explanation. I gave him back his guns, but asked him to have his crew use more discretion, as I didn't think

my crew should be thus endangered.

A few days later, the same thing happened. I did the same thing. That evening I was sitting in my office reading a *Reader's Digest* I had scrounged from somewhere, when the gunnery officer stuck his head in my door and asked, "Where's the mate on watch?"

"Up on the top bridge," I answered.

He left, and a few minutes later returned and said, "The second mate says you have the key to the saloon" (the officers' dining room).

"Yes, it's hanging there just inside the door. As soon as I finish this article I'll join you to see if the steward managed to get anything for the icebox," I said.

He grabbed the key and left. About five minutes later, I finished the article and went down to the saloon. The gunnery officer was sitting over a cup of coffee, eating a slice of bread and reading. I opened the icebox door to find only a can of milk with the top crusted over and a plate of curled-up, dry salami and a small fish in tomato sauce that had been there since day before yesterday.

I shut the door and said, "Aw, nuts!" and went back up to my office to read.

About five minutes later, the plate of salami and fish came sailing across my desk. The gunnery officer said, "There, that's what's in the icebox. Next time you want to come snooping around to see what I am up to, don't bother," and started down the passage to his room at the other end.

I picked up the fish and, going out into the passageway, threw it back at him, but he had stepped into his room and the plate went sailing out the aft door onto the boat deck. I went out on the boat deck by my office to stand at the rail and cool off a bit.

About ten minutes later, Captain Bieneman came out onto the wing of the bridge above me and said, "Mr. Chelemedos, I have just had a very interesting meeting with the gunnery officer. He told me that if I didn't get the mate taken off of the ship, he was going to take his crew and leave."

"Oh," I said.

"Do you know what I told him?" he asked.

"No, sir."

"I said, 'When you leave, be sure to take your entire crew with you.' "

The gunnery officer didn't go.

We lay there at anchor through October and November, and about the first week in December we finally heard rumors that we would be unloaded. The great day came, and we discharged the cargo of bombs and on December 10 sailed to Manila for orders. When we picked up the anchor, the barnacles on the anchor chain were four to six inches long.

I retrieved Juno and brought her back to the ship with some more cases of "C" and "K" rations. On December 14, we sailed from Manila to Panama. This is a 9,347-mile passage; at just over ten knots, it meant forty more days at sea.

After we cleared Manila and the Luzon Straits, I turned my crew to scraping the rust off the boat deck and giving it a coat of red-lead primer. As soon as they had applied the new coat of red-lead, the gunnery officer decided it was time to have a gunnery drill, since we had been in port for four months and his crew might be getting rusty.

I was at my emergency station on the foredeck when the bo'sun called my attention to the bridge. The gun crew found that, since they hadn't been in their gun tubs for four months, the rust and accumulated soot had plugged up the drain holes and there was six to nine inches of dirty rainwater accumulated. They proceeded to clear the drains and, besides their footprints tracking fresh red-lead up the ladders to the bridge,

the sooty water and junk drained down across the freshly painted deck.

We had a rope ladder hanging from the face of the bridge to the main deck for emergency escape route. I think I went up in three steps, for the next thing I knew I was on the wing of the bridge holding the gunnery officer by the necktie and describing my feelings of the moment. Then the thought struck me that it wouldn't be worth the trouble I would get into if I obeyed my impulses of the moment.

During these forty days of crossing the vast Pacific, we ran short of various items of food. Finally, the week before we got in, even the coffee was gone. When we arrived at Panama and got fresh stores aboard, we were in seventh heaven. We even got some Christmas mail addressed to the ship, but found it had been held for more than a year and was for the crew who had been on the ship in October 1944 and had gotten off in New York last March. We forwarded the first-class mail back home, but didn't think the fruitcakes would stand any more time or travel, so we added them to our diets.

I went down to the galley to get some scraps for Juno, and the steward gave me about five pounds of raw ground meat. When I brought it up and put it on Juno's plate, she sniffed at it and gave me a puzzled look. I took a small handful and held it out to her and told her, "It's good, try some." She stuck out a tentative tongue and, after a taste, went to work voraciously on the rest of the plate.

The next night when I came down from the bridge for dinner, she was standing there in the passageway prancing and wagging her tail as if to say, "Let's have some more of that wonderful stuff."

I went down to the galley and asked for a bit more, but the steward said, "I haven't got time. Here, give her this." He gave me a

Home again, before sitting for Master's License, March 1946

gallon can of army beef stew. When I brought it up to the boat deck and set out Juno's plate, she came up, her tail wagging wildly and she pranced around in joyous anticipation. When I poured the can on her plate, she came in and took one sniff. Stopped. Backed away and, pulling her tail between her legs, gave me a hurt look and slunk into my office, crawled under the desk, and hid her face beneath her paws. I couldn't have beaten that dog and got a worse reaction.

The chief engineer, when I told him of this, said, "I respect that dog's judgment."

We arrived at Galveston, Texas, on February 8, 1946, and lay at anchor. The gunnery officer went ashore on Monday and, as we lay there awaiting orders, we didn't hear from him for a few days, so all was quiet. His petty officer came up to me on Thursday and said, "You know, Mr. Mate, we have been waiting here since we got in. We all

have our points for discharge, and we haven't any money nor permission to even go ashore. I just got this note from our gunnery officer from one of the passing fishing boats. It reads: 'please bring two pounds of butter and some money to room # 2— at the ——— Hotel.' I can't go ashore without permission, so I can't do it, but what can I do?"

I said, "Get into a dress uniform and I'll take you ashore." I took him ashore to the Port Director's office and introduced him. Then I went back to the ship.

About two hours later, a navy boat was alongside and the gun crew was taken off the ship. When we turned the ship over to the lay-up fleet at Newport News the next week, the gunnery officer's personal effects were still aboard. We never did hear what happened to him.

I couldn't take Juno on the plane to bring home. One day, while she was tied up outside the store where I was telephoning Kay, I came out to find her being admired by three youngsters.

They asked if they could have her, as their dog had been run over the previous week. So they took me home with them to get permission from their parents. They then took Juno down to their place in the country.

I flew home, arriving in San Francisco on our third wedding anniversary, March 9, 1946.

During the stay at San Francisco, I sat for my Master's License with the Coast Guard, receiving it just a week short of seven years from the day I had received my Ordinary Seaman's papers in Boston. My feelings of elation at this accomplishment were unbounded. I felt like turning handsprings down the corridor of the Appraisers Building as I left with the long-sought license that read: "MASTER OF STEAM OR MOTOR VESSELS ANY TONNAGE, ANY OCEAN."

SERIAL NUMBER

007769

ISSUE NO.

8,11

UNITED STATES COAST GUARD

MASTER

LICENSE

This is to certify that   PETER CHELEMEDOS

having been duly examined and found competent by the undersigned, is licensed to serve as Master of United States Steam or Motor Vessels of any Gross Tons upon Oceans

ALSO, RADAR OBSERVER

for the term of five years from this date.

Given under my hand this   27TH   *day of*   APRIL   , 19   81 .

SEATTLE, WASHINGTON
Port

By direction of   *Officer in Charge of Marine Inspection*   LT.,USCG

Master's License

Part III

SETTLING
DOWN

Chapter 22

Ashore

1946

After a week or ten days at home, I stopped by the American Mail Lines office to thank the women there who had given blood transfusions to Peter Steven when he was so badly burned a few months back. Barbara Watson, the port manager, drove me out to her apartment on Nob Hill and asked me to estimate how much paint it would take to paint the entire interior one color. A ship chandler was going to mix the special color for her and, since she was in an apartment with no place to stow any left-over paint, she wanted just enough. I looked the place over and told her to arrange for seven gallons and one quart. Then I took Kay and the baby to the Santa Cruz Mountains to visit my Uncle Fred and Auntie Gudren for two weeks.

When I returned to San Francisco, I called the American Mail Lines office to ask Miss Watson how the painting made out. She asked me where the hell I'd been, as she was looking for me to come out and do some painting. But she had it done, and scraped the bottom of the quart can to paint the last light switch. "I've never seen anything like it," she said.

I said, "Remember that, Miss Watson. When I turn in a requisition for my ship's

stores, I figure quantities pretty close. I don't want anything cut out."

She said, "I'll remember that, believe me."

Miss Watson sent me over to join the CAPE NEWENHAM as Second Mate. I took a water-taxi out to where she was anchored in the bay to meet Captain Osterhaut. Before I could unpack my bags, we received a message calling me back to the office to be sent out to the OCEAN MAIL.

Apparently, Miss Watson had fired the chief mate on the OCEAN MAIL and I was to be his replacement. This didn't set well with Captain Axel Hvam as he and the fired mate were longtime buddies. The captain told me he would take care of things when we reached Seattle.

We brought the OCEAN MAIL to Seattle and temporarily moored her at Carmac Shipyard dock in Ballard, alongside the ISLAND MAIL.

It was beautiful weather in Seattle. I called Kay to come up to join me, as American Mail Lines would be headquartered in Seattle during the post-war years. When she came, she too enjoyed the weather and we set about finding a house to purchase. Kay then returned to San Francisco to ship our belongings up, and in August 1946 we moved into our first Seattle home. It rained that day, and we didn't see much of the sun again until the following May. Kay swears I had it in with the weatherman to lure her up here.

One day while Kay was house-hunting, I took Peter Steven down to the ship to spend the day with me. Since all the crew had been paid off, only the chief engineer, the captain and myself were aboard. I was standing on the top bridge talking with the captain over a cup of coffee, listening to the silence of the ship with all of the engines shut down except one generator. Suddenly, the earsplitting sound of the ship's fog signal started blaring over our heads, echoing against the steel shed alongside the ship and off the hills around Salmon Bay. I turned to find little Peter Steven had tried out the intriguing switch on the face of the bridge that activates the signal. He was frozen by the noise and the realization that he had brought this about, and I had to literally pry his little fingers off of the switch. He was one scared kid.

I bought a 1936 Chevrolet coupe from the chief engineer. He said it had only 100,000 miles on it and had never been in the shop. Since it was my first car, I didn't take this as a warning.

Two weeks after we moved in, we laid up the OCEAN MAIL at Everett in time for the 1946 Maritime Strike, which lasted from September 1 to December 10. Kay was expecting our daughter during these months, and I drove back to Massachusetts to bring her mother out to be with her if I had a chance to ship out as soon as the strike was over.

It was not an uneventful trip. The water pump expired one Sunday morning as I approached Davenport, Iowa. I hoped that my one-time pen pal, Beverly, would still be there, as she had been working in an auto

A beautiful wife to come home to, March 1946

parts dealer. Fortunately she was, and was able to get her boss to open the store to get me a new pump. After feeding me lunch and catching me up on all the family news, we said good-bye and I stopped over at Silvis for a visit with the Engholms before resuming my trip east.

While passing through New York City on the way up to the Connecticut turnpike on a rainy morning, a man ran across the street in front of me. When I turned sharply to miss him, I crumpled my fender on a fireplug. While I was trying to pull the fender out from the wheel where it was jammed, I could hear in the background a constantly ringing bell. It turned out to be the burglar alarm at the nearby gas station. Knowing this didn't help me as I pulled off the bent wheel and muttered under my breath at the callousness of the guy I had avoided who didn't even turn around to see that I hadn't been hurt.

More of the muttering later when the owner of the gas station came over to ask me if I had seen anyone around the station and I realized what had taken place.

Kay's mother decided she would rather come out by train, so I drove back across the country again, alone. Crossing this nation in those days was a long, long trip. The car radio wasn't working, so I had to make do with my own singing, such as it is. I was fortunate to only have one flat tire on the trip, except that it was in the Badlands of South Dakota, and my spare was low on air as the wheel had been bent against that curb in New York City.

Someone with a hand pump stopped to help, and I was able to get the car going again, only to find a service station just over the first hill from the place I had spent the past two hours.

When I started out of Spokane on the last leg homeward, the car wouldn't go up the first hill, so I coasted back to a level spot. It would run on the level, so I drove it to the Chevrolet garage to have it checked out and I booked into the hotel for some much needed sleep as I had been driving day and night to get home before my money ran out.

When I came back for the car at five o'clock, they said they couldn't find anything wrong with it. The shop manager went for a test run with me, and it ran fine on the level. But when I again tried to go up the hill again, it wouldn't make it. We drove back to the garage and checked again and found that the driveline splines were worn so that when I went uphill and the shaft slid back into the differential housing, the part still in the transmission did not have enough teeth left to engage the gears. He apologized and replaced the shaft at no charge for their error, which made me happy since I had barely enough money for supper that night.

I ate that supper at Moses Lake and, as I left, found that the fog had set down over the desert. I got behind an oil tank truck and, with my headlights dimmed, followed him all the way over Snoqualmie Pass, losing him at the toll plaza of the floating bridge leading into Seattle. I arrived home about two in the morning and slept until noon.

When I started to drive up to the market for some shopping that next afternoon, I found the steering wheel would just turn around and around to the left but the car kept going right. The brass steering sector had picked this time to give out. I thank my lucky stars that this hadn't happened the previous night while driving over the mountains in the fog.

I went up to the Master's Mates & Pilots hall, and turned in my card for a Third Mate's job on a Shell Oil Company tanker preparing for a voyage to Australia. The longshore strike was still on and no freighters were sailing, so I figured this would provide some much needed cash. When I went home to pick up some gear, however, I found Kay was quite ill, so I took her to the doctor and called the Union to find a replacement on the tanker.

Chapter 23

WILLIAM LEROY GABLE
December 1946 - August 1947

The long maritime strike ended December 10. "Smokey" Johnson called me to go Second Mate with him on the Grace Line Liberty ship SS WILLIAM LEROY GABLE, which was loading for Central and South America at Pier 20 in Seattle. The ship loaded general cargo below decks and, in those days, it took several days to load. Friday the thirteenth at about 2:00 a.m. I took Kay to Doctors Hospital and left her there in the care of the nurses. In the morning, while cataloging charts on the ship, I mentioned to "Smokey" and Captain Ellis Emberg this fact. After calling the hospital to be told she had given birth to our daughter, Penny, I was given the rest of the day off to visit her.

We shifted the GABLE to Everett for some pulp, and then to Tacoma for more cargo. On Christmas Day, I drove Kay, her mother, Peter Steven and baby Penny down to Tacoma. It was a freezing cold day, but the radiator on the '36 Chevy kept boiling over and the steam froze to the windshield, so every half mile or so I had to stop and scrape off the ice. To add to the glory of the day, it was so foggy that visibility was very short. By the time we arrived at Tacoma, I thought about driving the car right off the end of the pier, but refrained, since I would then have

no way to get the family home again.

After Christmas dinner on the ship, the world seemed all right again.

We loaded the GABLE with some railroad cars from the old narrow-gauge Alaska Railroad for delivery to Punta Arenas, Costa Rica, as a deck load, to top off the general cargo in the holds.

The first port of call after sailing from Puget Sound after New Year's Day was Manzanillo, Mexico. I picked up two books for studying my Spanish: "Capricito Rojo" and "El Raton Miguel" ("Little Red Riding Hood" and "Mickey Mouse"). It was surprisingly easy to learn conversational Spanish, when I remembered the pronunciation of the language spoken by the Mexican kids who worked with me at the messenger service in Tucson back in 1938.

I was pleased to be able to hold a conversation in the barber shop when we arrived at Punta Arenas.

The night we lay at the pier in Punta Arenas, a group of us were in the "Blue Moon" cafe and bar for our evening's entertainment, dancing with the señoritas and consuming cerveza. Sparks decided he would stay a while after the rest of us returned to the ship, so I talked him into giving me most of his money

SS WILLIAM LEROY GABLE, 1947

to take back with me.

The next afternoon, I was walking past the place and one of the girls started berating me. I gathered she was angry that, when she "rolled" Sparks, he didn't have the big roll of bills on him he had had earlier.

We proceeded on down to anchor in the river mouth at Guayaquil, Ecuador, to discharge a small lot of cargo to a barge. I was interested to note the launch used by the boarding officials looked like a cut-down steam-driven revenue cutter from rum-running days.

Leaving Guayaquil, our next port was Callao, Peru, where we discharged more of our general cargo.

I rode the streetcar up to Lima for the day, looking for more books or newspapers and just generally walking around the area.

At Mollendo, Peru, we anchored out and the cargo was discharged to lighters and ferried into the small basin-like dock to be discharged by a shore crane. The longshoremen at Mollendo worked to prevent a railroad being constructed at the new port of Matarani, a few miles up the coast, where the ships would be able to tie up to a pier. This would effectively put the bargemen out of work, which was scarce enough around there.

A trip ashore entailed riding the barge into a slip and being hoisted up by a crane in a net and deposited on the pier. The walk around the town's dry, dusty streets, between rusty sheet-metal-covered houses was just that, dusty and dry. It hadn't rained on the town in more than thirty years, and each of the metal houses was rusted through in the corners where the local dog population left their marks.

While on watch one day during the noon hour, I was sitting in the 'tween deck of Number Four hatch with an eye on the fenced-in special cargo in the wings. About 12:30, one of the longshoremen climbed down the ladder and, instead of proceeding on to the lower hold where his cargo was being worked, slipped off into the 'tween deck and made for the plywood partition around the special cargo.

When I called to him and pointed out his cargo was down below, he went on down. About five minutes later, a voice from on deck called down to him to ask what was stowed back there. He answered, in Spanish, "How can I find out when the piloto is in the hatch?"

I looked up to see official police gangway watchman duck back out of sight when he saw me looking.

At Antofagasta, Chile, I went with Smokey and chief engineer, W.P. Wolfe, out to the horse races. An English girl there, Judy Hescott, told us which horse to bet on as it was "his turn to win." The horse belonged to the local funeral director and pulled a hearse around on weekdays.

At Santiago, Chile, we discharged the last of our southbound cargo, then proceeded to Tocopilla to load back. Since the harbor had about twelve ships awaiting their turn to load the cargo of ore, we sat in the bay for several days.

At night, the light at the end of the gangway attracted some large squid. One of the crew caught one and managed to get it up on deck and laid it on the Number Three hatch.

A Liberty ship hatch is twenty feet wide, and this squid was placed at one edge. His body extended about five and a half feet and his tentacles reached clear across the hatch and onto the deck on the other side. We examined him carefully. The suction cups on his tentacles were more than an inch in diameter and contained many needle-like teeth, which penetrate the skin of a victim and hold it in place while the parrot-like beak tears it apart.

Sparks was sleeping off his previous night on the town. In order to test his sense of humor, I took the opportunity to cut the tentacles off the top of the squid and placed the base in the washbasin in Sparks' room. I draped the long tentacles around his room, over the medicine chest, reaching into his desk drawer, and so forth. I then took a four-inch-diameter eyeball and placed it in the sink at the center of the tentacles. A while later, while we were sitting in the chief engineer's room having coffee, we heard a

yell from above and, investigating, found Sparks with a fire-axe heading back to his room to deal with his visitor.

After we loaded our cargo of ore, we returned to Selby, California, for discharge of part of the cargo.

While at Selby, I took the day off and caught the bus down to Albany to visit my dad. While awaiting the bus to return to the ship, a young lady came around the corner and asked, "What time will the bus leave for Vallejo?"

"Four o'clock," I replied.

"Oh," she said. "I guess I'll have time for a drink, then."

When she went off, my dad looked at me and shrugged his shoulders. We resumed our conversation until the bus came.

As I boarded the bus, the girl also got on, so we sat together to talk during the hour or so ride to Selby. By the time we reached there, I invited her to get off and come aboard the ship for dinner.

By the time dinner was finished, the dark clouds had turned into a heavy California downpour. Since Selby is a "flag stop" on the bus line, we waited until the rain stopped before walking up to stand by the highway to wait for the bus. I used the time to show her around the ship, and we joined chief engineer Wolfe for some of his favorite drinks, Pisco Sours.

The rain didn't stop. Rather than send our new friend, Peggy, into the storm, we found a place for her to sleep aboard the ship for the night. After breakfast, we sent her on her way.

We sailed on to the Tacoma Smelter to discharge the balance of the cargo, arriving there in early March. Chief Wolfe received a letter from Peggy, thanking us for our hospitality and telling us her boyfriend, who had been waiting to meet her at Vallejo, had the police of Richmond, Vallejo and Martinez out looking for her that night.

For the next voyage, the GABLE proceeded to Portland, Oregon, to take a load of wheat from the grain elevators for Antofagasta, Chile. We made another visit to that port. Revisiting the places we had previously been was quite a change from going into a strange port for the first time. We were made to feel welcome as old friends by the girls in the club at 28 Bella Vista.

We discharged our load of wheat to a large pile on the pier. It hadn't rained on the coast for about thirty years, but after the grain was all unloaded and lying exposed on the pier awaiting railroad cars to take it to Bolivia, it rained. By the time we sailed, some of the wheat was sprouting.

We again went up to lay at anchor at Tocopilla, awaiting our turn at the nitrate loading anchorage.

While in port, the mates rotated the watches. Every day it would be eight hours on, then sixteen off. During my time off, I learned to play golf at the local course which, because it never rains there, was entirely of rocks with the "greens" smoothed-off areas. Hard on the clubs, believe me.

One day, the captain of one of the east-coast Grace Line ships was riding out in the launch with me and asked me what my position was on the ship, since every time he saw me I was heading out to the golf course. I told him, Second Mate. He said, "On my ship the mates work their eight hours a day."

I replied, "On our ship, the mates have their eight hours work to do, do it quickly, quietly and efficiently, and the rest of their time is their own." Since I had the twelve-to-eight watch and only played golf in the morning, on my own time, I didn't feel I was out of line. I later learned he had sent a letter to the home office recommending the overtime sheets for our ship be checked carefully.

While in Antofagasta, we all chipped in and hired a shore crew to paint the sides of the ship down to the waterline, black hull and red boot-topping. While awaiting cargo at Tocopilla, the deck gang worked day work and painted the rest of the ship in Grace Line colors, so it really looked spiffy. Fourth of July, we hosted a party of mine people for luncheon aboard. I think the east coast skipper was miffed because they didn't come out to his ship.

We sailed up through the Panama Canal and delivered our cargo of nitrate to the East Coast, then laid the ship up at the James River reserve fleet at Newport News.

Chapter 24

Ashore

Fall 1947

In October 1947, after having laid up the WILLIAM LEROY GABLE in Norfolk, I found that waterfront jobs were few and far between. I answered an ad in the *Seattle Times* for a warehouse clerk paying $175 per month. The job was at a central distribution center for a shoe company that had twenty stores in Western Washington. I was taking over the desk from a woman who was leaving to get married. The personnel manager told me women had held the job in the past, but since as soon as one got efficient at the job, she would leave to get married or have a baby. So, the company was changing the position to use a man at the task.

My predecessor spent the day copying the incoming orders onto delivery orders to send down to shipping, waiting for the completed orders to come back, and making out the bills of lading for the truck outfits. The next morning, she would post the shipments on the inventory cardex, and then start on the next day's orders. This would take her until about ten o'clock the next morning.

My first day on the job by myself, I made out the delivery orders first and sent them down to shipping, along with the appropriate bills of lading filled out except for the quantity in case of back-orders or additions,

and then posted the orders on the cardex. I was all finished by 2:30, and commenced reading the news paper while awaiting the "confirmed shipped" slips from shipping to note any changes or back orders on the cardex.

The manager came up and asked me why I was reading the paper when I had so much work to do. But when I showed him that it was all done and up-to-date he was astonished. He said, "You know, this is the first time all the shipments have gone out so early and no one has to work overtime to do it. But you must understand, the $175 per month includes overtime. The base pay for the job is only $135, and if you work so fast, that is all you get paid."

I asked him, "Why don't you make the base for the desk the $175? You will be saving the overtime all down the line."

He replied, "I'm sorry, this is the way it has to be."

I said, "Fine. You can run the desk yourself then, because I can't afford to spend the time here when I could be earning enough to feed my family." Then I left.

The next day, I answered an ad for someone to "cruise" Christmas trees. I had to drive over to Coeur d'Alene, Idaho, to meet my supervisor. Since my 1936 Chevy coupe hadn't been in desert country since before the war, I had to pull off the road to a farmhouse somewhere west of Moses Lake to add water, which I got from a horse trough under a windmill. While driving back to the road, the car bogged down in the soft sand.

I hiked out to the highway and finally flagged down a passing pickup truck, which hauled me out, but it cost the last five dollars I had with me. I still had enough gas to get to my destination, but it meant going without supper and breakfast.

The supervisor arranged for me to stay with a family at Coeur d'Alene, and stopped by for me early in the morning. We would drive around the countryside looking over the trees and, when we found a patch of young trees that looked good for Christmas trees, we would go back to the county seat to find out who owned that piece of property and drive out to find the owner, or farmer, timing it so we wouldn't interrupt his milking or plowing. Then the supervisor would start dickering for the trees. My pay was based on the number of trees we purchased, plus my mileage. This made for a rather long day. The supervisor always wanted to spend the evenings visiting the various taverns and roadhouses around the area between Thompson Falls and Coeur d'Alene and, since I didn't drink, wanted me to chauffeur him. I put in for mileage for this work, but also put in for overtime. This didn't sit too well with him, so I had to go back to Seattle on my own.

I then applied at Frederick & Nelson for Christmas time clerking, and was hired to work in men's haberdashery. While awaiting my interview, I met Eda Guzzie, who was also applying for parttime work. We teamed up for the interview and, since we were both new in the work, met to compare notes over coffee from time to time.

Standing on the marble floor of Frederick's from 9:25 in the morning until 5:35 in the afternoon six days a week was not the easiest thing for one who was used to the flexibility of steel decks. The hours were 6:40 per day, so it took six days to get in forty hours after which overtime may be paid. Not a chance!

I was not a very successful salesman of socks and gloves for the season, and was laid off Christmas Eve.

At least working there gave me the fifteen percent employee discount privilege, which was some help that Christmas, especially when Kay's mother offered to buy her a washing machine and we got our first Bendix. What a welcome device for a young mother with a four-year-old boy and a one-year-old baby girl.

That Christmas, Peter Steven asked for an electric train. I had to explain that I hadn't been working very regularly and couldn't afford an electric train at that time, but I promised, "As soon as I can get a job on another ship I'd be able to get one."

He said, "Okay," and went on about his world.

At the first part of February, he asked, "Say, Dad, when will you be getting that ship and saving the money for that electric train?"

I said, "I'll see what I could do." I had to go to Alameda, California, anyway, to the Maritime School to get the Radar endorsement now being required by the Coast Guard.

As I was waiting for the bus to take me to Oakland, I met Captain Beekin who had been my captain on the SS JOHN A. JOHNSON. He was now skippering the SS OREGON MAIL.

He said he would be in 'Frisco later on in the week and invited me aboard for lunch.

When I got to San Francisco, I checked into the American Mail Lines office, and paid my respects to Barbara Watson and the few others left over in operations who were still there. Then I went on to register at the radar school at Alameda.

The next day when I called the office to find out when the OREGON MAIL would be in, Miss Watson told me that Captain Beekin had left a message for me to meet him at the office the next day for lunch, that he had hit the wildest storm coming down the coast and blamed it on the bad luck I had brought him on the JOHN A. JOHNSON. Just the thought of my coming aboard was more than he wanted to chance.

The next day, I got a call from Miss Watson to get over to the office right away. She was sending me out as Second Mate on the Liberty ship SS HIRAM MAXIM. Captain Dick Williamson, with whom I had sailed on the ISLAND MAIL in 1943, was skipper. I missed out on the lunch with Captain Beekin.

The HIRAM MAXIM carried a load of salt to Pusan, Korea, that trip.

On the long days crossing the Pacific at the ten-knot speed of a Liberty ship, I got to thinking about Peter Steven's request for an electric train. I thought a four-year-old was a little young for an electric train, and it would probably be forgotten in a short time. Instead, I took a copy of the blueprints of the ship to the carpenter's shop and made a nine-inch scale model of the ship. Using medical swab sticks for masts and booms and painting it up with real ship's paints, it came out pretty well.

I returned home late one night in April. Since the children were asleep, I placed the model ship by Peter Steven's bed.

The next morning I was wakened by a gentle push, and found Steve standing by the bedside with the model cradled in his arm. He said, "This is an awfully nice ship, Dad, but where is the electric train?"

I went up to MacDougal & Southwick that day to buy a battery-operated model train.

Chapter 25

Ashore

1948 - 1952

When we returned in April 1948 from the trip to Korea, the HIRAM MAXIM went into idle status and I was home again. Shipping was slower than ever, so Kay suggested I go to an accounting school and learn a new way of making a living. I enrolled at Auerswald's in Seattle and spent the next six months or so learning the difference between debits and credits, a smattering of business law, typing practice, business English and related subjects. One day, I was called into the office and offered a job as assistant timekeeper at Young Iron Works.

Since our bank balance was quite low and Kay's job at an automotive dealer was taking its toll on her and the children, who were at Seattle Day Nursery, I took advantage of it, figuring to continue my studies at night school.

I went to work just before the winter business turndown at this plant, which made tools and equipment used in logging camps. About a month later, "Smokey" Johnson, my skipper on the GEORGE H. WILLIAMS, who was now a Longshore Foreman, called me and told me of a Second Mate's berth on the SS YANKEE STAR, which was hauling a load of supplies to Yokohama for the military while she was being operated by Fall River Navigation Company.

I hemmed and hawed trying to bring myself to tell the office manager of this offer I wanted to take up. At the same time, he was hemming and hawing trying to tell me he would have to let me go because of the slow business.

When I told him of the offer, he told me to take it and to get in touch with him when I returned.

The YANKEE STAR trip to Japan was rather brief. I plotted her westbound trip down along the low-powered steamer lanes, instead of going north on the modified great circle route. After all, it was December. What happened, though, is that we managed to be heading into the wind for most of the storms we ran into, while listening to radio reports from ships north of us that had fair winds.

After discharging our cargo at Yokohama, we started out light ship for Manila for a return load. Two days out of Yokohama we were diverted to Portland, Oregon, which meant we had to cross the North Pacific in March with a light ship with no ballast except what little sea water we could carry in Number Four and Number Five lower holds up to the top of the shaft alley.

We didn't have any wind for the first

week or so, but the swells kept getting larger and larger, running up to twenty-five feet and more. . . . Then the wind caught up with us. We tossed and rolled across the Gulf of Alaska in waves and troughs so deep that I could stand on the top bridge of the ship and look up at the crest of the next wave approaching.

When we arrived in Portland, we found that the ceiling boards in the holds had drifted loose and, floating on top of the ballast water, had shaved themselves to sawdust on the rolled-up metal on top of the shaft alley. This meant we couldn't pump out the holds with the ship's pumps as they would have filled with sawdust and shavings.

I paid off at Portland and returned home. I stopped by Young Iron Works and found that Louis, the timekeeper, was being drafted. I could have his position if I cared to return. I took the opportunity and, during the next two years, also took over as purchasing agent.

When Paul Isaacson sold the business to Isaacson Iron Works, the office manager went over to Wenatchee to start up the Columbia Tractor and Equipment business, and I was offered the office manager position.

When Louis returned from Korea, I rehired him as timekeeper.

Kay and I moved from the little house we had first purchased to a large old home on Gatewood Hill in West Seattle, with a view of Puget Sound and the Olympic Mountains.

Two weeks after we moved in, during a heavy rain, we awoke to find the cliff below the house had slid down the hillside from a point about two feet from the corner of the house.

Our next-door neighbor worked for a private power company, which had taken down an old water tower recently, and the twelve-

Office manager, Young Iron Works, 1952

by-twelve timbers were available. Together, we purchased some long piling and had a construction company bring its rigs over and drill for setting the piling in. We used the timbers to build a bulkhead to retain the remainder of our respective yards on the hilltop.

I joined the local chapter of AHEPA, the American Hellenic Education and Progressive Association, in order to meet members of the local Greek community. They promptly drafted me to be secretary. This was entertaining in a way, because the old expression "When Greek meets Greek, they start a restaurant" extends to read "and when they meet a third Greek, they start an argument.

Kay, 1952

Trying to keep minutes of the meetings was an experience. Once in a while, one of the old-timers would lapse into the Greek language, which I could not understand. I would just put down my pen and wait until he noticed that I wasn't recording his great words and resumed speaking in English.

During the years while I was secretary of AHEPA, one of the annual conventions was held at the Palace Hotel in San Francisco. One day, while I was a delegate there, I went across the bay to Albany and brought my father back to the hotel to meet some of my Greek friends from Seattle. Dad was wearing a hat. As we walked through the lobby, he took off his hat and held it in his hands for a few minutes. Then, when he wanted to shake hands with someone, he put it back on his head.

I asked, "Dad, why are you so nervous?"

"My hat. I don't know whether to leave it on or carry it," he answered.

"Leave it on, you'll just be in the lobby. But tell me, why are you so nervous?"

"You know, the last time I was in this hotel was May of 1907, after they rebuilt it after the earthquake. I applied for a dishwasher job here and didn't get it."

To pick up a bit of much-needed extra money in those years, I kept books for some of the Greek taverns and restaurants along skid row. The office for the area was upstairs in a storefront mission. The door at the head of the stairs was locked by a combination padlock.

One day, one of my clients started up the stairs carrying an armload of books to be worked on. The following conversation took place:

"Tom! Let me carry those books."

"No, Peter, it's all right. I can carry them."

"Tom! Give me those books."

"What's the matter with you? I can carry them."

"Tom, when you get to the top of the stairs with that armload of books, how are you going to open that padlock?"

Tom looked up at the lock, then, turning to me said, "You're not all Greek, are you?"

"No," I answered. "Why?"

"You can think that far ahead!"

I held the position at Young Iron Works while continuing night school for another year, until Henry Isaacson, the new owner, informed me that his wife's nephew was now out of school and would take over my position. When Paul Isaacson heard this, he gave me an extra two months' pay along with my termination pay.

Chapter 26

WANDO

July - August 1952

With the bonus money from Young Iron Works, I was able to buy our first new car, a 1952 Studebaker Champion, to use while looking for a new job. I thought about getting some trips on Puget Sound to obtain a Pilot's endorsement on my Master's license.

To try for the Pilot endorsement, I first went to the Coast Guard Inspector's office to get any information regarding the form of supporting data they might require.

I was told that either a letter listing trips, each signed by the Master of the vessel or the Pilot supervising the move, would suffice, and that I would need at least twenty trips on vessels the tonnage of my license.

In order to meet the requirements for large tonnage, it would necessitate my sailing as pilot observer or mate on freighters or tankers sailing in and around Puget Sound.

I then approached the Puget Sound Pilot Association for information as to sailing as an observer with the regularly assigned pilots. It was explained that, since the pilots were only on the ship in an advisory capacity, they could not take along an observer without permission of the Master of individual vessels.

The man suggested I contact the Steamship agencies and, perhaps, the Masters of individual ships for such permission.

I called at the office of the publisher of the shipping newspaper for the area and obtained a listing of ships due in and out of Puget Sound for the next three months or so. I then visited the Seattle office of Grace Lines and posed my problem there. Grace Lines referred me to the San Francisco office.

I called in at General Steamship Company, agent for many of the foreign flag ships that call at Puget Sound ports. Its office referred me to U.S. Customs, since foreign flag ships could not carry passengers between two American ports.

American Mail Lines attorneys advised they could not allow pilot observers to ride on their ships under the terms of their liability policies with insurance companies.

I then visited the U.S. Customs office and confirmed the information I had been given. After all this running around, I was no closer to my goal of Pilot time than when I had started.

I went to Puget Sound Freight Lines, which operated small ships around the sound. No openings there, unless someone dropped dead on one of their ships as no one would leave such a desirable job.

Thus I wound up at Puget Sound Tug

and Barge Company. John Lee, its dispatcher at the time, said that since I had a deep sea license he would rather use me on the deep sea tugs. A job is income, which was my primary object, so I accepted. My first assignment was on the NEPTUNE, with Ray Quinn as master. We made trips towing retired LSTs (landing ship tanks) from Indian Harbor near Port Townsend to Astoria for the laid-up fleet.

While returning to Puget Sound in a fog, I had my head out the pilothouse window listening for fog signals. Ray was glued to the new radar set, watching the sweep of the indicator. I thought I heard a ship's whistle off the starboard bow. Ray said, "No, it must be the fog signal on Point Wilson. I don't see anything on the screen."

After listening to a few more blasts on the whistle and giving answering blasts from our own whistle, I suddenly looked up and read the name on the bow of a Knot ship within about a hundred feet. I said, "I didn't know they had changed the name of POINT WILSON to SQUARE KNOT."

Ray said, "Oh, can you see her now?"

"Yes, right above me," I answered.

"Okay," he said, "you can change course now. We must be in the right position."

I would cheerfully have wrapped the radar antenna across his skull if I could have torn it loose.

When we finished that assignment, I was sent over to the tug ACTIVE to tow more of the LSTs down to Astoria.

When we reached Astoria on the second trip, we received word that our next assignment was to Beaumont, Texas.

The ACTIVE was a small tug, much smaller than the ships I was used to. She also rolled a lot and, worst of all, the head was on the main deck level and the cold sea water would back up through the system, so re-laxed comfort was not one of the attractions of using that necessary facility.

I opted not to make the trip, so returned to Seattle to be assigned to the tug WANDO for a trip hauling a converted LST barge to Bethel, Alaska, with supplies to build the new Alaska Native Hospital there.

Our trip up the Inside Passage in the calm, quiet waters was a welcome change from the rolling and tossing about the trips on the NEPTUNE off the Washington coast.

The WANDO was equipped with a large Fairbanks-Morse diesel engine. My room was not insulated for sound and was right on top of the engine. My dreams were of riding the outside of a gondola on a freight train crossing an endless trestle. We found ourselves praying for fog so we would have an excuse to anchor and shut the thing down to get some sleep.

The trip across the Gulf of Alaska was made on a flat, calm sea. The wake of our tug and barge left a clear, white streak to the horizon behind us on the blue surface.

The weather was so clear that we could see both Mount St. Elias and Mount Fairweather, 200 miles apart, at the same time. Their snow-covered peaks stood out in the clear air.

The good weather continued all the way through Unimak Pass and up Kuskokwim River to Bethel. This was fine with me but, without wind, I found that as I walked ashore from where we had shoved the barge onto the beach for unloading down to the main part of Greater Bethel, the no-see-ums were out in force. I noticed as I walked with two of the people who had preceded us by two weeks that the insects were concentrating on me. My companions pointed out the black swarm of them around me and commented, "They know fresh meat when it comes."

When we returned to Seattle, I was assigned as Chief Mate on the little tanker MV UNITED for a run out to Port Alberni on the west coast of Vancouver Island for one trip.

Since the fall shipping to Alaska had slacked off, I made the rounds of employment agencies and obtained a position as office manager at Fiberglas Engineering. Occasionally, for a vacation I would take a job on the VITANNIC, a small freighter serving the Ketchikan, Alaska, area.

Later, because of my experience with logging machinery, I shifted over to work as office manager/purchasing agent at Hansel Engineering Company. Hansel moved his office to Lynnwood and, since the commute from my home in West Seattle to Lynnwood on old Highway 99 was longer than I wanted to spend on the road, I moved my family to a house in the woods north of Lynnwood.

Peter Steven became active in the Boy Scouts and, through that contact, I became active in a Sea Explorer unit at the Lake Serene Community Club, and spent most of my spare hours either working on their boat, the 23 SKID-DOO or taking the boys on outings.

When I was laid off during one of the periodic recessions in the logging industry, I took a position in Seattle at PuttyStik, Inc. and re-joined the ranks of commuters. Because Kay was then isolated in the woods a mile from the highway and two miles from the Lynnwood center, I felt the need for an-

other car to leave with her. Kay had been making more and more pointed remarks about all the time I was spending with the Sea Scouts.

I had the opportunity to purchase a 1953 Studebaker Commander for seventy dollars. For that price, I knew it needed a bit of mechanical work and figured working on the car would give me an excuse to forego the Scouts and spend my weekends at a project at home, repairing the car.

When I had the car towed home and had a chance to look at it in the light of day, I found more problems than I had anticipated, so I spent the summer replacing the engine, overhauling the transmission, replacing the broken windshield, etc. Because the design of the car was a national prize-winner, Kay immediately christened her "Gloria, the Glamour Girl."

For some reason or another, Kay didn't think much of the car. When I pointed out to her that this year I had spent every weekend at home, she muttered something about only having seen the seat of my pants or the bottom of my feet sticking out from under the greasy car, and that wasn't what she'd had in mind.

Anyway, since Kay and the car didn't seem to be compatible, I used "Gloria" to commute to Seattle after I finally got her to run.

Chapter 27

WESTERN TRADER
1960

The depression days of the late Eisenhower administration gave thoughts to people from many walks of life to start over in a different environment. Not the least of these were those who picked up on the dream of Don Harrsch to build a self-sufficient colony in the Galapagos Islands off the coast of Ecuador.

Don's Island Development Company program proposed that if 100 families each put $2,500 into a fund, he could buy the necessary ships to transport them and to rebuild a lobster plant on one of the islands, which would furnish them a livelihood.

The first real details of this plan to come before the public eye was the adventures of the ALERT, the first of the ships he had purchased, as it made its way down the west coast to San Pedro. The ALERT was a wooden-hulled ex-Puget Sound Freight Line vessel, which had been used mainly in the waters of Puget Sound hauling paper and lumber products from the many small mills to main ports for further shipment.

When the ALERT met the waves and swells of the Pacific Ocean, her planking twisted and wracked, causing more leakage than her pumps were designed to handle. This necessitated repeated calls to the Coast

Guard for additional pumps and visits to nearly every "dog-hole" port along the coast to get her pumped out and rendered seaworthy again. These adventures were given great play in the daily newspapers.

One item told of the work being done on a second ship, the WESTERN TRADER. The WESTERN TRADER was a 130-foot steel-hulled ship that had been used in the Aleutian Island trade and suffered much abuse from the weather and lack of maintenance. She was being readied by a second group preparing to sail from Lake Union in Seattle for this land of dreams.

The members of my Sea Scout group had been casting about for a community assistance project for one of their requirements in the sea scouting program, and I felt this might be a natural, as it would give the boys the opportunity to work on a large, seagoing ship. We took on the project of breaking loose the lifeboat davits from their bed of rust, and overhauling the lifeboat and its launching equipment.

In conversations with the group of prospective colonists, I met a dam-site engineer, college students, farmers, lawyers, schoolteachers, and several others who were desperate often not being able to find employ-

WESTERN TRADEI
Lake Union,
April 1960

ment in their fields. The prospectus for the adventure outlined plans to start a school and design and build a community, using the old lobster plant as a freezing facility and engaging in fishing as well as farming the lush land of this tropical island.

The prospectus painted a rosy picture to be sure and, if each point had been followed, the colonists may not have had such a difficult time. Most of the people couldn't come up with the entire $2,500, instead putting in what they could and contributing their labors to work off the balance due. Each person tried to make up for the lack of cash by being very conscientious about his or her tasks, from overhauling the ship's plumbing system, cleaning the years of accumulated grease from the engine room, and learning the operation of the different pieces of equipment therein, all the while restructuring the insides to accommodate the sixty-five persons who would be traveling south with the ship.

Since the ship was documented in the Fisheries trade and was less than 200 feet long, many of the Coast Guard regulations for passenger-carrying vessels didn't apply. However, they were required to purchase

and install ship-to-shore telephone equipment as well as the proper lifejackets, etc. This made a deep dent in the monies they had for food and other amenities, but it had to be.

After the Sea Scouts finished their project, the next I heard from these people was a request to use my license to take the ship south, as a licensed captain was another Coast Guard requirement. I took a week off from my position as office manager at PuttyStik, Inc. to sail with them.

On March 25, 1960, we sailed out of Lake Union for San Pedro, California. The weather was clear and fine as we steamed up between the beautiful mountains of Puget Sound. The Olympics hadn't lost their winter coat of snow, and Mount Baker smiled at us from the northeast.

As we sailed out of the Straits of Juan de Fuca and turned south, however, the prevailing northwest wind and its accompanying sea and swell gave the ship an uneasy motion. The ship rolled sideways and pitched up and down, twisting at the same time. As a consequence, most of the sixty-six people aboard suffered seasickness. One woman

Galapagos Dream Ends For American Colonists

BY ROBERT COUR

IT IS ALL over for the rugged American colonists on the Galapagos Islands and the dream of a bright, new civilization under sheltering palms with the whole blue Pacific Ocean as a front yard is over, too.

Charles Harrison Jr., 40, and his family — last to leave the island dream — came home to Kenmore yesterday to tell a story of near-starvation under blistering heat.

"WE LIVED like animals ... It was like a nightmare," Charles Harrison, a tough man whose tenacity to make his dream come true exceeded all others, said in unmasked disillusionment.

"I am older and wiser—and poorer by about $10,000," Harrison said.

In the past year he has acquired an even tan and a small, walrus-type mustache. He has also turned gray and learned the real meaning of the word, worry.

"Everybody's gone from the Galapagos now," Harrison said. "We gave it our best but it was too much for us."

Gone from San Cristobal, main island of the Galapagos group, are all the hardy pilgrims that sailed from Seattle and San Pedro, Calif., in the Alert and Western Trader, two battered vessels re-rigged for the voyage 650 miles out into the Pacific Ocean.

"I want to warn anyone considering anything like this that the imagined and real are quite two different things," Harrison said.

HARRISON LEFT Seattle last March 25 aboard the Western Trader. Mrs. Harrison closed their house at 18424-73rd Ave. NE, Kenmore, and followed by bus with the couple's two children, Ronnie, now 15, and Mike, now 13.

"I paid $2,500 for the right to settle San Cristobal and I could afford it," Harrison said. "Plenty could not. They had scraped together every dime they could to make the trip."

While the Western Trader was scheduled to be in San Pedro only a few days, it was not until August 2 that the ship, with 50 colonists aboard, set sail.

"It was miserably hot and my wife worked like an animal in the galley. The long delay in San Pedro had depressed everyone but we had our money invested so we went along."

THE WESTERN TRADER arrived in San Cristobal on August 19 but nobody wanted to go ashore.

"We looked out from the ship and there was nothing there — just nothing. The colonists were frightened. I finally grabbed my family and went ashore," Harrison said.

Colonists from the Alert had already landed a few weeks before. They had found little of the new civilization they sought. About half of those aboard the Western Trader kept their berths. They went back to America with the Western Trader. The ship sailed loaded full; the empty berths were quickly taken by those from the Alert, already fed up with "community life."

"Some of the people who got off had as little as $20 on them when we landed and some of those had brought little children along," Harrison said.

THE ECUADORIAN government had issued visas to all but had stipulated that they could bring with them no stoves, no furniture, no equipment of any kind. The colonists were supposed to buy that at native stores.

"We lived in a shanty. The roof sagged and the boards were rotted. It was so hot you couldn't breathe. There was no running water, no electricity. We burned candles for illumination but you had to be careful that the candles did not bend double from the heat and start fire."

The Harrisons settled near Wreck Bay, aptly named, they soon learned. The city smelled of dead fish and lack of sanitary facilities. Drifters from all parts of the world dotted community life "human garbage," Harrison termed them.

There was no work to be obtained. No income for the colonists who had thought they might get wealthy in coffee, tuna, lobsters or in tourism.

No income but the cost of living was considerable. The natives slaughtered one steer each day, then cut it up with an ax.

"No steaks or chops or roasts," Harrison said. "They just hacked it up into chunks and sold it by the pound. A good portion of it was inedible."

MANY OF THE colonists had to sell the things they brought with them for food. The Harrisons, along with others, ate "baby food sandwiches." Canned baby food was plentiful for some reason.

Little or no supplies came from America. The Western Trader brought a second load of colonists and some food but there were so many waiting to catch a ride back that the Captain of the ship insisted on keeping most of the food for the return trip.

One by one the colonists left the island, bitter and broke. They sold tables and chairs, even clothing, to get back home to America.

Harrison hung on tenaciously.

"Why? Well, I wanted to give it everything I had. And it was an experience we would never forget. I wanted to see it through to the end."

THE END came on January 27 when the Harrisons left aboard a converted LST—the only ship to call on San Cristobal each month. After a brief stay in South America and in Florida, the Harrisons reached home.

Harrison reached first for a glass of cold Cedar River water, "the most underrated thing in the world." As colonists, they had to boil all water. Lois Harrison went first to her electric stove and refrigerator stocked full with fresh food. The children went to the games and books they'd left behind.

In a few days, they will have a turkey with dressing, gravy and cranberries — the works.

"It's for our Christmas," Mrs. Harrison said. "We missed it last December 25."

131

came up to me while we were passing San Francisco to remark, "I can now understand why the Pilgrims never went back. They swore no matter what hardships they had to face, they wouldn't set foot aboard ship again once they reached dry land."

When I tied the ship up at Pier 227 on Terminal Island, San Pedro, I left to return to Seattle. We had called United Air Lines and booked a seat on the 1:00 p.m. flight. By the time we reached the airport, however, the flight had already been called so the ticket agent wouldn't sell me a ticket. I said, "But I must get to Seattle in the worst way."

He looked at me, then picked up the telephone, talked a bit into it and, after putting it down said, "I have booked you on a Western Airlines coach flight which will depart at four."

I had less than one dollar with me so, instead of spending it for lunch, I sat in the waiting room reading newspapers I found on a seat. I figured I'd get a meal on the plane (if I could believe the advertising).

When I was finally aboard the propeller-driven plane and waiting for take-off, I rummaged through the seat pocket ahead of me and picked out a Western Airlines schedule. I found that Western had a jet flight direct to Seattle that departed at 4:00 and arrived in Seattle at 8:00. My flight wasn't due to arrive until nidnight considering all the stops en route. When I asked the stewardess what was on the dinner menu she said, "This is a coach flight. We don't serve meals."

You know, I did tell that United Air Lines ticket agent that "I had to get to Seattle in the worst way." I guess this was the worst way he could think of.

As for the Galapagos colonists, they had a long wait in San Pedro while awaiting their visas and a near-revolution took place in Ecuador between the governor of the islands and the president of the country. The governor didn't want the colonist invasion, and the president had made a political commitment to accept them. I am including here a clipping from the *Seattle Post-Intelligencer* by Robert Cour describing the further adventures of the group.

The WESTERN TRADER started a return voyage to the States from Galapagos, but in a storm off the Gulf of Tehuantepec, Mexico, she lost one propeller. The ship went into Salina Cruz, Mexico, to await the monies to be accumulated to pay for drydocking. It never came.

Few by few, the people left the ship to make their way home on their own. One family went down to Salina Cruz to join the ship and found it abandoned there. They heard rumors in town that the Mexican government was planning to seize it for unpaid dockage charges. I had left a couple of books on steamship operations aboard and, I understand, this family by dint of these was able to get the machinery started and slipped out of port about two a.m. and brought the ship into San Diego.

The next I saw of this ship was her stern lying on the pier of a dismantler's dock at Seattle many years later.

Chapter 28

MOHAWK to Hawaii
October - December 1960

I left PuttyStik, Inc. in October 1960 to resume a career at sea in order to get extra money toward Peter Steven's future in college. Toward this end, I applied at the Master Mates & Pilots Union to reactivate my membership.

When Kay received the call from Merle Adlum of the Local 6 Master's Mates & Pilots asking if I would be interested in a berth as Second Mate on a seagoing tug towing lumber barges to Honolulu, she replied, "That's just what he wants." I returned the call and was soon on my way to Portland to join the MOHAWK, formerly the EUGENIA MORAN, a 133-foot tug built at Orange, Texas, for convoy rescue work during the Second World War.

We picked up two converted LST barges being loaded at Portland with lumber and plywood, and started down the Columbia River for Astoria. As we progressed down the river, I suddenly noticed that the barges were getting far behind us. Investigating, I found the tow wire dragging bottom, and we were anchored by it. The barges had broken loose at the mounts, which had been welded on the deck to hold the chain bridle for towing. We picked up the tow wire and found the two mounts still shackled it to the chain. We retrieved the barges from where they had shouldered against a mud bank at the bend of the river and towed them to Astoria to make repairs.

After making the repairs to the tow wires and loading some more lumber on deck, we headed across the bar and set a southwesterly course for Honolulu. The northwest wind and beam sea gave us a pretty good roll to start off with. Since my bunk was 'thwart ship, I found it expedient to brace myself in with lifejackets head and foot.

The morning light gave us a view of one of the barges down a bit by the head and listing to one side. Sheets of plywood were being blown off the deck load. Examining it with binoculars, we noted a couple of the chain lashings had broken. Since it was too rough to pick up the chain and tow wire to go alongside, we changed course and entered Coos Bay for further examination and repairs. While we were picking up the tow wire in the shallow river water, the tide set us back and we managed to get a bight of the tow wire into the propeller. We spent an hour or two getting that cleared, then proceeded around to North Bend where we could dock at the city wharf.

We had to unload part of the deck load

133

to examine the deck area and re-weld a seam that was allowing water to enter one of the upper wing compartments. Then a couple of days to reload.

While there, I learned the local Toastmasters group was having its scheduled meeting, so I went to visit. I found a group of "professors" from the local high school, a very erudite and pedantic group. While I enjoyed their talks, I felt their critiques were a bit picayunish, and they showed very little sense of humor. When they called upon me, I looked around at all the serious countenances and retold the story I had heard concerning a fiftieth anniversary banquet of a private utility company back in the early thirties:

"At the fiftieth anniversary banquet, the speeches were long and, as usual, tended to be a bit repetitious and wearying. The president spent twenty-five minutes telling of how his company had grown by servicing their customers over the last fifty years. The auditor demonstrated with charts and graphs how much the company had grown by servicing their customers over the last fifty years, and by the time a third speaker, the retiring plant manager, had spent a half hour recounting how the company had serviced its customers over the past fifty years, they called on the featured speaker of the evening.

"This was a well-known Hollywood personality and humorist. He stood, looked at the weary faces and the dead cigar butts floating in the melted ice cream dishes and began: 'Ladies and gentlemen. With the rest of you good people, I have listened to these gentlemen tell of how they have watched their company grow by servicing their customers over the past fifty years.

" 'At first I was rather puzzled, but then I got to thinking about the time I was fourteen

Back to Hawaii, Tug MOHAWK, *1960*

years old and visiting my uncle's farm down in Oklahoma. Uncle told me to take our cow, Betsy, down to the neighbor's place for a while. I did, and the neighbor put our Betsy into a pasture with a dirty, mean old bull. Now, if what that dirty, mean, wicked old bull did to Betsy is what they call service, I can understand what your customers must have been going through these past fifty years.' "

As I finished, I watched the faces of my audience. At first they just sat there looking at each other out of the corners of their eyes, as though each was afraid to be the first to laugh. Finally, one of them started to chuckle and, as if on cue, the rest joined in.

We sailed for Honolulu and made it with no more untoward incidents. After discharging the lumber, we returned to Portland and then were sent to Olympia, Washington, to tow a pair of Liberty ships from the reserve fleet to Japan for scrapping.

Chapter 29

Mohawk to Japan
December 1960 - April 1961

December 16, 1960, was gray and cool as we departed Tacoma, Washington, with two Liberty ships from the Olympia reserve fleet in tow for scrapping in Japan. The two ships were the SS Joseph Jefferson (about which I could learn nothing at this time) and the SS Will R. Wood, whose files tell her story.

The story is complete beginning with the sunny day in October 1943 at Houston, Texas, where Captain E. Anderson accepted delivery from the builders in the name of American Export Lines for the War Shipping Administration, and took her into the war-torn North Atlantic.

The log books tell of slow convoys on the submarine- and aircraft-infested seas. "Keep a sharp lookout for the other steamers in the convoy. If the seas get rough again, call me. We don't want to lose any more lifeboats if we can help it," are words from the captain's Night Order book testifying to nominal hazards of the day (November 22, 1943).

The logs tell of air raids and cargo operations and mention names such as Anzio Beachhead, Naples, Oran, Algiers, Sicily and Marseilles.

Then the books tally long sunny days in the Pacific in 1945. They mention such places as Tacloban, Manila, Finschaven (New

Guinea), Brisbane, back to Manila, and up to that rainy morning in December 1945 when she arrived at San Francisco with the remnants of the 841st Engineering Battalion from whence they ended their war. Then the ship made her last passage to the laid-up fleet.

Other files hold letters indicative of the trials of those days: A letter from the mate to the home office complaining that the padlocks he was issued for his stores were of the same series as those issued to the Armed Guard. Consequently, master keys in possession of the Armed Guard gave them access to his equipment and stores (a constant cancer on the thin skin of amity between the merchant crew and the Armed Guard). Another of the mate's letters outlines the quantity of stores that had been checked off a truck alongside the ship but were missing when the supplies were stowed aboard.

Another file holds a listing of personal effects of a fireman, no reason given. (The only time we made such lists was in cases of death, desertion or removal due to illness.) Later on, in the engine room log, I found a notation that this man had been in a fight with the cook, and the radio files hold a request for an ambulance to remove a patient with knife wounds.

The crew lists included a man eighty years old who signed on as messman (Z#-1283). And on the last voyage, the second and third mates were twenty years old, and there were several seventeen- and eighteen-year-olds in the crew as Able Seamen and radio operator.

The radio files hold copies of messages relating to the storm warnings and the hazards to navigation such as floating wreckage, drifting mines, life rafts, etc. and also two which record history:

"MAY 8, 1400GMT (1945) OPERATIONAL PRIORITY FROM COMMANDER IN CHIEF.

"THE GERMAN HIGH COMMAND HAS BEEN DIRECTED TO GIVE THE FOLLOWING SURRENDER ORDERS TO U-BOATS: TO REMAIN ON THE SURFACE, FLYING A LARGE BLACK OR BLUE FLAG BY DAY AND BURNING NAVIGATION LIGHTS AT NIGHT. TO REPORT POSITIONS IN PLAIN LANGUAGE ON 500 KCYS EVERY EIGHT HOURS, AND TO MAKE FOR SPECIFIED PORTS UNDER ALLIED CONTROL. U-BOATS COMPLYING WITH THESE INSTRUCTIONS ARE NOT TO BE ATTACKED BUT SHOULD BE GIVEN A WIDE BERTH."

And: "SEPT 8, 080411 FROM PORT MORSBY RADIO:

"EFFECTIVE IMMEDIATELY ALL SHIPS WHETHER SAILING IN CONVOY OR INDEPENDENTLY ARE NOT TO ZIG-ZAG. GUNS NEED NOT BE MANNED. NAVIGATION LIGHTS TO BE BURNED AT FULL BRILLIANCY. BLACKOUT REGULATIONS ARE CANCELED" etc.

And the lights came on again in the world.

The hours I spent reviewing those files, sitting in the chartroom of the ghostly empty ship, proudly brought back memories of my own days in those ships and those years.

As I walked the decks of these silent ships, the many memories from the war years sailing on this type of vessel ran through my mind. I have tried to put some of my thoughts into words:

THE SHIP

They say a ship is a thing,
an inanimate piece of floating machinery,
a manmade vessel to carry commerce
across the oceans of the world.
Maybe so.
But they're wrong.
I know a ship is a live being,
has a soul, has a heart,
who cares for her crew.
I know.
My last ship told me so.

She whispered to me
in her creaks and groans
as she rolled down the northwest swell
of the Pacific on her way
to the breakers yards of far off Japan.

She whispered to me as I walked

across the boat deck.
The ghost of Dave Stockton
the young Second Mate stopped me
to show me how he died.
Murdered while preparing the lifeboats
while the ship was being strafed
by an enemy aircraft in a world at war.

In the radio shack,
the ghost of Sparks told me again
how he had to re-mount the big radio set
which had broken loose from the bulkhead
when the torpedo struck
and the ship started to break in two.

Boatswain Jacek's ghost was on the foredeck.
He told me of how the young chief mate
and he worked to run winch lines
across the crack in the deck
to hold the ship together
'til the ship could be towed in
to the cold, unfriendly Russian port
of Archangel
to deliver her cargo and be repaired
to sail again the stormy seas.

Hermann's ghost was
in the chief engineer's cabin,
pouring coffee into mugs
on the handmade table
where the officers gathered around each day.

Even the dog, Juno, was there,
lying under the table
wagging her tail occasionally
to tell us she was awake and listening
to the yarns we were spinning.

Back aft, in the carpenter shop,
young Jim Brady proudly
showed me his new tool kit.
He had put it together while
on his way to join the ship,

his first trip to sea.
He didn't know the machine gun bullet
that cut him down
would have his name on it.

Even the pans and pots hanging in the galley
talked as they swayed back and forth
with the roll of the ship,
Voicing stories of the past:
The cook who couldn't cook.
The fire that wouldn't burn.
The steward who was slow to learn his trade.

The crew's mess-room
echoed the voices of Glen and Dave,
of Frenchy and "Half-hitch,"
the young ordinary from Boston
who had joined the group from far inland
Missouri to enter the Merchant Marine
together to help fight the war.

Hebb's ghost stopped me on the foredeck
to show where he was at work
tightening lashings on the deck load
when the stray sea came over the rail
and smashed him into the hard, steel bitts.

And on the forepeak,
stowed under the gun-tub,
the Throne of King Neptune
lay where it was stashed
after the ceremonies crossing the Equator
the last time, so long ago.

Down in the Shaft Alley,
aft of the now-silent engine room,
I could hear the water passing
outside the hull whisper to me.
As if the ghosts of seamen
consigned to the deep
over the years were gathering
to bid farewell to another
of the ships which sailed the sea.

Yes, the ship is a live being
who knew the hands that cared for her
and guided her over the sea.
I know.
She whispered the story to me
as I walked her decks
for one last time.

And now we were hauling these ships back across the Pacific. Old, rusty, peeling gray paint, still mounting gun-tubs and other relics of their days of unsung glory. We will deliver them into the hands of those against whom they waged war . . . for the cutting torches of the junkyard.

They went reluctantly. They kept pulling sideways toward the shore as if they knew what was in store for them at the end of the journey.

In January 1961, we stopped in Honolulu for fuel and stores. I spent about five hours at Waikiki and various shops, getting a haircut and odds and ends. Then it was back to the ship and out to pick up our tows from the holding tug around midnight, and an uneventful twenty-day trip to Wake Island for fuel.

When we arrived off Wake Island, we had to wait for swells to go down before we could fuel. We tied up to a buoy and a long hose was floated out to us. The problem on the shore end is to keep it from rubbing against the sharp coral head at the end of their pipeline.

A few days later, our mail came aboard. For the next ten minutes or so, the ship was silent as each man curled into his own little shell to read his mail from home. When I awakened again to the world around me, I took the opportunity to examine the atoll through binoculars. The part I could see along the west shore was covered by small mushroom-shaped trees which hid any scars of the

Towing tandem two, SS Joseph Jefferson and SS Will R. Wood, to scrapyards of Japan

war. South of us, past the oil storage tanks and the one remaining pillbox, the bow of a Japanese merchant ship stood out of the water on the edge of the reef . . . rusting and battered by the endless waves of the blue Pacific.

The balance of the island visible was the runway of the airstrip. The planes landed and took off right over the ship as we lay at this buoy, depending on the wind, of course.

Over on the other side of the emerald-green waters of the lagoon, a community of some 1,300 people stationed there at the various facilities could be seen — PX, theater, barracks and family housing. Most of the people were with the airlines or radio station as well as Standard Oil Company.

The waters alongside the ship were lively with fish, and an ardent fisherman in our crew was out there scattering bread upon the waters, hoping for a fish in return. Deep down against the white coral bottom, the shadowy figure of a shark slunk out from the shadow of the ship to investigate a sinking morsel. Then darted back into hiding to consider. Then out again to gobble it and return to his lurking.

I rode over to one of our tows to check the running lights and see if I could get them lit again. Then over to the other tow. Since the chain ladders hanging down the side of the ships were installed while we lay alongside the dock at Tacoma, they were quite high out of the water to reach from the deck of the LCM, and the fact that of the lower four rungs on the ladder, three were either missing or broken. The difficulty of getting aboard was increased. However, calling upon the agility reserve I somehow had and timing the rise of the LCM on a swell, I managed to scramble up and pull myself to the good portion of the ladder to get aboard.

We sailed later that evening bound on a course that would give us a landfall at Farrallon de Pajaros, south of Iwo Jima, to keep in fair currents and good weather as long as possible while we repainted the tug on our trip to Osaka.

Three days out of Wake Island, we got change orders for Yokosuka in Tokyo Bay.

We turned up to head for Iwo Jima and, on February 10, in sight of the island, we had to shut down one of the diesel engines that drove our electric propulsion plant. In order to do this with these diesel electric drives, we had to stop the ship so the engineers could take one engine off the line, then start it again on one engine. When we stopped, the tow wires to our charges started to sink and, acting as a slingshot, pulled the tug and the tows together. Since the tug was then going astern, the propeller started turning in reverse. When we tried to go ahead on one engine, the electric drive wouldn't take.

While the ships were coming together, the wind, which had been ahead, turned the tug broadside to the oncoming Liberty ships we had been towing. We watched with mixed emotions the inevitable collision approaching while the engineers fought to get us going again. By the time they did get us started, we were hit, bounced off of and hit again by the ship. Fortunately, no one was injured and no holes were punched in the tug, though we had some bent rails and a section of the main deck in the way of a fuel tank. If the first blow had been aft a bit farther, in line with the stack, it might have gone right into the engine room.

Of course, this all happened just after the new coat of paint dried. The tug had been sparkling before then.

After we all stopped shaking and talking about what we did when we saw that thing approach, etc., shipboard life returned to normal. Sunbathing, reading, card playing, etc., and our current hobbies of growing mustaches and beards took over our spare time.

A companion tug, the SEA RANGER, towing two Knot ships, left Wake Island ahead of us. When she was within fifty miles of Yokosuka, on a course up the island chain, she was set out to sea some 180 miles by a combination of wind and current at the rate of thirty to thirty-five miles per day and held there until she was down to five days of fuel remaining.

For a week or so, we followed her "progress" and it was like a radio serial. You know, tune again in twelve hours for the latest word. Will she run out of fuel? Will the storm let up and allow her to make port with her tows? Will she have to drop her tows?

The weather finally moderated, and SEA RANGER approached to within eighteen miles of the entrance to lower Tokyo Bay.

The freighter SS AMERICAN BEAR had been giving us weather reports and acting as a contact with our agents while they were at the port of Yokohama. And again at Osaka.

As an aftermath to all the tensions regarding the SEA RANGER, the AMERICAN BEAR wound up in troubles of her own. She collided with a small Japanese freighter and cut it in two. They rescued the entire crew of the Japanese ship and made port themselves. They reported, however, that the Japanese ship did not sink, but both halves remained afloat, the section with the engines still turning in circles as the ship was abandoned so fast no one shut down the engines. It probably ran in circles until the fuel tanks were dry, meanwhile drifting without lights along in the current across shipping lanes.

Our radar blew a transformer while we were off Wake Island, so we didn't have the benefit of that instrument in our approach to Japan. Two days off the coast, in the dark current that drifts eastward along the south coast of Honshu, the radio direction finder also blew something. I changed all the tubes in it, but it still didn't work. Fortunately, good weather came upon us so we were able to use star fixes and sun lines in our approach to the coast.

The radio direction finder had been giving us variable errors of as much as nineteen degrees before it blew, so I don't think we missed much by not having it.

The currents in the area south of Japan are dominated by the Kushiro, a strong current similar to the Gulf Stream, which runs north and easterly along the contours of the Japan coast at a rate of five knots or so. Since our speed was five knots, we had to do some fine calculating to make progress across this stream to arrive at our intended destination. There is one spot where the charts indicate two undersea mountain peaks ranging from 6,000 to 9,000 feet from the sea floor. I expected that this would funnel the currents

between them, and since this was directly on our route, was not too surprised to find ourselves spending twenty-four hours in the same spot in spite of the calm seas. We changed course to the westward to finally break free of this uncharted current.

Reading material on a long, slow trip like this depended on the books put aboard by the American Merchant Marine Library Association, as well as paperbacks scrounged and traded along the way. I thought that if there were even one more Western aboard, I would expect someone to rig a saddle on a sawhorse for the helmsman to "ride" as he guides the ship. As it was, I noticed one of them mounted his stool by first placing one foot on a rung and swinging the other leg over.

Another trend in reading matter led to someone approaching the table to play solitaire or cribbage wearing a pleated shirt and a string tie, with a green eyeshade and black armbands. This was the first time I saw a deck of cards worn so thin that the numbers could be read from the back, if they weren't already worn nearly off.

As for the stories told in irregular session, some were quite interesting and well told, and covered many fields of experience. Jim Barkell, our second engineer, told of days on a halibut schooner . . . of hours in wind and rain bent over the rail pulling in 100- to 150-pound halibut on hand lines. Hands cut and calloused and cold and wet in salt water. Then going below for six hours' rest in the steamy atmosphere of the fo'c's'le.

A picture of wet clothes hanging on lines strung between tiered bunks; of boots and oilskins and a galley stove cluttering up the confined area with smells of cooking and sweat and damp clothing. The rattle of pots and dishes and the clank of chain in the hawse pipe as the ship ceaselessly rose and fell and rolled in the seaway. Then back on deck for another six hours.

Or stories like the one "Frenchy" told of his grandfather, who had had a farm in the wilds of Quebec and thirteen children: "Grandpa was an inventor of sorts. One day, he called his children to watch as he flew from the barn roof on wings he had built. He crashed into the rockpile below and was pretty badly banged up. The kids took over the farm chores for the months the old man was laid up. Finally, Grandma complained of the lack of meat on the table.

"Grandpa went out that night and the next day they had lamb roast. A few weeks later, another one.

"Then one night when Grandpa climbed the fence, he saw the glint of a steel bear trap his neighbor had placed near the fence. 'So, he thinks he is so smart,' says Grandpa. He proceeded to lower his pants and turned to spring the trap with one of nature's missiles, and did so.

"He had failed to consider, however, the length of the jaws of the trap. He hobbled home as best he could supporting the bear trap between his legs. It took Grandma, Momma, a fence rail and eight kids to spring him loose from his painful predicament.

Mount Fuji reared its snow-covered head above the hills to our left as we entered Tokyo Bay in late February. The SEA RANGER was about twenty miles south of us. The weather advisory said a storm was due to hit the Hachijo Jima area at two in the morning, and that was to be her port of refuge!

We felt our way into Tokyo Bay through fog. As I mentioned, our radar and radio direction finder were both out, so it was a matter of steaming along on estimated distances until finally a hilltop broke through the fog. Other ships passed us outbound, and we would guess by their heading which lighthouse they had passed last. When we saw the hill, it was a matter of guesswork as to which hill it was. Finally, the fog lifted enough that I caught a glimpse of a lighthouse and got a fix. Then we steamed on past the signal station. The pilot came aboard just as the fog changed into rain.

The pilot brought word that we were to anchor for the night about three miles outside the breakwater. Mail and Immigration would be aboard in the morning. Just after he came aboard, the MS TATEKAWA MARU came rapidly out of a fog bank to our starboard and, ignoring our signals, crossed in front of us. This put us in the awkward position of either running into her or being run into again by our tows if we slowed down. By some skillful maneuvering and answered prayers, we avoided both.

The barometer had been dropping all day. From 30.00 inches at midnight to 29.60 at 4:00 p.m. And still going down. At least both the SEA RANGER and ourselves were in a nearly safe haven from the expected storm.

The next morning at 8:45, the agent came aboard with mail, and once again the ship surrendered to the silence of introspection as each man curled into his individual shell to read his.

The agent also brought news that, instead of returning direct to the States, we were to return to Wake Island to pick up another pair of Liberty ships being brought out by the tug SALVAGE CHIEF. And, because of the weather, they wouldn't be taking our tows from us today. So we would be at anchor another night.

While anchored in Tokyo Bay, we encountered "bumboatmen," natives in small, unseaworthy craft who appear seemingly from nowhere around a vessel at anchor. They offer for sale everything from beadwork and basketry to whiskey. Their liquor is sold under many guises, from plugged coconuts to refilled genuinely labeled bottles (usually counterfeit Johnny Walker labels), but all having the same result of getting two or three of the crew intoxicated enough to be noticed by the captain. His only method of discipline was to restrict the entire crew to the ship when we reached a pier as well as log the offenders for watches missed. Tokyo Bay was no exception.

As the day at anchor progressed, the wind picked up a bit more, pulling our tows out on their wires and, consequently, straining our anchors. We called for a tug to come out to either take one of them or to put a line on us and help ease the strain on our anchors, as we were steaming full ahead on our usable engine to merely hold our position with the anchor down. (Back near Iwo Jima, we had discovered a water leak in the other engine.)

We stood around in the cool winds checking the anchor bearings and watching the strain and waiting. A navy tug came out to stand by us, but couldn't be given authorization to put a line aboard unless it became a matter of safety. Meanwhile, the agent and Harbor Control worked to get a commercial tug out to us.

Twice during the evening, we got reports of tugs underway to us, but after standing expectantly alert for an hour or so, we checked and found it to be another false alarm. About ten o'clock that night, the wind seemed to moderate a bit, so we released the navy tug to go stand by inside the breakwater.

Midnight brought a clear sky, and a wind that had shifted to north-northwest on a rising barometer. By one o'clock the wind had risen again to about thirty-two knots. RPMs on the engine were at ninety-five or so, and we seemed to be holding position while our charges strain at their respective leashes.

Finally, at 8:00 a.m., tugs came out and we spent the morning getting the wires and chains picked up from the bottom of the bay. The workmen had gone aboard the tows and, with burning torches, cut off the surge chains and let them drop. This would have been okay except that we were on anchor chain stretched out at full length and we had to drag some twenty tons of wire and chain out of mud and water a hundred feet deep and stretched some five to 1,500 feet astern of us. Besides, chain and wire, we brought up a tangle of fish nets.

At least the bitter cold wind of the previous night had died down, and the sun shone brightly. We finally got the end of one chain pulled up to the rail, and pulled the wire up to the end of the 1,000-foot pendant (two-inch wire). We then got a crane barge alongside to pick the chains up and away from us. This proved very fortunate for us as our winch broke down at that time. I saw through binoculars that the two-inch wire from one pendant was wrapped around the chain so we would probably have been struggling with it for the next thirty-six hours.

Bidding farewell to our charges, we scooted up to Yokohama Harbor and tied up to a buoy. Speaking of bumboatmen, the lower passageways and messroom and even the crew's lavatory looked like a branch of a combination of Sears Roebuck, Woolworth's and National Dollar Store with the displays of watches, dishes, radios, silks, dolls, music boxes, wallets, binoculars, toy boats, fishing gear, etc.

At noon the next day, we shifted from the mooring buoy at Yokohama to the Hitachi shipyard at Kawasaki, about six or eight miles north. We were boarded by a small army of shipyard workers, rigging scaffolds of poles tied at crazy angles and seemingly hanging from the sky alongside the outside of the ship. More of them were in the engine room, tearing into the floorplates and main engine and its electrical connections to the propeller shaft. Even more were in my room working on the radar.

When the latter went home, I showered, locked up my room, and, together with Doug Maas (chief mate), Dave Doyle (chief engineer) and Ralph Slusher (wiper), went out to the main gate of the shipyard and headed for Yokohama.

The gateman gave us a strip of paper with the name and location of the shipyard written both in English and in Japanese. This proved quite handy when we tried to find our way back to the shipyard.

We waited for a taxi about ten minutes, and felt the temperature drop. Fortunately, I had thought to pad myself with an extra T-shirt and topcoat. When the taxi arrived, we were quite ready for its warmth. The taxi was a small Datsun, and the four of us piled in somehow. The chief engineer sat forward with the driver and six-foot-six Doug, six-foot-one Ralph, and six-foot-one me sat in back. I still have an impression of an elbow in my ribs. Thus we rode to Yokohama.

We were dropped off at a sukiyaki parlor and started by having a sukiyaki dinner. This was rather an interesting arrangement for the four of us, as the table was smaller than a card table. What with waitress/cook working over the hibachi (a small cook stove) in the center of the table; a plate of raw meat, bean sprouts, etc.; settings for four of us; and a couple of bottles of beer, our little booth was more than a bit crowded.

While we ate, we looked around. It seemed to be a typical "greasy spoon" type place with a bar and television and tables. The clientele included everything from local workers to a pair of army sergeants. An or-

chestra of three or four played one or two songs before the jukebox and the television took over. The television show on when we started was an episode of the Jungle Jim series, except the dialogue was dubbed in Japanese. This was also true of the next show, which also had Perry Mason and Della Street conversing in Japanese.

We also noted the "housepets," which came over to visit the booth and survey the dinner. The first roach we saw came crawling over the small wall separating our booth from the next. He perched on the wall, walked along surveying our table from all angles, then walked down the gas line to the hibachi and stood up as though to sniff the cooking. Apparently finding it not to his taste, he left to seek more savory fare.

When we left the restaurant, we walked down the street looking in the shops along "tourist alley." We lost track of Dave and Ralph, so Doug and I looked at sextants and bought a couple of circular slide rules. Then we went down to the canal to a tailor shop where Doug got fitted for a topcoat. I got so engrossed in watching Perry Mason and Della Street talking Japanese that I forgot about the weather and left my topcoat to be lined.

We wandered about for a while longer. When the shops started closing and it began getting rather cool, we took a taxi down to the Silk Hotel and booked a room.

Then we went down to the cocktail lounge for a couple of hot buttered rums before going to bed. Soft beds, still beds, no engine noise, no roll, no bookcase to bang our heads on when sitting up — it was wonderful.

We awakened to the sound of steamer whistles in the busy harbor below us, and watched the ship movements for a few moments.

Then I left Doug to come out to the ship. I took a taxi to the railroad station and for sixty yen (sixteen cents) bought a ticket for Kawasaki. I was told to take a train on track eleven at 8:08. The agent didn't tell me what color to look for. Since I missed the train that was at the platform, I took the 8:11, an orange and green one that looked somewhat like the Key System trains in the East Bay area of San Francisco, except for the double car arrangement.

To say I caught it is not quite accurate. I should say I stood near it on the platform and was carried into it on the tidal current of humanity. I spent the next twenty minutes as one of a group of thirty-six people standing on the vestibule section of the car, four feet wide by nine feet long. I do not think a drop of water falling from the light fixture would have stood a chance of hitting the floor. And, being more than a head taller than the others in the compartment, I felt I was looking over a sea of black coconuts with smiling faces.

The train did not stop at Kawasaki. I wound up at Shinosaki (like going to San Leandro and winding up at Hayward, or to Lynnwood and winding up at Lake Serene.) I made like I was lost and was directed to track five. Before getting on a train this time, I asked. So instead of the Express to Yokohama, I caught the local to Kawasaki.

This time I stood in the wrong place and wound up in a second-class car (the same as first-class except for wooden benches instead of upholstered). Anyway, it wasn't too crowded, so when I got to Kawasaki I wandered through the vast station looking at merchandise in the shop windows. Then I took the bus out to the shipyard. This time, I showed the written Japanese instructions to a bus conductor before I got on so I made the right one the first time.

The next day, I met Doug around noon at the Silk Hotel, and we toured the silk museum after lunch. An interesting, informative hour or so reviewing the history of the silk industry in Japan, followed by a half-hour color film on the modern-day silk industry.

After that, we walked back across the waterfront to the train depot and took the local to Kawasaki. We spent an hour or so there walking around the department store in the railroad station. It was quite a mart — six or seven floors of everything one could seek for home or office. Then we took a bus back out to the ship to eat our steaks to dinner music provided by an air hammer chipping on the steel hull outside.

The following day, I visited the ship behind us, the SS NATIONAL FORTUNE. She was a Greek-owned Liberty ship under the flag of Liberia. What was interesting about her was that she had been cut in two and another hatch installed between Number Two and Three holds. The captain said this increased her speed from eleven to fourteen knots for the same engine RPMs.

Then their second mate and radio operator returned the visit. They had been away from home two years and had no idea when they would return. They said they were scheduled to go to the Philippines for a load of copra (dried coconut meat) for West Europe, then to Chicago via the St. Lawrence Seaway for a load of scrap iron for Japan.

In the evening, after listening to the shipyard noises all day, Doug and I took the bus to uptown Kawasaki to price bicycles and wander around in the relative quiet of the shops before they closed.

We decided on another "real" Japanese-style dinner. So we asked a taxi driver to take us to a "first-class Japanese hotel." He took us to a reasonably nice-looking place. (He didn't understand any more English than

Mate on Tug MOHAWK, summer 1961

we did Japanese.) All we recognized from his talk was the word "hotel."

The two women at the hotel looked rather surprised that two Americans were there without girls. When they showed us to bedrooms and we saw no sign of a dining room, our suspicions were confirmed.

We tried to explain to the women we wanted to eat and were getting nowhere until, in trying to explain food, I used the word "sukiyaki." Then we couldn't get that idea out of their heads. One of them led us along several alleys and down the street to an elaborate Japanese restaurant. Again, we found no English spoken. (We sure missed the little translation books we had left back at the ship.) We tried to explain that we wanted something to eat, but couldn't get a word in past our guide who, apparently, was telling the hostess we wanted sukiyaki.

They apparently catered to large parties

and didn't know what to do with just the two of us. The hostess sent us off again with the guide, who took us to a street corner and flagged down a taxi. Again, no English spoken. The taxi driver listened to the guide a bit, said "Ah, so," and took us to a "Number One Sukiyaki House" about two blocks from the railroad station.

Here again, no English. So we ate sukiyaki; by that time we were resigned to the fact that it was all we would get no matter what else we said.

The lesson learned: Take your translation book with you.

We returned to the ship about 9:30 p.m. and, to the song of a riveting gun, slept fitfully until 3:00 a.m. when everything quieted down for the night.

The next morning, pre-sailing activities got into full swing, The pilot and radio men were aboard to take us out of the harbor, and the fuel barge was alongside. The skipper was back to sign forty or so copies of invoices, documents, etc. Shipyard workers were busy slapping a coat of primer paint over the steel they had built in to replace our stove-in railings.

At 2:30 p.m., we left dock and went to an anchorage where the radio men were calibrating the RDF.

By 5:15, all the shipyard people had left and we hoisted anchor to proceed to the open sea again and Wake Island, 1,740 miles ahead.

A week later, we arrived off Wake Island, and tied up alongside the SS CANADA BEAR overnight. Her skipper (Butch Iverson) and ours (Jean Daly) had been shipmates years ago. Among the reminiscences that evening I heard about a chariot race in rickshaws through the streets of Calcutta, and of the two girls they met at a dance in New York in 1939 and how the promise of the evening was spoiled when they decided to take the parachute jump at the New York World's Fair. Butch's girl had an accident when the parachute dropped and both herself and Butch were soaked in a warm fluid.

The first engineer and the cook acquired somewhere more liquor than they could handle. They were "poured" aboard around 1:00 a.m. The cook was up for breakfast, however.

The next day, we took over the two Liberty ships from the tug SALVAGE CHIEF and, after having spent the day taking on fuel from her (we tied up to her tow wire and passed a hose so she could pump it over), we sailed. The SALVAGE CHIEF then went back to the fuel buoy to replenish her supply. This arrangement was made so we wouldn't have to wait for the CANADA BEAR to sail.

This arrangement worked to our advantage. The next day we received a radio message from the SALVAGE CHIEF that the shore supply was so low they had to rig pumps to pump the fuel aboard and it took them the entire day instead of the two hours as planned. We were well on our way by then.

For the next three weeks, we sailed nearly the same track as the previous month, except we went past Farallon de Pajaros before turning north to pass Iwo Jima.

We listened with interest to radio reports of Typhoon Tessie, which was making up near Yap Island and heading our way. About the time we were computing its track and speed of approach and the time we had to go the remaining distance to shelter, we ran into a local storm which the weather maps had not plotted.

This storm, coupled with the strong current past the undersea mountains, kept us back somewhat. We steamed by engines 140 miles west in twenty-four hours, at the end of which time we were sixteen miles east of our starting point.

The wind dropped by noon and in the next twenty-two hours we made fifty-five miles against the current (steaming at 5.5 knots).

Our sister tug, the COMACHE, left Wake Island on March 16 with two Liberty ships and, if she kept on her course, would have met Typhoon Tessie head-on around Iwo Jima. So she reversed course to head southeast out of the path.

Twelve hours later, the typhoon changed its course and headed for the COMACHE. From where we were, it looked as if the COMACHE's crew would have some well-chewed fingernails before the week was over.

We arrived at Osaka at 5:00 p.m. on March 31. We approached the Sakai breakwater as instructed in Yokohama, but in the fog we ran afoul of a new breakwater under construction across the lane we were traveling. We passed between two barrel-shaped buoys, which we discovered were wired together.

I stopped the propeller for a minute as we passed over it so it wouldn't foul our propeller but, with those ships on the tow line following us, didn't hesitate too long to re-engage it. After we had passed over the wire, dragging the ships along behind, we passed a crane barge anchored in the fog. All the crew of that barge were excited and hollering at us, but we didn't want to change course in the fog even though our charts indicated no obstructions in that area.

When we got our mail aboard, we also picked up the Notices to Mariners that had been issued since we had left Honolulu. In one, I found the report that a new breakwater was being constructed across the entrance to Osaka, which told us just what we had dragged ourself and two liberty ships (all of

BAR SEVEN SEAS

ALWAYS OFFERS

NEW, AND, FRESH, MOOD, AND, ATTRACTION EXCELLENT, PLACE.

FOR REST. MUSIC. AND, DANCING, WITH, CHARMING, GIRLS TRY, ONCE, AGAIN, AND, AGAIN.

TRY ONCE !
DRINKS MUSIC & WOMEN

SEXY MOOD !!

CALL ALL BOYS !
WHICH ONE IS BEST ? = BAR AGAIN
ENJOY YOURSELF LIKE HOME

Bar cards, Osaka, Japan

us drawing sixteen feet) across. No wonder the crew of that dredge had been so excited.

Typhoon Tessie seemed to be dissipating, so the COMACHE was again on her way.

After spending most of the day picking up our tow chains off the bottom of the bay, we moved into the harbor. We waited for about half an hour for the pilot off the end of the breakwater and, when one didn't come, we came on in without one with the aid of a Japanese chart of the harbor.

After the usual leisurely preparations (five minutes to shower and dress), we sat in the shore taxi for the trip in to the pier with the skipper and the second and chief engineers. When we arrived on the pier, we were besieged by touts for the local bars, each giving us cards advertising the attractions of their establishment and offering free taxi service to them.

I collected a few of their cards before the

Skipper and I went to the agent's office. Then we took a taxi to uptown Osaka, foregoing the "attractions" advertised.

I left the agent and skipper at Osaka New Grand Hotel and found my way to the right railway station through miscellaneous passageways and purchased a ticket to Awaji to look up the parents of one of the young ladies I had worked with at PuttyStik in Seattle. I had again taken the precaution of having someone in the agent's office write the address in Japanese.

The railroad station at Osaka seemed to take up a good two city blocks, and the area in front of the station seemed to be another square block devoted to taxi and bus stands. A series of underground passageways about thirty feet wide were provided for pedestrians to cross under the area. These passageways were lined with shops of all sorts as well as advertising posters.

Awaji Station provided no problem, having shown my ticket to the brakeman before I boarded the train and every stop where I tried to get off he would motion me to stay aboard. "Not right," he said until we arrived at the proper station. After looking in vain for street signs along the narrow streets parallel to the station, I showed it to a passerby who confidently took me in tow. But he couldn't find it either.

He took me to the police precinct station about three blocks from the depot, and turned me over to the guidance of the policeman on duty. While that gentlemen examined his chart of the area (a plat of all property listing all residents) and a big file drawer of residents in alphabetical (Japanese) order, a young Japanese lad stopped by to try his command of English on me, and did quite well as an interpreter.

The policeman took us with him and inquired at several business houses in the neighborhood for Mr. Shinomi, my friend's father. The druggist directed us to an appliance shop up the block. The people there said the Shinomis had lived there, but had left for America on March 22, ten days before. So maybe "Snookie" got her babysitters — I mean parents — without my help.

The young Japanese then invited me to his home. So I spent the evening with him and his family. His father, Kanji Takada, operated a metal shop where he made pots, pans and kettles. Mother Kieme was a housewife. Sister Yumiko was attending her last year at college. Brother Kazuaki was a seventeen-year-old high school student. And my benefactor, Masumichi Watanabe, who was the English speaker in the family.

When Kazaki came in, he dug up a record for the stereo so I could translate the song for him. It was "Santa Lucia" in Italian, so I wasn't much help. Later, he put another record of dinner music on. I ate a Japanese-style dinner (fox, tuna, egg rolled over rice, tangerines, raw ginger, etc.) to the tune of "The Persian Market Song" (shades of 1937 and my mandolin lessons). Everything was quite delicious.

Then Kanji brought out his pride and joy, a sword some 300 years old, to show me. It was a real beauty.

Kazaki showed me his coin and currency collection. I showed them a U.S. five-dollar bill. They were surprised that it was so small. I explained all denominations of American money are the same size. In Japan, the larger the denomination, the larger the bill.

Then they brought out a geography book and Yumiko showed me around Japan by map, with Masumichi translating. In return, I gave them a tour of the U.S. on a Japanese map of the States.

About 11:00, after shifting my legs from position to position to relieve the cramps from the hours of squatting at the low table, I found my way back to Osaka-ko and the ship by the 00:30 launch.

The next morning, I relieved Doug at 8:00 a.m. and was relieved by skipper at 1:00 p.m. I took a trip back over to Awaji to get Masumichi to guide me around Osaka. I arrived there about 3:00 p.m. to find he was in Osaka-ko, the port area, where he was probably looking for me.

All day, I had the feeling someone was trying to get in touch with me.

I visited with the Takada family again for the afternoon, having brought some U.S. stamps and U.S. coins for Kazuaki. We went through photo albums of the family and of Japan, and talked. They sent for a friend of Masumichi's to be interpreter. I waited until 6:00 but, when Masumichi didn't show up, I went back to Osaka by bus.

I walked down from bus stop near the railroad station to the Osaka Grand Hotel and rousted the agent, Ted Harris, from his nap. We went in search of supper, but wound up spending the remaining evening hours in a nightclub trying to converse in Japanese with the geishas who were assigned to us. We never did get supper.

When the place closed, I took a cab back to pier in time to catch the 00:30 launch to the ship, to relieve the skipper for watch.

The next day, we were to move into drydock to have our bent propeller blades straightened. When the pilot came aboard, we picked up the anchor and started under his directions down the channel. He seemed to be disturbed by the fourteen-foot-six-inch draft of the ship. He had not brought an interpreter with him, so we took him to the small-scale harbor chart we had and he pointed out that the depth of the channel to the shipyard was only twelve feet. We need more water than that to stay afloat. So we returned to anchorage.

Since we had canceled the water taxi service, we could not get a water taxi to stop. After an hour or so, the dockyard's boat came alongside to find out what the trouble was. The skipper sent me ashore to the agent's office to make other arrangements.

Since all the English-speaking members of the agent's staff were at the dockyard awaiting us, I spent an hour or so translating our problem into Japanese with the help of an English-Japanese dictionary, so that when the agent called to find out if they had heard from us, he could be given the information.

Translating into Japanese presented a little problem. First, I printed in English my message, and I read it slowly to the agent, pointing to each word as I went along. Then, I referred to the English-Japanese dictionary. This gave the English word and its equivalent Japanese characters. I had him read the characters and listen to the sound. Then we looked up the word in the Japanese-English dictionary, which lists words in English letters in alphabetical order of Japanese pronunciation, in order to determine which combination of characters expressed my intent.

Since I wanted to tell him to get our towing chains *and* our laundry back to the ship today *and* arrange for drydocking at Yokohama since the river at Osaka was too shallow, I spent some time at it.

While he was studying, I walked back to the pier and sent a note out to the skipper and dismissed the shipyard boat. Then I returned to the agent's office to learn the English-speaking staffers had called and were on their way back from the shipyard.

As I waited, I was given a book of Japanese ghost stories (written in English) to read. Talk about Grimm's Fairy Tales!!! Goblins in the form of humans by day but, when they sleep, their heads detach from their bodies and float about doing their wicked work, eating people, etc.

When the agents finally showed up, I explained the problem. Mr. Harris, the agent, called Hitachi Shipyard and a couple of others in the Yokohama area, but was told they were booked for three weeks or more. One other yard at Osaka would be free the seventh or eighth of April, and it was accessible to us. We tentatively reserved that.

After a short trip out to consult the skipper, Mr. Harris took a plane to Yokohama to see if he couldn't scare up anything else sooner.

The remainder of the day I spent at the agent's office, taking crew passes over to immigration for extension. I listened while the agent tried to find a diver to come out to examine the bottom of the ship to determine if there was any damage other than the bent propeller blades.

I waited another hour and a half for a water-taxi. It stopped and I visited aboard the ISLAND MAIL to arrange for weather broadcasts from "Sparks."

I had many memories of the ISLAND MAIL as I spent over a year on her as Junior Third and Second Mate in the South Pacific campaigns in 1943 and 1944. She was a new ship then, sparkling and rarin' to go.

Now the ISLAND MAIL looked old and tired. It was my understanding that she was scheduled for the "boneyard" the next year. (That was before she found the charted rock west of Smith Island for one of Puget Sound's better known pilots.)

I returned to the MOHAWK for supper and had a few minutes to shave before the agent was finished with his business.

When I went ashore and back out to Awaji for the evening, I brought along pictures of the MOHAWK taken the previous August when she was icebound near the

149

MacKenzie River (about 1,000 miles east of Point Barrow, Alaska), as well as pictures of my own family and home area.

I spent some time with Kazaki and his bout with the English language while awaiting Masumichi and their parents to finish the evening's work in the shop.

During the evening, Mrs. Takada showed me their family albums, one for each person. One was of the ten-year-old daughter, Sachiko, who had died in December. The album even contained a complete photographic record of the funeral — decorations of the house and room as well as of the procession and rites. These pictures filled the last pages of Sachiko's album and closed the book on her short life.

Before I left, Mrs. Takada gave me a Japanese doll and case to take to my own daughter. It had belonged to Sachiko. I didn't know how to accept this gift, or what I should do in return. I know that under similar circumstances, I would have had to think much and long before giving such a keepsake to a stranger, let alone a foreigner.

The boys escorted me as far as Osaka Station and I found the right streetcar to take me to Osaka-ko in time for the 00:30 launch.

On April 4, I received the message that my son, Steven, had passed away April 1.

The next few hours were spent arranging transportation for me to Yokohama to catch the night plane to Seattle.

Since air travel was booked solid, I was sent by train, leaving Osaka at 4:30 p.m., arriving at Yokohama at 10:30 p.m. My seatmate spoke no English, but let me look at his Japanese magazine. My beard seemed to attract quite a bit of interest from the youngsters both aboard and on the platform of the stations we stopped at.

The countryside we passed during the remaining daylight hours was mostly farms nestled in every accessible area of hill and valley.

I was met at Yokohama by our agent and driven to the Haneda airport to catch the midnight flight to Honolulu, arriving there six hours later. Then a four-and-a-half-hour flight to San Francisco, and another three hours to Seattle. There is something about rapid air travel that takes away the feeling of accomplishment one achieves from taking sixty days to cross the ocean on a ship.

Chapter 30

MOHAWK to Alaska

May - August 1961

The MOHAWK returned to Portland on May 1; three days later, I rejoined her as Chief Mate to let Doug Maas have his trip off. I was told about their trip out to tow the COMACHE and her tow of two Liberties into Yokohama on account of her engine room being flooded by sea water during the storm. The MOHAWK then went to a shipyard in Sendai province to get her propeller straightened. The port they visited there was a small fishing village and they encountered a hospitality often dreamed of. The stories I heard of this visit made me feel I really missed something.

After moving my gear into the Chief Mate's room, I met my new crew as they came aboard. We took stores aboard at Swan Island on May 5.

The cook didn't show up, so we stowed what we could of his stuff, meats, milk, etc. in the refrigeration box, and stacked so many cases of canned goods in the crew's quarters (until he could direct the stowage) that it looked like a grocery warehouse.

The cook didn't show on Saturday either, so I had the crew stow everything in the storeroom, and then we set about splicing new mooring lines. We shifted to the fuel dock and took on more stores. It seemed the longer we lay, the more items we found lacking from stores, such as fresh vegetables, fruits and potatoes.

The chief engineer's wife and Kay fixed sandwiches and salad for the crew, with the assistance of George, the German messman with some distinctive ideas about cooking. The chief's wife made the comment during the process: "No wonder George isn't married. No woman would put up with him."

On Saturday night, we shifted back to Swan Island to lay over Sunday. I sent Kay home on Sunday morning's train and walked uptown Portland to a show, after which I bused and hitchhiked the last two miles back to the shipyard, arriving in time for a steak dinner George had cooked up.

Monday, we returned to the fuel dock. After topping off, went to the company's (Columbia River Navigation Company) new dock at Stebco Mill, about three miles down river from Vancouver, Washington, to lay another thirty-six hours awaiting orders.

Wednesday, we picked up barges 546 and 508 and took them to Astoria, where we made up a tow of barges 546 and 510 for sea.

Thursday morning, we sailed up the coast with an ear to the radio for orders to Seattle. Late at night, as we neared Umatilla

Lightship, we got the word to proceed to Dutch Harbor, Alaska. As we turned to leave the coast, a last-minute check of the radar showed that the three days and money spent on it at Portland hadn't got it working properly. So we turned up the straits to Port Angeles for more repairs.

As we docked at Port Angeles, three injectors on our port engine gave out. We suspected water in the fuel we had taken at Portland. So we lay at the dock until midnight, getting all the injectors cleaned and the fuel filters purchased and installed.

Friday, we pulled the heavy surge chain out of the hold and rigged it to Barge 510, after transferring the small chain to Barge 546.

When evening came, I got a ride up to see the sights of the center of town, all six square blocks. There I met Ralph, the wiper, and we shuttled between two joints, each on opposite ends of the business district, waiting for "later when the joint starts jumping." It must have been much later, for the only jumping we saw was one of the three couples in the place jitterbugging on the small dance floor. The remaining ten or so beer drinkers sullenly looked at each other along the bar, relating their problems to the bartender or neighbor, whoever would listen.

We walked back to the ship at 11:30 and got the rest of the crew rounded up from the beer joint at the end of the pier and sailed.

Saturday, we were to head up inside of Vancouver Island, the tug getting shipshape and ready to cross the Gulf of Alaska.

As the week progressed, our trip across the Gulf went well. One by one, the colds everyone had come down with since leaving Astoria faded. Occasional glimpses of sun through the overcast gave us our position to check the LORAN equipment we had just had installed, and we got the spare tow gear over-

hauled. The only ship we passed was a Russian trawler heading eastward.

The night of May 21, we came through Unimak Pass last night and into a fifty-mile gale. We bucked a bit then decided to anchor up in Akutan Bay until it blew over as Dutch Harbor would be on a lee shore and we did not have a schedule to meet.

When we tried to anchor, however, we found too much wind to hold position, as the anchor kept dragging. So we hove up and spent the day steaming up and down the bay, past the Indian village of Akutan (population eighty-six) up to the abandoned whaling station and back, finally anchoring again during a lull in the wind about sunset.

We received by radio word that our schedule would take us up to Dutch Harbor, Naknek, St. Paul Island, and up to Teller, north of Nome.

When we got underway from Akutan in the morning, we still had a twenty-knot breeze. But since the forecast was for a new storm making up, we figured maybe we should take advantage of this lull to steam the forty miles over to Dutch Harbor.

As we were leaving, I had left the towing winch drum turned off and the brake on, when I went forward to work on getting the anchor secured. The skipper speeded up, and the big barge started unreeling the wire from the winch. Skipper noticed it in time to stop when there were still two turns of wire left on the drum, and saved a day's work trying to pick up ninety feet of 2½-inch chain and about 1,600 feet of two-inch wire from the bottom of the bay to get the end I nearly lost. When I leave that winch now, I make sure the "dog" is in.

We arrived in Dutch Harbor and tied the barges up to an old pier on the north side of the bay just as the southeast wind started to pick up. So we felt fairly secure at our berth.

About 5:30 we got a radio call from the fishing vessel BERNIE, who had lost her rudder about five miles off the harbor entrance. So we got underway and went out to find her. She was a boat the size of our lifeboat with a cabin over her. We towed her in before dark, with the strong forty- to fifty-knot gusts of wind we encountered. Her owner was happy to get to shelter, as he would have spent the night drifting out into the Bering Sea with no control.

The morning of May 24 dawned with patches of blue in the sky overhead. The snow-capped hills around the harbor surrounded quiet waters. The barometer was dropping, from 29.90 the previous noon to 29.47 at 4:00 a.m. After shifting about the harbor to help the WINQUATT with the monstrous Barge 539, we refueled.

While the vessel lay at the fuel dock for a few hours, nearly all of the crew including myself went over to visit the town of Unalaska. We were driven over on the back of a truck through the abandoned streets of the wartime naval community. The vacant buildings, featuring paint-peeled signs such as "Harbormaster," "Fleet Post Office," "Ships Services," etc., were the only traces of this once active harbor.

On the Unalaska side, we got the postmistress from home to open up to accept mail and sell stamps, money orders, etc. Then we walked down the main street to the general store next to the Williwaw Theater ("Walls of Jericho," no soundtrack) for our shopping for all the little odds and ends we forgot at Portland and Port Angeles. Then walked around to look over the town.

The new church was being re-roofed; it apparently had just been painted. As a matter of fact, it seemed to be the only building in town with a coat of paint less than twenty years old, and that was because the old church burned down a few years ago. It was a Russian Orthodox church, founded around 1800 when the area was a Russian settlement.

While we were at Dutch Harbor, the crew finished painting nearly all the outside of the hull — black, to cover nearly all the splotches of red lead left over from the last voyage. Then the ship didn't look so much like a refugee from a Taiwan junkyard.

We moved Barge 510 to and then away from the tanker HILLYER BROWN for her cargo of JP4 jet fuel.

After leaving Dutch Harbor, we encountered a fine sea but overcast skies. We passed a Japanese factory ship about twenty-five miles north of Port Moller, constructed from an old "Hog Island" freighter, built during World War I the Hog Island yards near Philadelphia. Their main distinction was they were designed by a bridge builder and, since there were no curves in her lines, had the appearance of "being built by the mile and cut off to lengths."

The present crew had bamboo structures mounted over the entire afterpart of the ship; "four-story tenement" would about describe it. Hundreds of faces peered out at us as we passed. A fleet of small tenders hung in the davits all along her sides, and another small vessel (about 125 feet) worked the line of crab traps to the north of us.

We threaded our way through about eight miles of crab pots in the vicinity of this ship.

The next morning, we shortened our tow wire preparatory to entering the shallower waters at the mouth of the Kvichak River.

The long approaching storm reached us about 3:00 the next morning. After dragging anchor a bit, we heaved it up and steamed up and down the bay for a while. Then, as the current slacked at the change of tide, we anchored again and steamed against the anchor for another eight hours until the fifty-five-knot wind dropped.

Kvichak Bay (Naknek) is a shallow bay with swift-running currents from Naknek and Kvichak rivers and a twenty-five-foot rise and fall of the tide. It is surrounded by low tundra country. Its main purpose commercially is the support of nine or ten salmon canneries here and down the coast a bit at Egekik.

We turned Barge 510 over to WINQUATT and the 546 to the NEZ PERCE, then went alongside Barge 539 to top off fuel and spend the night. Did I say the 539 was monstrous? Two hundred ninety-nine feet long, seventy-five feet wide, twenty feet deep and, besides carrying more than three million gallons of bulk fuel, it was stacked thirty feet high with cargo ranging from trailer vans to drums of gasoline. Towering over all this were three large cranes giving the appearance of an island more than a barge.

Two days later, we left Naknek and steamed for a beautiful, sunny cruise over to St. Paul Island in the Pribilof group. At daybreak on June 2, I saw the mountain of the island for a short while before the rain hid it. We made our approach by radar and anchored half a mile off the snow-splotched beach.

A fair breeze blew over a small southwest swell, which formed large breakers across the mouth of the village cove.

I went ashore to meet the contractor, John Long, and to look over the cargo we were to load. I was shown several piles of miscellaneous construction equipment, knocked-down buildings, trucks, bulldozers, timbers, lumber, tar plant, batch plant, etc. I had mentally figured we could get it all on our thirty-one-foot-by-110-foot single-deck barge with little trouble at all, until I was shown into a Quonset hut about one-third full of boxes,

building sections, etc., which were also to go. My mind stacked these in the space left from my previous mental calculations. Then, as we walked over to the hotel for some coffee, he pointed out the fourteen pieces of heavy equipment, generators, a thirty-three-foot trailer, a cement truck, and various items like some four-foot-by-eight-foot plywood boxes full of cased canned goods.

By the time I got them all measured and had sketched out a loading plan, I found it too late to get back to the ship, as the swells past the dock made it impossible to launch a boat. So I made arrangements to stay at the local hotel.

After more work drawing out a stowage plan with Mr. Long, I went down to the radio station to witness a ham radio operator in action. He had a rather powerful station and went into much technical detail of explanation, and turned his set on to demonstrate his power and directional antenna, which he designed by rigging a "V" antenna with each leg 688 feet long. His second attempt picked up a Seattle ham who patched in a call home for me. He tells me he can talk to South Africa with this set-up.

On June 3, we spent all day pulling our barge the 2,000 feet from the anchorage to the pier, using tractors and other equipment to pull in our rope hawser. The main obstacle was the shallowness of the water, which didn't permit the MOHAWK to get in closer. So we not only pulled in the barge, but also 2,100 feet of 1¾-inch tow wire, which, of course, dragged along the bottom. This was necessary in case the wind shifted and the tug had to haul her out in an emergency.

We got to within 100 feet of the pier by 10:00 p.m., so left it there for the night, the tow wire holding it off and the two hawsers holding it too the pier.

We went in at 5:00 a.m. the next day to

pull the last 100 feet to bring the barge along-side. After breakfast, I brought my crew in to start loading and stowing heavy timbers on deck, and the construction equipment on top. This went on board little by little and, as the days progressed, the barge took on the appearance of a "Grapes of Wrath" type vehicle rather than a shipshape, seagoing enterprise. It had to be loaded in such a way that we could push her nose on the beach, unload the bulldozer to bulldoze a drive-ramp, and bring the pieces off on the vehicles we carried.

Loading progressed at twenty hours per day until Wednesday midnight. About 1:00 a.m., after singling up the mooring lines and sending the crew out to the ship, I got the signal from the ship to let go. I rode the barge for an hour or so as it was towed over the shallow spots and around the island to the lee side, where I could safely transfer to the tug to a nice, warm bed. I slept for eight straight hours for the first time in a week.

During the loading, we would take time out once in a while to watch a pair of medium-size whales play about the bay, and one huge old-timer who stayed about the bay all week blowing and spouting a fishy-smelling fountain occasionally.

After lashing the cargo as best we could, we sailed for Point Spencer, on a course that passed within a mile of Walrus Island, where we could watch the hundreds of huge sea lions basking on the rocks. The island was nearly covered with a moving brown mass of life.

On June 10, the fog which had been over us all day lifted about 4:00 p.m. and revealed the ice chunks, bergs and fields all around us. We navigated the last fifty miles or so dodging through and around them, arriving in Port Clarence at 10:30 p.m. Sunset did not arrive until 11:15 p.m. and the bay was more than seventy-five percent covered with ice.

We unloaded the barge at one of the most isolated parts of the United States. During World War II, this base had been used to transfer bombers to the Russians, but had since been abandoned. The buildings, outside of having no window glass, were in remarkably good condition, no rot in the wood, just plain air-dried and solid.

The spit of land that was Point Spencer was about seven miles long and from one-tenth to three-quarters of a mile wide. The air strip was serviceable and the contractor's chartered planes landed at periodic intervals. The weather had been clear. The ice in the bay shifted back and forth with the change of tide, and light winds blew until Wednesday, when the sky became overcast and a strong southerly wind and a light rain covered us as we finished unloading the barge.

We had beached the barge in an area bulldozed out just north of where we unloaded, tying it to the old beachmaster's tower and a concrete "deadman" set in the ground.

The contractor's crew didn't waste much time setting up a campsite, as the temperature hovered around thirty-seven degrees. Monday there was nothing but a desolate, barren strip and by Wednesday a village of about thirty men had sprung up — Quonset-type insulated tents, a mess hall, repair shop, each occupied as fast as it was assembled.

We headed south for Dutch Harbor and were diverted to Naknek. We stopped at Naknek only long enough to pick up Barge 539, then headed again for Dutch Harbor.

We docked the 539 at the Standard Oil pier and started filling our own hungry fuel and water tanks.

On the voyage over, Bill Stanton, the sailor on my watch (from Coos Bay, Oregon) kept me semicaptivated with his stories of the waterfront over the past forty years, and his acquaintanceship with the writer Matt Peasley and his "Cappy Ricks," a character based on the life of R. Stanley Dollar. He also told of old Captain Oliver Olson of the Olson Steamship Company, whose steam schooners hauled lumber from the dog-hole ports of Washington and Oregon to California for many years.

One of the tales was of the funeral of young shipowner Lawrence Phillips, Captain Olson officiating. It seemed Lawrence wanted to be cremated and his ashes sprinkled on the waters off Point Conception, outside Los Angeles Harbor. All participants in the service were standing at respectful attention on the boat deck. Captain Olson read the service and, as the ship swung into position off the point, he signaled the mate to open the box of ashes. At that moment, a vagrant gust of wind emptied the box and blew the ashes back to cover the well deck aft.

The bo'sun quietly called two of his crew to rig a hose and started washing down the well deck.

Captain Olson walked down from the bridge. Head bowed, he walked aft in dignified fashion through the standing mourners. He stopped short when he saw what was going on below. He said, "My God, bo'sun, what are you doing?"

"I'm washing Larry overboard, sir."

"Okay, bo'sun, be gentle with him." Then he returned to the bridge.

The fuel we had taken aboard from Barge 539 proved to be about thirty-five percent water, and contaminated the fuel we had, so we spent the night pumping it back into 539 and in the morning shifted around to the dock to take fuel from Standard Oil.

After spending the morning overhauling the boom and rigging a new wire fall, we shifted over to Ballyhoo dock across the harbor to pick up Barge 510 and departed for Naknek.

The next day, we pulled into Port Heiden area and transferred Barge 510 to PEYAKA. PEYAKA is an LSM converted into a combination tug and freight-handling landing craft. She has a wheelhouse built high enough to see over ramp and appears to be a good craft, handy for this beach work. I would like to look into the operating costs for such a craft and, with a couple of LCMs, look to a lighterage business in Alaska. There seems to be plenty of room for such a business.

We picked up Barges 537 and 520 from TIGER and, after delivering their mail to PEYAKA and TIGER, pulled out for our destination.

After a hectic weekend at Naknek with a fresh to strong southwest wind blowing up the bay, both with and against the flow and ebb of the tide, we left early on June 27. Our only damage was a bent section of rail up near the starboard bow received the previous afternoon when we were not quick enough to slip out of the way of the barge that had been hanging upstream on the tow line. It set down upon us as we swung to the change of tide. As we sought to slip away, we backed over our tow wire, getting it in the wheel.

After dropping the anchor on the barge, we finally drifted away from the barge to spend the next two hours swinging the wheel back and forward trying to shake the wire loose. It finally came loose on its own accord — the worse for wear, but loose. Then we drifted down to anchor.

During the time the skipper and crew were working aft to clear the wheel, I was working forward to clear a long piece of ⅜-inch chain from the anchor. It had a round turn around our anchor and I had to snag it from on deck and pull it up with the winch, hold what I got, then snag some more to pull up. When I finally got enough up to drop the bight free over the anchor, I found I not only had about 100 feet of heavy chain, but also a 450-pound anchor from some barge.

Apparently it had lain for months, judging by the rust and sea growth. However, it could be cleaned up, painted and used. Not the chain, though; it was too badly pitted with rust. So I managed to get it aboard and secured it on the after deck until I get a chance to work on it.

We headed back to Dutch Harbor with Barge 537 in tow for a load to take to Shemya. Also some work on our engines and tow wire.

Two days later, we docked our barge at Dutch Harbor after limping in on one engine. Apparently, we had a broken camshaft on the starboard engine. So it was a few days' wait until parts could be flown up from the States.

We found the Canadian icebreaker CAMSELL at the pier when we arrived and, before long, we were visited by several of the Canadian crew members. They invited our crew over to a few drinks and a movie. Since I was on watch and had to mind the store, a quartermaster from the CAMSELL stayed to visit with me. He had the foresight to bring a small sample jug with him. He left about 9:00, and the skipper and second mate returned from the movie about 10:30.

The visitor told me of having gone over to Unalaska with a couple of shipmates earlier in the day, looking for a bootlegger in this "dry" community, only to be referred to be the local missionary. They got a fifteen-minute sermon on their evil ways, and no jug. They seemed to have been doing quite well with supplies they had laid in at Victoria, though, so didn't need any sympathy.

The following day, we worked for a couple of hours with hydraulic jacks and a sledge to straighten the bulwark and rail bent by the barge. Tough stuff, this steel.

We then cut off a hundred feet of tow wire to get the portion cut and kinked by the propeller. The barge captain of 537 came over and replaced the "D" fitting on the new section.

The crew then borrowed a truck and went scrounging in the airport dump for some large tires to use for fenders. In the evening, I went over to the Unalaska side to the store.

The storekeeper told us of the costs of getting supplies: freight from Seattle to Kodiak by Alaska Steamship, storage charges at Kodiak waiting for the supply ship EXPANSION's monthly voyage, freight charges on the EXPANSION, loading and unloading costs and transportation from the ship to the store. This all added at least fifty percent to the original cost of a case of canned goods from the Seattle wholesale house.

A week later, we took time off for Independence Day. Unalaska celebrated the holiday with foot races for the younger set, and Monday (July 3) the EXPANSION paid its monthly visit, bringing among its cargo, fresh watermelons ($2.68 each) to the local market.

In the evening, the movie "African Queen" was shown, after which a record player was brought out for a dance, the first since December. Members of our crew, the barge, the RANDE A (a sub-chaser hull that brought up a load of sheep, horses, and a cow from Seattle) brought attendance up to about thirty persons. The bashful Aleut girls had to be literally pried out of their seats to dance with the strangers, but got into the "swing" of things as the evening progressed.

We left when the dance was over and got back to the ship in time for me to stand my watch until 8:00 a.m.

Thursday, July 6, we shifted over to the

fuel dock and loaded our barge. Topped off our fuel and water tanks. The SALVAGE CHIEF came in with her barge, and I met again with the skipper I had first met at Wake Island last March.

We returned to our berth at Ballyhoo dock around midnight. The chief engineer traded our old DC washing machine to the LUPE for an MG set to power our new AC model. However, since the MG set was only good for 0.7 amps and the machine needed three amps, we were still without the convenience.

The parts came Tuesday afternoon, July 11. The engineers spent most of the night and all day Wednesday putting together the starboard engine. The crew finished painting the foredeck and everything on it, and installing the new washing machine in which the engineers had installed a new DC motor. So, after going over to Unalaska to top off our water tanks and pick up our ship's laundry, we took the Barge 537 in tow and sailed at midnight.

I hired Ken Radike, an Able Seaman who worked on the converted sub-chaser RANDE A. He told us of the trials they had on their way up to Alaska with a load of sheep. The pilot had gotten off at Juneau and no one else on the ship had been to sea except Ken, and his experience was mainly on the Great Lakes.

Ken got them out to Dutch Harbor, after running aground once and being driven aground another time when their anchors dragged during a storm.

The passage was foggy and hazy along the north side of the Aleutian chain and inside (south) of Semisopochnoi Island (now there is a name for you). The wind was from the northeast, shifting to northwest and threatening to give us quite a "lump" in Shemya Harbor. However, it then shifted to the west and flattened out.

Tug MOHAWK off Point Barrow, Alaska, August 1960

We docked at Shemya, having made our approach by radar in the almost perpetual fog. Fortunately, the wind held in the west-southwest, so we had only a minimum of surge at the dock.

The harbor around us was spotted with reefs, rocks and wreckage. The beach was littered with broken pilings from the dock, which at one time extended about 500 feet farther than at present. Also, the hulk of one of Puget Sound Tug's big oil barges was on the beach. She had snapped her mooring lines while at the pier, and also broken her tow wire when WANDO tried to pull her to safety. A large swell from a sudden storm put her across the reef, tearing out her bottom and leaving her stranded.

I took the cook over to the big air force "composite" building to have a dentist pull the teeth he had been complaining about since we were in Honolulu last trip, but never could take time out from drinking enough to have them cared for.

In the evening, we learned that the SALVAGE CHIEF's orders had been changed and she was to meet the QUINNETT. But since the

COMACHE had headed for Seattle and we were the only large tug up here, it looked as if we would meet the SALVAGE CHIEF or one of the Seattle-chartered tugs to trade barges at sea and head north again.

We finished unloading at 1:00 p.m. July 19. After listening to Captain Royall (USAF) comment favorably on the condition of the cargo (except for some diesel oil stains on some cartons) and for the cooperation and coordination that made rapid discharge possible (in spite of breakdown of their fork-lift in the warehouse), we sailed.

We made a rapid passage over to Attu and docked at Massacre Bay about 9:30 p.m.

The next morning, we started unloading some odds and ends into the two old trucks we had brought along. And, since unloading is going slowly as we wait for these trucks to return after hauling their loads up the hill, I got a chance to look around.

The hillsides were dotted with remnants of Quonset huts and buildings from the once active naval station which, as in Dutch Harbor, had been abandoned. Coast Guard had about twenty-five people here at the Loran Station, and that was about the size of the population.

While at Shemya awaiting the mail the other evening, I visited with the General Electric man. He was a former Chief Engineer from the Norwegian Merchant Marine. He told me about that work and events, including being interned by the Germans at Dakar when France was taken over. He was left aboard his ship with his crew for about three months, at which time the Germans came and told them the owners had sold the ship and the crew was to turn it over to them.

The Germans had taken essential parts of the engine ashore to prevent the crew from taking the ship to sea. The crew told the Germans that they wanted proof of the sale before they would turn over the ship. So the Germans took the crew off and put them aboard an Italian passenger ship for transportation to an internment camp at Casablanca. Before they sailed, however, the Germans came to the chief engineer and accused him of having sabotaged his ship since they could not get it started.

The chief answered that it hadn't been sabotaged, and that if the Germans would return the parts from the engine they had taken, he, with one of his men, would be happy to start it to prove it.

He and one of his oilers were take back to the ship and supervised the re-installation of parts. Then he proceeded to start the engines, having instructed the oiler to open and close every valve in the engine room, leaving only the proper ones in position for the start in such a way that the German observer couldn't keep track.

When the engines started and shown to the German as not having been sabotaged, the chief shut them down again, having the oiler make motions with many odd valves in the process of securing the plant.

When the German protested his stopping the engines, the chief reminded him he was only brought over to prove it would run. Since he had done this, he had shut her down and was ready to re-join his crew in internment.

A year or so later, he ran across his brother who said the ship was still at Dakar. When he was released and went back to get it at war's end, he found the Germans had never been able to get it started. She had so many barnacles she could only do three knots to the shipyard.

The second to fourth days of our stay at Attu gave us beautiful summer weather, from clear sunrises against the green hills to golden sunsets and warm clear nights.

We loaded our barge with a cargo of rusty landing mats, left in the fields since the days of the war when this island was a base for some 100,000 men. Only a Loran navigation aid manned by some twenty-five people still remained.

We sailed before sunset and got a view of the entire island from offshore (no fog), the snow-capped mountains standing purple and white over the flat sea.

We passed Shemya around midnight, and "hove to" long enough to put Ray Waters, our beachmaster, ashore to catch a plane for Adak to prepare for our arrival there.

We stopped at Adak for half an hour to pick up a few items from the pier. Then away again to sail through Great Sitkin Sound in the sunshine. The mountains touched with snow and clouds towered above the bay and channels as we proceeded eastward to Dutch Harbor.

Sea otters playing around the bay held our attention. One mother was floating backwards with her baby across her chest, feed-ing it fish she held up with her flipper like a bunch of grapes. All the while she watched us with a wary yet nonchalant eye.

We docked at Dutch Harbor to pick up a cargo of oil for Cold Bay to be delivered on our way to Seattle. The weather had been overcast and a brisk breeze blew across the bay in the evening. Brisk, though warm — seventy degrees or so. It portended rain as the night progressed.

We steamed eastward past Akutan Island. Mount Shishalden rose, snow-capped and majestic, above the blue horizon off our port bow as we headed into Unimak Pass. The song the vibration of the propeller far below us sang, echoing the feeling in our hearts — "We're going home."

At Cold Bay, snow-capped tiers of volcanos peeked out above the fog blanket surrounding them. A stiff southerly breeze blew all day. It did not delay the pumping out of our cargo of fuel oil. At 11:00 p.m., we were underway again. Our next stop, Puget Sound country. Seattle or Tacoma, we weren't sure yet which it would be. But home.

Chapter 31

MERCATOR

September 1961

During the six weeks at home, while looking for a new berth, I accepted a two-week relief job on a crab packer at Kodiak Island.

After a rather bumpy plane ride over Kodiak Island in a Kodiak Airways six-passenger seaplane, and after landing and taking off from some fishing ports and canneries tucked into some of the many bays around this mountainous island, I arrived at Jap Bay and boarded the MERCATOR about 4:30 p.m.

The MERCATOR was a ship about 210 feet long and 1,235 tons, built in San Francisco in 1925 as an oil tanker ALASKA STANDARD. She had been converted to a cannery tender while I was working at Fiberglas and was now a crab packer with facilities for freezing crab within minutes after they are taken from the water. Vic Hanson, the skipper I relieved, gave me a "Cook's tour" of the vessel.

The next afternoon, four or five boats came in and I learned to operate the cranes to unload them into the big "wet" tanks on deck. By nine o'clock, we had about 2,500 crabs crawling restlessly around their new home awaiting their fate. They were really large, measuring about ten to twelve inches across the backs and twenty-six to thirty inches across the extended legs.

The cook was capable, and the crew

looked well-fed and well-bearded. The MERCATOR stayed up there from about June to March, with a trip home for Christmas. Its regular overhaul is March to June as that was the crab's moulting period.

Vic didn't get off as scheduled the next day. The wind came up about an hour before the plane was due, so it turned back. The wind gusts hit eighty miles an hour by 1:00 p.m., so we dropped another anchor and sat tight. All the tenders came slipping into the bay during the afternoon in the heavy rain as the wind steadied to about forty- to sixty-knot gusts. Being anchored in this nearly enclosed bay with anchors big enough to hold sure made "living" easy when compared with the troubles with the MOHAWK's small anchors and large barges.

The wind died down about nine that night, so I got some sleep until midnight when it shifted and whistled in from the other direction. I spent the next four hours watching and listening to radio reports from those vessels still out in the fury of the blow, including the MOHAWK and the COMACHE, as well as a power barge REEFER II, which was dragging toward a beach nearby. None of the small boats were able to face the wind to go out to her and the Coast Guard was around the other side of the Island.

The wind was still blowing the next afternoon. Even though we were protected from heavy seas in the small bay, the wind would shoot down the slopes of the hills and hit the water hard enough to pick up spray and blow it in white sheets across the harbor.

The stormy weather seemed to scatter the crabs so the boats had trouble finding them in good quantities. It was possible I would have to get the ship underway and move to another anchorage up the coast or over on the mainland before Vic returned. Since it was quite a narrow harbor to maneuver a strange ship in, I'd have preferred to have made at least one run with Vic's guidance before such a shift. But he assured me the crew was quite capable.

I trusted the wind would diminish enough for Vic to make his plane the next day. The bush plane couldn't land with so much wind. As a matter of fact, the pilot couldn't even take off from Kodiak.

After several days, the sun broke through the clouds to shine on the rapidly browning hillsides surrounding the bay.

The crew got the processing line going and started packing crab meat like mad. Then, due to the weather, our tenders began scouting the area again for trace of the crab "herd" as it moves rapidly with weather changes.

I heard the COMACHE and the MOHAWK on the radio fighting weather and barges along the beaches and felt somewhat smug in the quiet anchorage. I figured I would probably have to move the ship over the weekend if the tenders didn't find anything nearby.

I was looking over the other possible anchorages on the west coast. I was reluctant to leave the one I was in; it was the most protected harbor in Alaska that I knew of.

A few days passed, and all was quiet on the Kodiak front. The crabs had apparently moved because of the weather and my boats were busy searching. I was getting the ship ready to move, though that involved having the dry boats (our small tenders) bring most of their pots aboard for us to carry as the pots are rather bulky. Since the tenders could only carry a few of their thirty-some aboard at any one time, it took about twenty-four hours of good weather to pick up.

Meanwhile, we were getting odds and ends of repair and maintenance work done.

Movies aboard, besides "Mr. Roberts," were "High Noon" and "Kiss Me, Kate." Unfortunately, we didn't have a color projector.

Late in the month, I started to take the MERCATOR around to the other side of the island, my first experience with the true direction radar. This type of radar shows north always at the top so the ships head on the screen in the direction of the course they are is steering. Once one is used to it, it is the same as steering down the chart. Trouble with the engines brought me back into Jap Bay after anchoring overnight in Kaguak Bay. I had to wait for engine parts from the States before I could sail my ship.

By the time the new cylinder liners for the diesel engines reached us, it was the end of Vic Hanson's vacation, so he was back in time to make the shift around the island, and I caught the plane back to Kodiak and Seattle.

Chapter 32

Tug CHARLES

November 1961 - January 1962

After using up my compensating days (for weekends at sea on the MOHAWK), I was looking for another berth. On Monday, November 6, 1961, the call came. Captain King of Alaska Freight Lines had apparently gotten my name from Merle Adlum of the Master's Mates & Pilots Union (Local 6). I was told to report aboard the tug CHARLES at Duwamish shipyard to look it over and take it for one of their scheduled trips to Alaska.

The CHARLES was a small (compared to the MOHAWK) "miki"-class tug. The "miki"-class tugs were wooden-hulled tugs builts during World War II, and saw much service hauling barges for the Army in Alaska. Since the war, the CHARLES had been run steadily between Seattle and Anchorage for Alaska Freight Lines.

I walked across the boat deck, observing the old-fashioned radial davits, from which a sailor was chipping out rust. No lifeboat, but one of those new "containerized" life rafts, which is supposed to inflate when it is thrown overboard.

The small wheelhouse was crammed to capacity with two radar sets, engine room telegraph, radio direction finder, loran, ship-to-radio and a hallicrafter radio. The charts were stacked on a hanging table under the

deckhead in the after corner of the wheelhouse and were used one at a time in sequence on the way north, then stowed under the chart desk. Getting to the chart desk necessitated a climb over the "skipper's seat," a small bench-like affair between the GE radar set and the port door.

The passageway behind the wheelhouse led to Captain's quarters and down a ladder to the messroom and galley area on the main deck.

I sampled a cup of coffee. Then, seeing no one around to report to, I continued my tour.

By climbing down through the hatch forward, I came upon the crew's fo'c's'le with bunks lining both sides of the ship, three high, with stowage lockers beneath for some of the ships dry stores.

The door through the "collision" bulkhead opened into the forepeak store room, lined with shelves for canned goods and containing the electric motor for the anchor winch.

Aft, through a passageway between two fuel tanks, was the engine room, where I passed between two well-painted Fairbanks Morse diesels, each driving its own propeller. The overall appearance of the engine

Tug CHARLES, *Seattle to Alaska, fall 1961*

room was of general cleanliness and care. Aft of the engines was the large electric panel, and behind this and again between fuel tanks, were passageways that led aft to the "lazarette," where spare lines, ropes, wires, etc. were stowed.

There appeared to be no watertight subdivision aft of the "collision" bulkhead in the forward end of the fo'c's'le.

I didn't find a skipper or mate aboard, so I drove up to the office to find Captain King and report in to him.

On Tuesday, I spent the day about the ship, looking alert and wise as I read through the publications I could find pertaining to the equipment aboard. I stowed my gear in the cabin I'd share with the chief mate on the boat deck aft of the skipper's quarters and just forward of the smoke stack.

The skipper, E. (Al) Cox, showed up, and later the mate came over from the tug alongside to move into the cabin with me. We learned we wouldn't be sailing until at least the next day, so everyone left the ship by 4:30 except for the chief engineer, who was asleep in his cabin, his son who awaited him and myself.

Wednesday morning, we shifted out of the Duwamish shipyard and out into Elliott Bay where we dumped our two cables into the bay before proceeding to Union Oil dock for stores and fuel for the voyage.

In the afternoon we shifted back to Duwamish Waterway to the company's dock to put a new tow cable aboard and to make up to our tow, a wooden barge #1601.

The mate took me over the barge to show me where the soundings were to be taken and, in general, where and what the machinery aboard was and how it operated. This, in general terms: "The engineers will start it and you push this lever."

Since it was after 4:00 p.m. by the time we got "made up," we had to wait at the dock until 6:00 before we could get through the Spokane Street Bridge. We shifted barges around the dock while waiting, then waited an extra hour while the engineers did some last-minute work on a battery bank.

At 7:00 p.m., we got underway and rounded West Point at 8:24 for our trip up the inside passage to Alaska.

The Thursday morning watch (midnight to 4:00 a.m.) was overcast, calm waters from Hein Bank and up the passage east of San Juan Islands, past Deception Pass, Rosario Strait and up past Clark Island. I was secretly happy there were no gillnetters to worry my way through.

The afternoon watch was a long straight

stretch in Georgia Straits, approaching Cape Lazo, and supper relief brought me inside of Cape Mudge past Campbell River.

I couldn't seem to stay awake to watch passage through Seymour Narrows.

Friday morning watch, black and windy took me through the upper part of Johnston Straits, past Alert Bay where wind and currents played havoc with my courses, but once past Alert Bay I had no more difficulty passing through Broughton Strait and rounding Pulteney Point into Queen Charlotte Sound.

The afternoon watch, I watched for the drifting logs in Fitzhugh Sound from Addenbrooke Light up to make the sharp turn around Pointer Island into Lama Passage.

Supper relief, we were passing Bella-Bella and making the turn into Seaforth Channel then into Millbank Sound.

Saturday morning watch found us in the upper end of Graham Reach through Fraser Reach, from the Waterfall and Elephant Head (a mountain formation whose silhouette resembled that of an elephant) around through McKay Reach.

Afternoon watch, we passed through the upper part of Malacca Passage and across Chatham Sound, mostly open water. I was passing the Alaska Steamship Company vessel TANANA while approaching Herbert Reach. I signaled by one blast that I wished to pass to starboard, but she maintained course across my bow without an answering signal so I had to swing to port to pass, contrary to the "rules of the road," keeping fingers crossed that ship would clear my tow.

Sunday morning, I came up in time to pass Ketchikan and out into a stormy crossing of Behm Canal Entrance and pitched up Clarence Strait with a following wind and sea. The tossing nearly dislodged the sextant and charts from the chart bins as well as the

pots and pans in the galley.

In the afternoon, we made the turn at the upper end of Sumner Strait into the lower part and around Cape Decision.

Going past Cape Decision brought to mind the day in November 1943 when I joined the MS CAPE DECISION at Beaumont, Texas, and Mr. Murray, the second mate, and Harry Shafter and "Tiny," the cadets. Shafter, the cadet from Brooklyn who was so proud to be a cadet in the United States Merchant Marine and whose eagerness to learn was a target for our sense of humor, and gave him the privilege of getting most of my third mate's and Mr. Murray's second mate's work done for us.

Monday morning watch, we were still proceeding up Chatham Straits, past places with names like "Whitewater Bay," "Kasuyku Bay," "Kootsnahoo Inlet," etc. Afternoon we rounded into Icy Strait and slipped into Idaho Inlet to anchor and wait out the storm which was putting twenty-five-foot swells on the beach at Cape Spencer.

While in Idaho Inlet, we put the surge chain on the tow and pumped it, preparing for the long haul across the open waters of Gulf of Alaska.

Tuesday noon, we got underway and resumed courses through Icy Strait and around Cape Spencer. In the evening relief period, we headed the ship for Yakutat.

Wednesday morning watch, we headed west from Yakutat. The southwesterly swells were still running about ten feet and the wind from the southeast gave us a small push to go along with the roll.

Thursday afternoon, we were running between Cape Cleare and Cape Hinchinbrook. Gradually increased speed as the swell and sea moderated.

Friday morning watch, we were in Prince William Sound. Sailing down between

Latouche and Erlington Passage in relatively calm water on a black, starry night.

Afternoon we were running down past the Pye Islands. I got my sextant out and took first sights of the trip. They still come out in line with shore bearings so, I guess, its fall that night out of Ketchikan didn't hurt it too much.

Saturday morning, we rounded Cape Elizabeth into Cook Inlet and in the afternoon made the turn through the forelands into the upper reach of Cook Inlet.

We slowed a bit to time our entry at Anchorage with the high tide Monday morning, and spent 24 hours at slow speed.

About 1:30 a.m. Monday, we ran through slush ice, which became more and more dense as we approached Fire Island, the entrance of Knik Arm (the bay Anchorage Port adjoins). The flood current set us sideways toward Turnagain Arm as we had to proceed at slow speed through the ice. We could barely make headway or hold our own position. Each time we'd get up to the light on Fire Island, the engine room would have to stop an engine to clear the ice from the cooling water intake.

Finally, we reversed course entirely and steered back down the inlet to clear water. In the afternoon, we brought the barge alongside and started through the ice again, but when we got to a clear place the waves surged the barge so much that it broke the mooring lines. We dropped it astern to tow it on a "bridle" and made our way into Anchorage.

The WESTWIND, a converted LCI (landing craft) took our barge (1601) from us to dock and we pulled Barge 1602 clear of the pier so she could. We then tied up Barge 1602 alongside 1601 and lay quiet overnight.

During the night, the crew put a "soft patch" of cement and plywood over the hole

stove in our bow while coming alongside the barge that afternoon.

I spent the Tuesday morning watch making up log abstracts of the voyage to date and watching the fields of ice flow past the ship on the incoming tide.

We sailed at 7:30 a.m. for Seattle and plowed our way around and through ice drifts until about noon, when we were in water clear enough to drop our barge astern and make our way down Cook Inlet at full speed.

The waters of Cook Inlet were so laden with glacial sand that no one had ever managed to stay afloat in them. One's clothing pick up an estimated 100 pounds of sand in the first minute and the freezing temperature shocks the fight of anyone unlucky enough to fall in.

I came on watch Wednesday after an evening of tossing around in my bunk to find a heavy southwest swell and a strong northwest winds and sea. The winds were getting stronger. The skipper decided that, in view of weather forecast for gale winds, we would go into Port Chatham for anchorage to await a break in the weather.

That evening we got word we were to go to Seward to pick up another barge to tow in addition to ours back to Seattle. They were to fly a 1,000-foot tow pendant to Seward for us.

This was a hell of a time of year for towing two barges across the exposed waters of Gulf of Alaska, when we could barely make headway with one.

While we lay at anchor Thanksgiving Day in a quiet bay among the snow-covered hills, we listened to radio search for the seventy-foot fishing schooner RUTH L, which was overdue on a voyage across Cook Inlet on the night we came in. Planes and ships had turned up no trace.

The way we were tossed around that night, I wasn't surprised, for those waves would strain the seams on many boats.

When we sailed from Port Chatham for Icy Straits, we were passing south of Cape St. Elias we heard a fish boat calling the lighthouse on Cape Hinchinbrook to ask him how far off he should pass. When the Coast Guard asked him how it is that he was out on such a stormy night without a chart on board, the answer in Scandinavian accent was: "Ve haf a chart, but some idiot left a can of linoleum cement in the veelhouse and you should see the mess."

We got in past Cape Spencer, anchored our barge at Hoonah, and tied up at the fuel dock for a quiet night. A couple of years back while I was on a long cruise with the Sea Scout boat 23 SKID-DOO, I managed to lose our family cat, Inky, while tied up alongside the Bellingham Sea Scout boat at Bellingham. On our return from the long cruise, we met the Bellingham ship at Sucia Island and asked if our cat was still aboard. They said they had put her ashore before they sailed, and that there were several fish boats tied up near their dock.

We took the SKID-DOO into Bellingham, but on the way in we passed several fish boats en route out and I noted that they were registered at Hoonah, Alaska. Needless to say, I didn't find the cat and really caught heck from my family when I returned home without her.

So now that I found myself at Hoonah, I went to the general store at the end of the dock and asked the woman there if she knew if any of the boats had a black cat aboard. She gave me the name of one, so the next few moments found me walking down the snow-covered floats calling for the cat while carrying a piece of leftover turkey.

A black cat with a white spot on her chest came out from the wheelhouse of the boat the woman had identified. When I picked her up, she sniffed me a bit, then suddenly relaxed in my arms. I was pretty sure it was Inky but, since no one was around, I couldn't bring myself to take her away from someone who had given her a home for the past two years to take her back out on another stormy crossing of the Gulf of Alaska on my tug.

We traded barges with another tug and, after putting charcoal heaters in some of the vans of perishables, headed back across the Gulf of Alaska for Seward. The seas had calmed down and the skies cleared. When I approached the corner at Renard Island light to head up into Resurrection Bay toward Seward, the sea was covered with wisps of ice-fog.

As we turned the corner, I watched the thermometer drop from thirty-five degrees to twenty degrees below zero. The steam from our breathing froze to the inside of the wheelhouse window, so I found myself in the position of navigating by radar on a clear, sunny afternoon as we approached Seward. When we came up to the pier, it was after five o'clock and the longshoremen who were to take our lines to tie up were at supper. So we had to lay off for an hour in a forty-knot wind to await their six-o'clock turn-to time before they could get us tied up.

It was while waiting on that cold, windy deck that I asked myself, "Just what are you doing here? There must be a better way to make a living," and promised myself that on our return to Seattle I would try to find one.

Chapter 33

RICHARD
February - March 1962

After returning from Seward on the CHARLES in February 1962, I resumed my casting about for another position with little luck. I accepted the Chief Mate's job on another "miki"-class tug, the RICHARD.

Our assignment was to take one of the wooden ex-army barges down to San Pedro to pick up a load of used cars from the National Steel dock on Terminal Island, and some more from San Diego to take to Alaska.

When I learned we would be heading for San Diego, I remembered that when I had first met Beverly she had been on her way to San Diego and had mentioned that her father was there. My hopes built up in anticipation that I would again have news of her, as she, as a pen pal, had really been an influence in my life when I was wandering about the world in the late thirties.

The first thing I did ashore was to find a phone book to look up Fulwider (her father's name). The only one I found I called and learned I had reached her father's second wife, who was now a widow. She told me that Beverly, her mother, and her sister Ruth had all moved to Chula Vista, a southern suburb of San Diego, and that her mother and sister were still there. Beverly had been killed in an auto accident in the fall of 1960.

I called Beverly's mother and was invited out to her home on Penelope Drive to meet Beverly's children, David and Kathy, and to renew my acquaintance with Mrs. Nichols, Beverly's mother, who was also now a widow.

On our return to Seattle, I paid off the ship and started again to find a place ashore. The loss the previous year of Peter Steven had been weighing heavily upon me, and now this latest news really added more emotions than I felt I wanted to handle without having the love of Kay and Penny nearby.

I remembered that, years ago, "Smokey" Johnson had mentioned going to work on the Seattle waterfront, so it was there I turned.

After a few years as a stevedore superintendent and a year with a custom's broker, I managed to get on the books of the ILWU Checkers union.

For the next twenty-four years until I retired, I was able to work checking and supervising the loading of the deep sea ships that called at Puget Sound ports. I watched my daughter, Penny, grow into a fine young career woman in the financial field, and was proud when she was named "Woman of the Year" by her Business and Professional

Women's group.

As I received my retirement presentation, my mind quickly went back over the years since the days I had walked along the highways of Texas chewing cotton bolls for a bit of nourishment, the years on ships of the sea, the war years, and all the many people I had met along the way who were helpful in making this life possible. To all of them, I say "Thank you."

APPENDIX I
AMERICAN SHIPS SUNK DURING WORLD WAR II IN CHRONOLOGICAL ORDER
Excerpted from *A Careless Word, A Needless Sinking,* by Captain Arthur Moore

U = German   I = Japanese   ? = Unknown

Note: The first five were sunk before the attack on Pearl Harbor.

Ship	Year	Mo	Day	Location		Cause
MS CITY OF RAYVILLE	1940	11	09	CAPE OTWAY, AUST		MINE
SS ROBIN MOOR	1941	05	21	06-10N	25-40W	U-69
SS STEEL SEAFARER	1941	09	05	GULF OF SUEZ		G-AIR
SS LEHIGH	1941	10	19	08-26N	14-37W	U-126
SS ASTRAL	1941	12	02	NEAR ARUBA		U-43
SS CYNTHIA OLSON	1941	12	07	33-42N	145-29W	I-26
SS PRESIDENT HARRISON	1941	12	07	YANGTSE RIVER		GROUNDED
SS VINCENT	1941	12	12	22-41S	118-19W	HOKOKU MARU
SS MANATAWNY	1941	12	13	MANILA, P.I.		J-AIR
SS MANINI	1941	12	17	18-18N	157-52W	I-175
SS PRUSA	1941	12	19	16-45N	156-00W	I-172
SS EMIDIO	1941	12	20	40-33N	125-00W	I-17 SHELLED
SS MONTEBELLO	1941	12	23	35-30N	121-51W	I-21
SS ADM. Y.S. WILLIAMS	1941	12	25	HONG KONG		SCUTTLED
SS RUTH ALEXANDER	1941	12	31	01-00N	119-10E	J-AIR
SS MALAMA	1942	01	01	26-21S	153-24W	J RAIDER
SS CITY OF ATLANTA	1942	01	09	35-42N	75-21W	U-123
SS LIBERTY	1942	01	11	08-54S	115-28E	I-166
SS ALLAN JACKSON	1942	01	18	35-57N	74-20W	U-66
SS FRANCES SALMAN	1942	01	18	47-30N	52-25W	U-522
SS FLORENCE LUCKENBACH	1942	01	19	12-55N	80-33E	I-64
SS NORVANA	1942	01	22	35-15N	75-30W	U-66
SS WEST IVIS	1942	01	26	EAST COAST, U.S.		U-125
SS FRANCIS E. POWELL	1942	01	27	37-45N	74-53W	U-130
SS ROYAL T. FRANK	1942	01	28	20-34N	155-33W	I-171 DD-339
SS ROCHESTER	1942	01	30	37-10N	73-58W	U-106
SS W.L. STEED	1942	02	02	38-25N	72-43W	U-103
SS INDIA ARROW	1942	02	04	38-48N	73-40W	U-103
SS CHINA ARROW	1942	02	05	37-44N	73-18W	U-103
SS MAJOR WHEELER	1942	02	06	EAST COAST, U.S.		U-107
MS DON ISIDRO	1942	02	19	11-00S	130-00E	J-AIR
SS FLORENCE D.	1942	02	19	11-18S	130-51E	J-AIR
SS PAN MASSACHUSETTS	1942	02	19	28-27N	80-08W	U-128
SS PORTMAR	1942	02	19	PORT DARWIN, AUST.		J-AIR DAMAGED
SS MAUNA LOA	1942	02	19	PORT DARWIN, AUST.		J-AIR
SS MEIGS	1942	02	19	PORT DARWIN, AUST.		J-AIR
SS DELPLATA	1942	02	20	14-45N	62-10W	U-156
SS AZALEA CITY	1942	02	20	38-00N	73-00W	U-432
SS LAKE OSWEYA	1942	02	20	43-14N	64-45W	U-96
SS EMPIRE SEAL	1942	02	20	43-14N	64-45W	U-?
SS REPUBLIC	1942	02	21	27-05N	80-15W	U-504
SS WEST ZEDA	1942	02	22	09-13N	69-04W	U-129
SS W.D. ANDERSON	1942	02	22	27-09N	79-56W	U-504
SS CITIES SVC EMPIRE	1942	02	22	28-00N	80-22W	U-128

SS LIHUE	1942	02 23	14-30N	64-45W	U-161
SS NORLAVORE	1942	02 24	35-02N	75-20W	U-432
SS MARORE	1942	02 26	35-33N	74-58W	U-432
SS OREGON	1942	02 28	20-44N	67-52W	U-156
SS R.P. RESOR	1942	02 28	39-47N	73-26W	U-578
SS MARY	1942	03 03	08-25N	52-50W	U-129
SS MARIANA	1942	03 05	27-45N	67-00W	U-126
SS COLLAMER	1942	03 05	44-18N	63-10W	U-404
SS STEEL AGE	1942	03 06	06-45N	53-15W	U-129
SS CARDONIA	1942	03 07	19-53N	73-27W	U-126
SS BARBARA	1942	03 07	22-10N	73-05W	U-126
SS GULF TRADE	1942	03 10	39-50N	73-55W	U-588
SS TEXAN	1942	03 11	21-34N	76-28W	U-126
SS CARIBSEA	1942	03 11	34-35N	76-18W	U-158
SS OLGA	1942	03 12	21-32N	76-24W	U-126
SS JOHN D. GILL	1942	03 12	33-55N	70-39W	U-158
SV ALBERT PAUL	1942	03 13	26-00N	72-00W	U-332
SS LEMUEL BURROWS	1942	03 14	39-20N	74-20W	U-404
SS ARIO	1942	03 15	34-37N	76-20W	U-158
MS AUSTRALIA	1942	03 16	35-07N	75-22W	U-332
SS PAPOOSE	1942	03 18	34-17N	76-39W	U-124
SS W.E. HUTTON	1942	03 18	34-25N	76-40W	U-124
SS E.M. CLARK	1942	03 18	35-50N	75-35W	U-124
SS LIBERATOR	1942	03 19	35-05N	75-30W	U-332
SS OAKMAR	1942	03 20	36-22N	68-50W	U-71
SS MUSKOGEE	1942	03 22	28-00N	58-00W	U-123
SS NAECO	1942	03 23	34-00N	75-40W	U-124
SS DIXIE ARROW	1942	03 26	35-00N	75-33W	U-71
MS CITY OF NEW YORK	1942	03 29	35-16N	74-25W	U-160
SS EFFINGHAM	1942	03 30	70-28N	35-44E	U-435 PQ-13
SS T.C. McCOBB	1942	03 31	06-50N	49-00W	It-CALVI
SS MENOMINEE	1942	03 31	37-34N	75-25W	U-754 SHELLED
BARGE ALLEGHENY	1942	03 31	37-34N	75-25W	U-754
BARGE BARNEGAT	1942	03 31	37-34N	75-25W	U-754
SS TIGER	1942	04 01	36-55N	75-59W	U-754
SS DAVID H. ATWATER	1942	04 02	37-46N	75-05W	U-552 SHELLED
SS WEST IRMO	1942	04 03	02-10N	05-50W	U-505
SS OTHO	1942	04 03	36-25N	72-22W	U-754
SS COMOL RICO	1942	04 04	20-46N	66-46W	U-154
SS BYRON D. BENSON	1942	04 04	36-08N	73-32W	U-552
SS CATAHOULA	1942	04 05	19-16N	68-12W	U-154
SS SELMA CITY	1942	04 06	17-11N	83-20E	J-AIR
SS BIENVILLE	1942	04 06	17-48N	84-09E	J-AIR & CRUISER
SS EXMOOR	1942	04 06	19-52N	86-25E	J CRUISER SHELLED
SS WASHINGTONIAN	1942	04 07	07-25N	73-05E	I-5
SS EUGENE V. THAYER	1942	04 09	02-35S	39-55W	It-CALVI
SS ESPARTA	1942	04 09	31-00N	81-10W	U-123
SS ATLAS	1942	04 09	34-27N	76-16W	U-552
SS MALCHACE	1942	04 09	34-28N	75-56W	U-160
SS GULF AMERICA	1942	04 10	30-10N	81-15W	U-123
SS TAMAULIPAS	1942	04 10	34-25N	76-00W	U-552
SS EDWARD B. DUDLEY	1942	04 11	53-00N	39-00W	U-615 HX-232
SS DELVALLE	1942	04 12	16-51N	72-25W	U-154
SS ESSO BOSTON	1942	04 12	21-42N	60-00W	U-130 SHELLED

SS LESLIE	1942	04	12	28-35N	80-19W	U-123
SS MARGARET	1942	04	14	EAST COAST, U.S.		U-571
SS ROBIN HOOD	1942	04	15	38-39N	64-38W	U-575
SS ALCOA GUIDE	1942	04	16	35-34N	70-08W	U-123
SS STEEL MAKER	1942	04	19	33-48N	70-36W	U-654
SS WEST IMBODEN	1942	04	20	41-14N	66-00W	U-752
SS SAN JACINTO	1942	04	21	31-10N	70-45W	U-201
SS PIPESTONE COUNTY	1942	04	21	37-43N	66-16W	U-576
SS CONNECTICUT	1942	04	23	23-00S	15-00W	MICHEL
SS ALCOA PARTNER	1942	04	26	13-32N	67-57W	U-66
SS MOBIL OIL	1942	04	29	23-35N	66-18W	U-108
SS FEDERAL	1942	04	30	21-12N	76-07W	U-507
SS JOHN ADAMS	1942	05	02	23-30S	164-35E	I-21
SS NORLINDO	1942	05	03	24-57N	84-00W	U-507
SS EASTERN SWORD	1942	05	04	07-00N	58-12W	U-162
SS TUSCALOOSA CITY	1942	05	04	18-25N	81-31W	U-125
SS MUNGER T. BALL	1942	05	04	25-17N	83-57W	U-507
SS JOSEPH M. CUDAHY	1942	05	04	25-57N	83-57W	U-507
SS DELISLE	1942	05	04	27-05N	80-05W	U-564 REPAIRED
SS AFOUNDRIA	1942	05	05	20-00N	73-30W	U-108
MS GREEN ISLAND	1942	05	06	18-25N	81-30W	U-125
SS HALSEY	1942	05	06	27-14N	80-03W	U-333
SS ALCOA PURITAN	1942	05	06	OFF MISSISSIPPI		U-507
SS OHIOAN	1942	05	08	26-31N	79-59W	U-564
SS OKLAHOMA	1942	05	08	31-18N	80-59W	U-123
SS ESSO HOUSTON	1942	05	12	12-12N	57-25W	U-162
SS VIRGINIA	1942	05	12	28-53N	89-29W	U-507
SS NORLANTIC	1942	05	13	12-13N	66-30W	U-69
SS GULFPENN	1942	05	13	28-29N	89-12W	U-506
SS DAVID McKELVEY	1942	05	13	28-30N	89-55W	U-506
SS NICARAO	1942	05	15	25-20N	74-19W	U-751
SS RUTH LYKES	1942	05	16	16-36N	82-25W	U-103
SS GULFOIL	1942	05	16	28-08N	89-46W	U-506
MS CHALLENGER	1942	05	17	12-11N	61-18W	U-155
SS PEISANDER (Br)	1942	05	17	39-08N	69-57W	U-?
SS FOAM	1942	05	17	43-20N	63-08W	U-432
SS QUAKER CITY	1942	05	18	15-47N	53-45W	U-156
MS MERCURY SUN	1942	05	18	20-01N	84-26W	U-125
SS WILLIAM J. SALMAN	1942	05	18	20-08N	83-46W	U-125
SS OGONTZ	1942	05	19	20-30N	86-39W	U-103
SS HEREDIA	1942	05	19	28-53N	91-03W	U-506
SS CLARE	1942	05	20	21-35N	84-43W	U-103
SS ELIZABETH	1942	05	20	21-36N	84-48W	U-103
SS GEORGE CALVERT	1942	05	20	22-55N	84-26W	U-753
SS HALO	1942	05	20	28-42N	90-08W	U-506
SS PLOW CITY	1942	05	21	39-08N	69-57W	U-588
SS SAMUEL Q. BROWN	1942	05	23	20-15N	84-38W	U-103
SS BEATRICE	1942	05	24	17-23N	77-00W	U-558
SS ALCOA CARRIER	1942	05	25	18-45N	79-50W	U-103
SS CARRABULLE	1942	05	26	26-18N	89-21W	U-106
SS SYROS	1942	05	26	72-35N	05-30E	U-703 PQ-16
SS JACK	1942	05	27	17-36N	74-42W	U-155
SS ALAMAR	1942	05	27	74-00N	20-00E	G-AIR PQ-16
SS MORMACSUL	1942	05	27	74-40N	20-00E	G-AIR PQ-16

SS ALCOA PILGRIM	1942	05 28	16-28N	67-37W	U-558
SS NEW JERSEY	1942	05 28	18-32N	82-28W	U-103
SS CITY OF FLINT	1942	05 28	73-41N	21-58E	G-AIR PQ-16
SS ALCOA SHIPPER	1942	05 30	37-49N	65-15W	U-404
SS KNOXVILLE CITY	1942	06 01	21-15N	85-30W	U-158
SS HAMPTON ROADS	1942	06 01	21-18N	75-48W	U-106
SS ILLINOIS	1942	06 01	24-00N	60-00W	U-172
SS WEST NOTUS	1942	06 01	34-10N	68-20W	U-404
SS CITY OF ALMA	1942	06 02	23-00N	62-30W	U-159
SS M.F. ELIOTT	1942	06 03	11-59N	63-33W	U-502
MS BEN & JOSEPHINE	1942	06 03	GEORGES BANK		U-432
SS STEEL WORKER	1942	06 03	KOLA INLET		MINED
SS VELMA LYKES	1942	06 04	21-21N	86-36W	U-158
SS DELFINA	1942	06 05	20-22N	67-07W	U-172
MV AEOLUS	1942	06 05	CAPE ANN		U-432
SS L.J. DRAKE	1942	06 05	CARIBBEAN		?
SS MELVIN H. BAKER	1942	06 06	21-44S	36-38E	I-10
SS STANVAC CALCUTTA	1942	06 06	SO. ATLANTIC		STIER
SS EDITH	1942	06 07	14-33N	74-35W	U-159
SS GEORGE CLYMER	1942	06 07	14-48S	18-37W	MICHEL
SS SICILIEN	1942	06 07	17-30N	71-20W	U-172
SS COAST TRADER	1942	06 07	48-19N	125-40W	I-26
SS FRANKLIN K. LANE	1942	06 08	11-27N	66-56W	U-502
SS MERRIMACK	1942	06 09	19-47N	85-55W	U-107
SS AMERICAN	1942	06 11	17-58N	84-28W	U-504
SS HAGAN	1942	06 11	22-00N	77-30W	U-157
SS F.W. ABRAMS	1942	06 11	34-57N	75-56W	MINED
SS GRIJNSSEN (Du)	1942	06 11	CARIBBEAN		U-? LEBORE
SS SIXAOLA	1942	06 12	09-24N	81-25W	U-159
SS CITIES SVC TOLEDO	1942	06 12	29-02N	92-00W	U-158
SS SCOTTSBURG	1942	06 14	11-48N	63-06W	U-161
SS COLD HARBOR	1942	06 14	11-52N	63-07W	U-?
SS LEBORE	1942	06 14	12-53N	80-40W	U-172
SS WEST HARDAWAY	1942	06 15	11-50N	62-15W	U-502
SS KAHUKU	1942	06 15	11-52N	63-07W	U-126
SS ARKANSAN	1942	06 15	12-07N	62-51W	U-126
MS CHANT	1942	06 15	36-24N	11-40E	G-AIR WS-19Z
SS CHEROKEE	1942	06 15	42-11N	69-25W	U-87 XB-25
SS MILLINOCKET	1942	06 17	23-12N	79-58W	U-129
SS SEATTLE SPIRIT	1942	06 18	50-23N	42-25W	U-124 ON-102
SS WEST IRA	1942	06 20	12-04N	57-35W	U-128
SS ALCOA CADET	1942	06 21	KOLA INLET		MINE
SS E.J. SADLER	1942	06 22	15-36N	67-52W	U-159
SS MAJOR GEN. H. GIBBINS	1942	06 23	24-35N	87-45W	U-158
SS RAWLEIGH WARNER	1942	06 23	28-53N	89-15W	U-67
SS MANUELA	1942	06 24	34-30N	75-40W	U-404
SS JOHN R. WILLIAMS	1942	06 24	38-45N	74-50W	MINE (U-373)
SS POLYBIUS	1942	06 27	11-00N	57-30W	U-128
SS POTLATCH	1942	06 27	19-20N	53-18W	U-153
SS SUWIED	1942	06 27	20-00N	84-48W	U-107
SS TILLIE LYKES	1942	06 28	19-00N	85-00W	U-502
SS SAM HOUSTON	1942	06 28	19-21N	62-22W	U-203
SS SEA THRUSH	1942	06 28	22-38N	60-59W	U-505
SS RAPHAEL SEMMES	1942	06 28	29-30N	64-30W	U-332

SS WM. ROCKEFELLER	1942	06	28	35-11N	75-02W	U-701
SS RUTH	1942	06	29	21-44N	74-05W	U-153
SS THOMAS McKEAN	1942	06	29	22-00N	60-00W	U-505
SS EXPRESS	1942	06	30	22-00S	38-00E	I-10
SS CITY OF BIRMINGHAM	1942	06	30	OFF BERMUDA		U-202 DD-180
SS WARRIOR	1942	07	01	10-54N	61-02W	U-126
SS EDWARD LUCKENBACH	1942	07	02	24-56N	81-53W	AM. MINE
SS NORLANDIA	1942	07	03	19-33N	68-39W	U-575
SS ALEXANDER MACOMB	1942	07	03	41-48N	66-35W	U-215
SS CHRISTOPHER NEWPORT	1942	07	04	75-49N	22-25E	U-457 PQ-17
SS WILLIAM HOOPER	1942	07	04	75-55N	27-14E	G-AIR PQ-17
SS JOHN RANDOLPH	1942	07	05	66-34N	23-14W	A-MINE QP-13
SS PETER KERR	1942	07	05	74-30N	35-00E	G-AIR PQ-17
SS FAIRFIELD CITY	1942	07	05	74-40N	39-45E	G-AIR PQ-17
SS HONOMU	1942	07	05	75-05N	38-00E	U-456 PQ-17
SS DANIEL MORGAN	1942	07	05	75-08N	45-06E	U-88 PQ-17
SS WASHINGTON	1942	07	05	76-14N	33-44E	G-AIR PQ-17
SS CARLTON	1942	07	05	76-14N	40-00E	U-88 PQ-17
SS PAN KRAFT	1942	07	05	76-50N	38-00E	G-AIR PQ-17
SS HEFFRON	1942	07	05	ICELAND		A-MINE QP-13
SS MASAYA	1942	07	05	ICELAND		A-MINE QP-13
SS HYBERT	1942	07	05	ICELAND		A-MINE QP-13
SS JOHN WITHERSPOON	1942	07	06	70-30N	52-30E	U-255 PQ-17
SS PAN ATLANTIC	1942	07	06	70-30N	52-31E	G-AIR PQ-17
SS OLOPANA	1942	07	07	70-30N	53-30E	U-255 PQ-17
SS ALCOA RANGER	1942	07	07	71-20N	51-00E	U-255 PQ-17
SS SANTA RITA	1942	07	09	26-11N	55-40W	U-172
SS BENJAMIN BREWSTER	1942	07	09	29-05N	90-07W	U-67
SS HOOSIER	1942	07	10	69-45N	38-35E	G-AIR PQ-17
SS TACHIRA	1942	07	12	18-15N	81-54W	U-129
SS SANTORE	1942	07	12	37-06N	75-53W	U-701
SS R.W. GALLAGHER	1942	07	13	28-48N	91-00W	U-67
SS ARCATA	1942	07	14	53-35N	157-40W	I-7
SS CHILORE	1942	07	15	34-47N	75-22W	U-576 KS-520
SS WILLIAM F. HUMPHREY	1942	07	16	05-37S	00-30E	MICHEL
MS GERTRUDE	1942	07	16	23-25N	82-03W	U-126 SHELLED
SS FAIRPORT	1942	07	16	27-12N	64-30W	U-161 AS-4
SS KESHENA	1942	07	19	35-00N	75-45W	A-MINE
SS COAST FARMER	1942	07	20	35-23S	151-00E	I-11
SS HONOLULAN	1942	07	22	08-41N	22-12W	U-582
SS WILLIAM DAWES	1942	07	22	36-47S	150-16E	I-11
SS ONONDAGA	1942	07	23	22-40N	78-44W	U-129
SS STELLA LYKES	1942	07	27	06-46N	25-00W	U-582
SS EBB	1942	07	28	43-24N	59-20W	U-754 SHELLED
SS CRANFORD	1942	07	30	12-17N	55-11W	U-155
SS ROBERT E. LEE	1942	07	30	28-40N	88-30W	U-166 TAW-7
SV WAWALOAM	1942	08	06	39-18N	55-44W	U-86
SS KAIMOKU	1942	08	08	56-30N	32-14W	U-379 SC-94
SS CALIFORNIA	1942	08	13	09-24N	33-02W	It-GIULIANI
SS CRIPPLE CREEK	1942	08	13	04-55N	18-30W	U-752
SS DELMUNDO	1942	08	13	19-55N	73-49W	U-600 TAW-12
SS R.M. PARKER, Jr.	1942	08	13	28-37N	90-48W	U-171
SS ALMERIA LYKES	1942	08	13	36-40N	11-53E	E-BOAT
SS SANTA ELISA	1942	08	13	36-47N	11-20E	E-BOATS WS-21S

SS BALLADIE	1942	08	15	55-23N	24-32W	U-705 SC-95
MS LOUISIANA	1942	08	17	07-24N	52-33W	U-108
SS JOHN HANCOCK	1942	08	18	19-41N	76-50W	U-552 TAW-13
SS WEST CELINA	1942	08	19	11-45N	62-30W	U-162 TAW-S
SS CHATHAM	1942	08	27	51-50N	55-45W	U-517 SG-6
SS ARLYN	1942	08	27	51-53N	55-48W	U-165 SG-6
SS TOPA TOPA	1942	08	29	10-45N	52-55W	U-66
SS WEST LASHAWAY	1942	08	30	10-30N	55-10W	U-66
SS STAR OF OREGON	1942	08	30	11-48N	59-45W	U-162
SS JACK CARNES	1942	08	30	45-35N	28-02W	U-516 & U-705
MS AMERICAN LEADER	1942	09	10	SO. ATLANTIC		MICHEL
SS PATRICK J. HURLEY	1942	09	12	23-00N	46-15W	U-512
SS JOHN PENN	1942	09	13	67-00N	10-15E	G-AIR PQ-18
SS WACOSTA	1942	09	13	76-05N	10-00E	G-AIR PQ-18
SS OREGONIAN	1942	09	13	OFF NORTH CAPE		G-AIR PQ-18
SS MARY LUCKENBACH	1942	09	14	76-00N	16-00E	G-AIR PQ-18
SS COMMERCIAL TRADER	1942	09	16	10-30N	60-15W	U-559
SS MAE	1942	09	17	08-03N	58-13W	U-515
SS KENTUCKY	1942	09	18	CAPE KANIN, RUSSIA		G-AIR PQ-18
SS WICHITA	1942	09	19	15-00N	54-00W	U-516
SS SILVER SWORD	1942	09	20	75-41N	03-12W	U-255 QP-14
SS CORNELIA P. SPENCER	1942	09	21	02-08N	50-10E	U-188
SS PAUL LUCKENBACH	1942	09	22	10-03N	63-42E	I-29
MS ESSO WILLIAMSBURG	1942	09	22	53-12N	41-00W	U-211
SS BELLINGHAM	1942	09	22	71-23N	11-03W	U-435 PQ-14
SS ANTINOUS	1942	09	23	08-58N	59-33W	U-515
SS VENORE	1942	09	23	34-50N	75-20W	U-66
SS PENNMAR	1942	09	23	58-12N	34-35W	U-432 SC-100
SS WEST CHETAC	1942	09	24	08-05N	58-06W	U-175 TAW-14
SS LOSMAR	1942	09	24	07-40N	74-15E	I-165
SS JOHN WINTHROP	1942	09	24	56-00N	31-00W	U-619 ON-131
SS STEPHEN HOPKINS	1942	09	27	28-08S	11-59W	TANNENFELS/ STIER
SS ALCOA MARINER	1942	09	28	08-27N	60-08W	U-175
SS ALCOA TRANSPORT	1942	10	02	09-03N	60-10W	U-201
SS CARIBSTAR	1942	10	04	08-30N	59-37W	U-175
SS CAMDEN	1942	10	04	43-43N	124-54W	I-25
SS ROBERT H. COLLEY	1942	10	04	59-06N	26-18W	U-254 HX-209
SS WILLIAM A. McKENNEY	1 942	10	05	08-35N	59-20W	U-175
SS LARRY DOHENY	1942	10	05	42-40N	125-02W	I-25
SS CHICKASAW CITY	1942	10	07	34-15S	17-11E	U-172
SS JOHN CARTER ROSE	1942	10	08	10-27N	45-37W	U-201
SS SWIFTSURE	1942	10	08	34-40S	18-25E	U-68
SS EXAMELIA	1942	10	09	34-52S	18-30E	U-68 ZAANDAM
SS COLORADAN	1942	10	09	35-47S	14-34E	U-159
SS STEEL SCIENTIST	1942	10	11	05-48N	51-40W	U-514
SS SUSANA	1942	10	12	53-41N	41-23W	U-221 SC-104
SS ANGELINA	1942	10	17	49-39N	30-20W	U-618
SS STEEL NAVIGATOR	1942	10	19	49-45N	31-20W	U-610 ON-137
SS REUBEN TIPTON	1942	10	23	14-33N	54-51W	U-129
SS ANNE HUTCHINSON	1942	10	26	33-10S	28-30E	U-504
SS PRESIDENT COOLIDGE	1942	10	26	ESPRITU SANTO		MINE
SS GURNEY E. NEWLIN	1942	10	27	54-51N	31-04W	U-436
SS BIC ISLAND (Br)	1942	10	28	55-05N	23-27W	U-224

SS WEST KEBAR	1942	10 29	14-57N	53-37W	U-129
SS PAN NEW YORK	1942	10 29	54-58N	23-56W	U-624 HX-212
SS GEORGE THACHER	1942	11 01	01-45S	07-40E	U-126
SS ZAANDAM (Du)	1942	11 02	01-17N	36-40W	U-?
MS EAST INDIAN	1942	11 03	37-23S	13-34E	U-181
SS HAHIRA	1942	11 03	54-15N	41-57W	U-521 SC-107
SS WILLIAM CLARK	1942	11 04	71-05N	13-20W	U-354 BX-35
SS METON	1942	11 05	12-21N	69-21W	U-129 TAG-18
SS NATHANIEL HAWTHORNE	1942	11 07	11-34N	63-26W	U-50 TAG-19
SS LA SALLE	1942	11 07	40-00S	21-30E	U-159
SS WEST HUMHAW	1942	11 08	04-21N	02-42W	U-161
SS MARCUS WHITMAN	1942	11 08	05-40S	32-41W	It-daVINCI
SS EDGAR ALLEN POE	1942	11 08	22-14S	166-30E	I-21 RETRIEVED
SS YAKA	1942	11 11	57-07N	38-26W	U-624 ONS-144
SV STAR OF SCOTLAND	1942	11 13	26-30S	00-20W	U-159
SS EXCELLO	1942	11 13	32-23S	30-07E	U-181
SS PARISMINA	1942	11 18	54-07N	38-26W	U-624 ON-144
SS ALCOA PATHFINDER	1942	11 21	26-45S	33-10E	U-181
SS PIERCE BUTLER	1942	11 21	29-40S	35-35E	U-177
SS CADDO	1942	11 23	42-25N	48-27W	U-518
SS JEREMIAH WADSWORTH	1942	11 27	39-25S	22-23E	U-178
SS ALASKAN	1942	11 28	03-58N	26-19W	U-172
SS SAWOKLA	1942	11 29	28-00S	54-00E	MICHEL
SS JAMES McKAY	1942	12 07	57-50N	23-10W	U-600 HX-217
SS CAPILLO	1942	12 08	CORREGIDOR, P.I.		JAP AIR
SS COAMO	1942	12 09	OFF BERMUDA		U-604
SS LAHAINA	1942	12 11	27-42N	147-38W	I-9
SS ALCOA RAMBLER	1942	12 12	03-51S	33-08W	U-174
MS DONA AURORA	1942	12 25	02-02S	35-17W	It-TAZZOU
SS ANDREW JACKSON	1942	07 12	23-32N	81-02W	U-84
SS ARTHUR MIDDLETON	1943	01 01	35-35N	00-45W	U 73
SS BIRMINGHAM CITY	1943	01 09	07-12N	55-37W	U-124 TB-1
SS COLLINGSWORTH	1943	01 09	07-12N	55-37W	U-124 TB-1
SS BROAD ARROW	1943	01 09	07-23N	55-48W	U-124 TB-1
SS MINOTAUR	1943	01 09	07-40N	55-18W	U-124
SS LOUISE LYKES	1943	01 09	56-15N	22-00W	U-384
SS C.J. BARKDULL	1943	01 10	NO. ATLANTIC		U-632
SS BENJAMIN SMITH	1943	01 23	04-05N	07-50W	U-175
SS CITY OF FLINT	1943	01 25	34-47N	31-40W	U-575 UGS-4
MS CAPE DECISION	1943	01 27	23-00N	47-29W	U-105
SS JULIA WARD HOWE	1943	01 27	35-20N	29-10W	U-442 UGS-4
SS CHARLES C. PINCKNEY	1943	01 27	36-37N	30-55W	U-514 UGS-4
SS SAMUEL GOMPERS	1943	01 30	24-21S	166-16E	I-10
SS JEREMIAH RENNSELAER	1943	02 02	54-40N	28-55W	U-456 HX-224
SS HENRY R. MALLORY T	1943	02 02	55-18N	26-29W	U-402 SC-118
SS DORCHESTER (TROOP)	1943	02 03	59-22N	48-42W	U-223 SG-19
SS GREYLOCK	1943	02 03	70-50N	00-48W	U-255 RA-52
SS WEST PORTAL	1943	02 05	52-00N	33-00W	U-413 SC-118
SS ROGER B. TANEY	1943	02 07	22-00S	07-45W	I-160
SS ROBERT E. HOPKINS	1943	02 07	55-14N	26-22W	U-402 SC-118
SS STARR KING	1943	02 12	34-15S	154-20E	I-21
MS ATLANTIC SUN	1943	02 15	51-00N	41-00W	U-607
SS DEER LODGE	1943	02 17	33-46S	26-57E	U-516
SS ROSARIO	1943	02 21	50-30N	24-38W	U-664 ON-167

SS EXPOSITOR	1943	02 22	46-53N	34-22W	U-606 & U-303
SS CHATTANOOGA CITY	1943	02 22	46-54N	34-32W	U-606 ON-166
SS ESSO BATON ROUGE	1943	02 23	31-15N	27-22W	U-202 UC-1
SS JONATHAN STURGES	1943	02 23	46-15N	38-11W	U-707 ON-166
SS MADOERA (Du)	1943	02 23	46-15N	38-11W	U-707 ON-166
SS HASTINGS	1943	02 23	46-30N	36-23W	U-186 ON-166
SS NATHANIEL GREENE	1943	02 24	37-02N	03-40E	U-565
SS WADE HAMPTON	1943	02 28	59-49N	34-43W	U-405 HX-227
SS FITZ-JOHN PORTER	1943	03 01	12-20S	37-11W	U-518 BT-6
SS STAGHOUND	1943	03 03	16-44N	36-03W	It-BARBARIGO
SS HARVEY W. SCOTT	1943	03 03	31-54S	30-37E	U-160 DN-21
SS JAMES B. STEPHENS	1943	03 08	28-53S	33-18W	U-160
SS THOMAS RUFFIN	1943	03 09	07-50N	52-10W	U-510 BT-6
SS PUERTO RICAN	1943	03 09	66-49N	10-41W	U-586 RA-53
SS JAMES SPRUNT	1943	03 10	19-49N	74-38W	U-185 KG-123
SS VIRGINIA SINCLAIR	1943	03 10	20-11N	74-04W	U-185
SS RICHARD D. SPAIGHT	1943	03 10	28-00S	37-00E	U-182
SS ANDREA LUCKENBACH	1943	03 10	51-20N	29-29W	U-221 HX-228
SS WILLIAM C. GORGAS	1943	03 10	51-35N	28-30W	U-444 & U-757 HX-228
SS RICHARD BLAND	1943	03 10	66-53N	14-10W	U-225 RA-53
SS CITIES SVC MISSOURI	1943	03 14	14-50N	71-46W	U-68 GAT-49
SS KEYSTONE	1943	03 13	38-45N	39-00W	U-172 UGS-6
SS EXECUTIVE	1943	03 15	72-44N	11-27E	U-255 RA-53
SS BENJAMIN HARRISON	1943	03 16	39-09N	24-15W	U-172 UGS-7
SS JAMES OGLETHORPE	1943	03 16	50-38N	34-46W	U-758 HX-229
SS MOLLY PITCHER	1943	03 17	38-21N	19-54W	U-167 UGS-6
SS WILLIAM EUSTIS	1943	03 17	50-10N	35-02W	U-435 & U-91 HX-229
SS IRENEE DUPONT	1943	03 17	50-36N	34-30W	U-600 HX229
SS HARRY LUCKENBACH	1943	03 17	50-38N	34-46W	U-91 HX-229
SS WALTER Q. GRESHAM	1943	03 19	53-39N	27-53W	U-221 HX-229
SS MATTHEW LUCKENBACH	1943	03 19	54-23N	23-34W	U-527 & U-523 HX-229
SS WILLIAM P. FRYE	1943	03 29	56-57N	24-15W	U-610 HX-230
SS GULFSTATE	1943	04 03	24-22N	80-18W	U-155
SS SUNOIL	1943	04 04	58-16N	34-14W	U-563 HX-231
SS JOHN SEVIER	1943	04 06	20-48N	74-00W	U-185 GTMO83
SS JAMES W. DENVER	1943	04 11	28-52N	26-30W	U-195 UGS-7
SS JOHN DRAYTON	1943	04 21	32-10S	34-50E	It-daVINCI
SS LAMMOT DUPONT	1943	04 23	27-10N	57-10W	U-125
SS ROBERT GRAY	1943	04 23	57-30N	43-00W	U-306 HX-234
SS SANTA CATALINA	1943	04 24	30-42N	70-58W	U-129
SS LYDIA M. CHILD	1943	04 27	33-08S	153-24E	I-178
SS McKEESPORT	1943	04 29	60-52N	34-20W	U-258 ONS-5
SS PHOEBE HEARST	1943	04 30	20-07S	177-35W	I-19
SS MICHIGAN	1943	04 30	OFF ALGERIA		U-565 UGS-7
SS WEST MAXIMUS	1943	05 04	55-00N	42-58W	U-264 ONS-5
SS WEST MADAKET	1943	05 05	54-47N	44-12W	U-707 ONS-5
SS SAMUEL J. KIRKWOOD	1943	05 06	15-00S	07-00W	U-195
SS PAT HARRISON	1943	05 09	GIBRALTAR		LIMPET MINE
SS NICKELINER	1943	05 13	21-30N	76-42W	U-176
SS WM. K. VANDERBILT	1943	05 16	18-41S	175-07E	I-19
SS H.M. STOREY	1943	05 18	17-30S	173-02E	I-25
SS AGWIMONTE	1943	05 28	CAPE AGULHAS		U-177

SS FLORA MACDONALD	1943	05 30	07-20N	13-20W	U-126 TS-41
SS MONTANAN	1943	06 03	17-54N	58-99E	I-27
SS WILLIAM KING	1943	06 06	30-25S	34-15E	U-198
SS ESSO GETTYSBURG	1943	06 10	31-02N	79-17W	U-66
SS SOLON TURMAN	1943	06 13	10-45N	80-24W	U-159
USAT PORTMAR	1943	06 16	COFFS HARBOR, AUST.		I-174 GP-35
SS HENRY KNOX	1943	06 19	00-01N	71-15E	I-37
SS SEBASTIAN CERMENO	1943	06 27	29-00S	50-10E	U-511
SS BLOODY MARSH	1943	07 02	31-33N	78-58W	U-66
SS ELIHU B. WASHBURNE	1943	07 03	24-05S	45-25W	U-513
SS MALTRAN	1943	07 05	18-11N	74-56W	U-759 SC-1279
SS THOMAS SINNICKSON	1943	07 07	03-51S	36-22W	U-185 BT-18
SS WM. BOYCE THOMPSON	1943	07 07	04-00S	36-00W	U-185 BT-18
SS JAMES ROBERTSON	1943	07 07	04-00S	36-00W	U-185 BT-18
SS ELDENA	1943	07 08	05-50N	50-20W	U-510 TJ-1
SS SAMUEL HEINTZELMAN	943	07 09	09-00S	81-00E	U-511
SS ALICE F. PALMER	1943	07 10	26-03S	44-20E	U-177
SS ROBERT ROWAN	1943	07 11	GELA, SICILY		G-AIR
SS AFRICAN STAR	1943	07 12	25-46S	40-35W	U-172
SS ROBERT BACON	1943	07 13	15-25S	41-13E	U-178
SS ONEIDA	1943	07 13	20-17N	74-06W	U-166
SS TIMOTHY PICKERING	1943	07 14	AVOLA, SICILY		G-AIR
SS RICHARD CASWELL	1943	07 16	29-22S	46-34W	U-513
SS JOHN A. POOR	1943	07 28	42-51N	64-55W	U-119 REPAIRED
SS HARRISON G. OTIS	1943	08 04	GIBRALTAR		MINED
SS FRANCIS PETTYGROVE	1943	08 13	36-08N	02-13W	G-AIR MKS-21
SS BENJAMIN CONTEE	1943	08 16	OFF ALGERIA		G-AIR
SS RICHARD HENDERSON	1943	08 26	37-11N	08-21E	U-410 UGS-14
SS JOHN BELL	1943	08 26	37-11N	08-21E	U-410 UGS-14
SS JAMES W. MARSHALL	1943	09 13	SALERNO, ITALY		G-AIR REPAIRED
SS BUSHROD WASHINGTON	1943	09 14	SALERNO, ITALY		G-AIR
SS THEODORE D. WELD	1943	09 20	57-03N	28-08W	U-238 ON-202
SS FREDERICK DOUGLAS	1943	09 20	57-03N	28-08W	U-238 0N-202
SS WILLIAM W. GERHARD	1943	09 21	OFF SALERNO		U-593
SS RICHARD OLNEY	1943	09 22	37-25N	09-54E	MINED
SS STEEL VOYAGER	1943	09 23	53-18N	40-24W	U-952 ONS-18
SS ELIAS HOWE	1943	09 24	11-35N	45-50E	I-10
SS METAPAN	1943	10 01	37-20N	10-35E	MINED
SS YORKMAR	1943	10 09	56-38N	20-30W	U-645 SC-143
SS JOHN H. COUCH	1943	10 11	GUADALCANAL		J-AIR
SS JAMES RUSSELL LOWELL	1943	10 15	37-18N	07-10E	U-371 GUS-18
SS DELISLE	1943	10 19	47-19N	52-27W	MINE WB-65
SS TIVIVES	1943	10 21	36-55N	01-36E	G-AIR UGS-19
SS JAMES IREDELL	1943	10 23	NAPLES, ITALY		G-AIR
SS SANTA ELENA	1943	11 06	37-13N	06-21E	G-AIR KMF25A
SS CAPE SAN JUAN	1943	11 11	22-08N	178-13W	I-21
SS ELIZABETH KELLOGG	1943	11 23	11-10N	80-42W	U-526
SS MELVILLE E. STONE	1943	11 24	10-36N	80-19W	U-516
SS SAMUEL J. TILDEN	1943	12 02	BARI, ITALY		G-AIR
SS JOHN BASCOM	1943	12 02	BARI, ITALY		G-AIR
SS JOHN L. MOTLEY	1943	12 02	BARI, ITALY		G-AIR
SS JOSEPH WHEELER	1943	12 02	BARI, ITALY		G-AIR
SS JOHN HARVEY	1943	12 02	BARI, ITALY		G-AIR M-GAS
SS SAGADAHOC	1943	12 03	21-50S	07-50W	U-124

SS TOUCHET	1943	12 03	25-50N	86-15W	U-193
SS McDOWELL	1943	12 16	13-08N	70-02W	U-516
SS JOSE NAVARRO	1943	12 26	08-00N	74-00E	U-178 MULES
SS ALBERT GALLATIN	1944	01 02	21-21N	59-58E	I-26
SS WILLIAM S. ROSECRANS	1944	01 06	40-40N	14-15E	MINED
SS DANIEL WEBSTER	1944	01 10	36-04N	00-14W	G-AIR KMS-37
SS SUMNER I. KIMBALL	1944	01 16	52-35N	35-00W	U-960 ON-219
SS WALTER CAMP	1944	01 25	10-00N	71-40E	U-532
SS PENELOPE BARKER	1944	01 25	73-22N	22-30E	U-278 JW-56A
SS ANDREW G. CURTIN	1944	01 25	73-25N	25-16E	U-716
SS SAMUEL HUNTINGTON	1944	01 29	ANZIO BEACH		G-AIR
SS EDWARD BATES	1944	02 01	36-38N	00-50E	G-AIR UGS-30
SS ELIHU YALE	1944	02 15	41-27N	12-38E	G-AIR ANZIO
SS PETER SKENE OGDEN	1944	02 22	37-18N	06-59E	U-969 GUS-31
SS GEORGE CLEEVE	1944	02 22	37-18N	06-59E	U-969
SS E.G. SEUBERT	1944	02 23	13-50N	48-49E	U-510 PA-69
SS DANIEL C. FRENCH	1944	03 06	37-18N	10-22E	MINE UGS-33
SS VIRGINIA DARE	1944	03 06	37-21N	10-13E	MINE UGS-33
SS CLARK MILLS	1944	03 09	37-18N	10-13E	G-AIR
SS WILLIAM B. WOODS	1944	03 10	38-36N	13-45E	U-952
SS H.D. COLLIER	1944	03 13	21-00N	63-50E	I-26
SS MAIDEN CREEK II	1944	03 17	37-08N	05-27E	U-371 SNF-17
SS SEAKAY	1944	03 18	51-10N	20-20W	U-311 CU-17
SS JOHN A. POOR	1944	03 19	13-58N	70-30E	U-510
SS RICHARD HOVEY	1944	03 29	16-40N	64-30E	I-26
SS THOMAS MASARYK	1944	04 16	32-51N	23-00E	U-407 UGS-37
SS MEYER LONDON	1944	04 16	32-51N	23-00E	U-407 UGS-37
SS PAN PENNSYLVANIA	1944	04 16	40-05N	69-24W	U-550 CU-21
SS JAMES GUTHRIE	1944	04 17	40-34N	14-16E	MINED NV-33
SS PAUL HAMILTON	1944	04 20	37-02N	03-41E	G-AIR UGS-38
SS WILLIAM S. THAYER	1944	04 30	73-52N	19-10E	U-711 RA59
SS ARTEMAS WARD	1944	06 08	GOOSEBERRY BREAKWATER		
SS VICTORY SWORD	1944	06 08	GOOSEBERRY BREAKWATER		
SS COURAGEOUS	1944	06 08	GOOSEBERRY BREAKWATER		
SS GALVESTON	1944	06 08	GOOSEBERRY BREAKWATER		
SS GEORGE S. WASSON	1944	06 08	GOOSEBERRY BREAKWATER		
SS GEORGE W. CHILDS	1944	06 08	GOOSEBERRY BREAKWATER		
SS JAMES W. MARSHALL	1944	06 08	GOOSEBERRY BREAKWATER		
SS WEST GRAMA	1944	06 08	GOOSEBERRY BREAKWATER I		
SS WILSCOX	1944	06 08	GOOSEBERRY BREAKWATER I		
MS WEST HONAKER	1944	06 08	GOOSEBERRY BREAKWATER II		
SS CHARLES MORGAN	1944	06 10	UTAH BEACH		G-AIR
SS WEST CHESWALD	1944	06 11	GOOSEBERRY BREAKWATER I		
SS CHARLES W. ELLIOTT	1944	06 28	JUNO BEACH		MINES
SS JOHN A. TREUTLEN	1944	06 29	50-07N	00-47W	U-984 EGM-17
SS H.G. BLASDEL (Tr)	1944	06 29	50-07N	00-47W	U-984 EMC-17
SS JAMES A. FARRELL	1944	06 29	50-17N	00-47W	U-984 EGM-17
SS ESSO HARRISBURG	1944	07 06	14-00N	71-00W	U-516
SS WEST NILUS	1944	07 07	GOOSEBERRY BREAKWATER		
SS WEST NOHNO	1944	07 11	GOOSEBERRY BREAKWATER		
SS KOFRESI	1944	07 14	GOOSEBERRY BREAKWATER		
SS WILLIAM GASTON	1944	07 22	26-27S	46-13W	U-861
SS ROBIN GOODFELLOW	1944	07 25	20-03S	14-21W	U-862
SS ILLINOIAN	1944	07 28	GOOSEBERRY BREAKWATER		

SS EXMOUTH	1944	07 31	56-33N	02-12W	MINED
SS LENA LUCKENBACH	1944	08 04	GOOSEBERRY BREAKWATER		
SS PENNSYLVANIAN	1944	08 04	GOOSEBERRY I BREAKWATER		
SS WILLIAM L. MARCY	1944	08 07	49-23N	00-26W	E-BOAT
SS EZRA WESTON	1944	08 08	50-42N	05-03W	U-667 EBC-66
SS KENTUCKIAN	1944	08 12	GOOSEBERRY BREAKWATER		
SS ALCOA LEADER	1944	08 13	MULBERRY A BREAKWATER		
SS RICHARD MONTGOMERY	1 944	08 20	THAMES ESTUARY		G-AIR
SS SAHALE	1944	08 24	MULBERRY A BREAKWATER		
SS EXFORD	1944	08 26	GOOSEBERRY BREAKWATER		
SS JOHN BARRY	1944	08 28	15-10N	55-18E	U-859
SS JACKSONVILLE	1944	08 30	55-30N	07-30W	U-482 CU-36
SS ROBIN GRAY	1944	09 18	GOOSEBERRY BREAKWATER		
SS EDWARD H. CROCKETT	1944	09 29	72-57N	24-32E	U-310 RA-60
SS AUGUSTUS THOMAS	1944	10 24	LEYTE ANCHORED		J-AIR
SS JOHN A. JOHNSON	1944	10 30	29-36N	141-43W	I-12
SS FORT LEE	1944	11 04	27-35S	83-11E	U-181
SS LEE S. OVERMAN	1944	11 11	LeHAVRE, FRANCE		MINED
SS WILLIAM D. BURNHAM	1944	11 23	CHERBORG, FRANCE		U-978
SS GUS W. DARNELL	1944	11 23	SAMAR ISLAND		J-AIR
SS FRANCES ASBURY	1944	12 03	51-21N	03-00E	MINED TAM-6
SS ANTOINE SAUGRAIN	1944	12 05	09-42N	127-05E	J-AIR
SS DAN BEARD	1944	12 10	51-56N	05-29W	U-1202
SS WILLIAM S. LADD	1944	12 10	DULAG, LEYTE		KAMIKAZI
SS STEEL TRAVELER	1944	12 18	51-25N	03-21E	MINED ATM-16
SS ROBERT J. WALKER	1944	12 24	36-35S	150-43E	U-862
SS JAMES H. BREASTED	1944	12 26	MINDORO, P.I.		J-AIR
SS JOHN BURKE	1944	12 28	MINDORO, P.I.		KAMIKAZI
SS ARTHUR SEWALL	1944	12 29	50-28N	02-28W	U-772 TBC-21
SS BLACK HAWK	1944	12 29	50-28N	02-28W	U-772 TBC-21
SS HOBART BAKER	1944	12 29	MINDANAO		J-AIR
SS LEWIS L. DYCHE	1945	01 02	MINDORO, P.I.		KAMIKAZI
SS HENRY MILLER	1945	01 03	35-51N	06-24W	U-870 GUS-63
SS ISAAC SHELBY	1945	01 06	41-10N	13-21E	MINED
SS JONAS LIE	1945	01 09	51-45N	05-27W	U-1005 ON-277
SS ROANOKE	1945	01 11	53-19N	04-48W	U-1005
SS MARTIN VAN BUREN	1945	01 14	44-27N	63-26W	U-1232 BX141
SS GEORGE HAWLEY	1945	01 21	50-00N	05-45W	U-1199 TCB-43
SS PETER SILVESTER	1945	02 06	34-19S	99-37E	U-862
SS HENRY B. PLANT	1945	02 06	51-22N	02-00E	U-245 TAM-71
SS HORACE GRAY	1945	02 14	69-21N	33-43E	U-711 JW-64
SS THOMAS SCOTT	1945	02 17	69-30N	34-42E	U-968 RA-64
SS HENRY BACON	1945	02 23	67-00N	07-00E	G-AIR RA-64
SS NASHABA	1945	02 26	51-22N	02-55E	MINE TAM-91
SS SORELDOC	1945	02 28	52-15N	05-35W	U-?
SS ROBERT L. VANN	1945	03 01	OSTEND, BELGIUM		MINED ATM-76
SS THOMAS DONALDSON	1945	03 20	68-26N	33-40E	U-968 JW-65
SS HORACE BUSHNELL	1945	03 20	69-23N	37-17E	U-995 JW-65
SS JOHN R. PARK	1945	03 21	49-56N	05-26W	U-399 TBC-102
SS JAMES EAGAN LAYNE	1945	03 21	50-13N	04-14W	U-1195 BTC-103
SS CHARLES D. McIVER	1945	03 23	51-22N	03-05E	MINED ATM-100
SS HOBBS VICTORY	1945	04 06	OKINAWA		KAMIKAZI
SS LOGAN VICTORY	1945	04 06	OKINAWA		KAMIKAZI
SS SWIFTSCOUT	1945	04 18	37-30N	73-03W	U-548

SS CYRUS H. McCORMICK	1945	04 18	47-47N	06-26W	U-1107 HX-348
SS CANADA VICTORY	1945	04 27	26-35N	127-41E	KAMIKAZI
SS EDMUND F. DICKENS	1945	05 02	MANILA, P.I.		MINED
SS BLACK POINT	1945	05 05	41-19N	71-25W	U-853
SS HORACE BINNEY	1945	05 08	OSTEND, BELGIUM		MINED TAM-62
SS COLIN P. KELLY, Jr.	1945	06 04	51-20N	02-50E	MINED TAM-89
SS JOSEPH CARRIGAN	1945	09 10	05-15N	115-00E	MINED

1939-09	SEP	1	GERMANY INVADED POLAND
1939-09	SEP	3	SS ATHENIA SUNK BY U-BOAT
1939-10	OCT	17	HMS MOHOWK DAMAGED AIR ATTACK
1939-11	NOV	21	GERMAN RAIDERS "SCHARNHORST" & "GNEISENAU" ENTERED ATLANTIC
1939-11	NOV	25	BRITISH ARMED MERCHANTMAN "RAWALPINDI" ENGAGED GERMAN POCKET BATTLESHIPS
1939-12	DEC	17	G. LEIPZIG & NURENBERG TORPEDOED & DAMAGED BY HMS SALMON
1939-12	DEC		HMS AJAX & HMS ACHILLES BATTLE G. GRAF SPEE IN SOUTH ATLANTIC
1939-12	DEC	25	G. GRAF SPEE SCUTTLED AT MONTEVIDEO
1940-04	APR	8	BRITISH MINE NORWAY WATERS ON NARVIK ROUTE
1940-04	APR	9	BRITISH AND FRENCH FORCES LAND IN NORWAY
1940-04	APR	14-19	GERMANS INVADE NORWAY
1940-04	APR	9	HMS DEVONSHIRE, HMS GLASGOW, HMS SOUTHAMPTON FAMMAGED NORWAY - AIR
1940-04	APR	9	KARLSRUHUE (Ger) TORPEDOED NORWAY HMS TRIUMPH
1940-04	APR	9	LUTZOW (Ger) DAMAGED NORWAY HMS SPEARFISH
1940-04	APR	11	G. LUTZOW TORPEDOED OFF NORWAY BY HMS SPEARFISH
1940-04	APR	14	G.BLUCHER SET AFIRE IN OSLOFJORD BY NORWEGIANS
1940-04	APR	14	HMS GURKHA SUNK OFF NORWAY, AIR
1940-05	MAY	03	NORWAY CAPITULATED, QUISLING GOVERNMENT TAKES OVER
1940-05	MAY	05	HMS SEAL CAPTURED BY G. AIRCRAFT NORTH SEA
1940-05	MAY	10	GERMANS INVADE BELGIUM & NETHERLANDS
1940-05	MAY	15	NETHERLANDS CAPITULATED TO GERMANS
1940-05	MAY	24	GERMANS OVERRUN BELGIUM & NETHERLANDS
1940-05	MAY	25	FRENCH SHIP CHACAL SUNK AT DUNKIRK
1940-05	MAY	26	EVACUATION OF BRITISH COMMENCES FROM DUNKIRK
1940-05	MAY	27	ADEN & COTE d'AZUR (Fr) SUNK AT DUNKIRK
1940-05	MAY	28	BELGIUM CAPITULATED TO GERMANS
1940-05	MAY	28	SS KING ORRY & SS LORINA SUNK AT DUNKIRK
1940-05	MAY	29	HMS HEREWARD & HMS IMPERIAL SUNK DUNKIRK
1940-05	MAY	29	SS FENELLA & SS NORMANIA SUNK DUNKIRK
1940-05	MAY	29	SS QUEEN OF THE CHANNEL SUNK OFF DUNKIRK AIR
1940-06	JUN	2	"ARANDORA STAR" SUNK. 1,600 INTERNEES & POWS ABOARD NORTH ATLANTIC
1940-06	JUN	14	GERMAN FORCES ENTER PARIS, FRANCE
1940-06	JUN	17	"LANCASTRIA" SUNK BY BOMBERS WITH 6,000 REFUGEES FROM FRANCE
1940-07	JUL	4	SS FOYLE BANK DAMAGED AIR ATTACK CONVOY OA 178 AIR
1940	JUL		U.S. FORCES ESTABLISHED BASES IN GREENLAND
1940-07	JUL	25	"MEKNES" (FRENCH) SUNK WITH FRENCH REPATRIATES BY "E" BOAT

1940-09	SEP	2	U.S. & BRITAIN SIGN 99-YEAR LEASE IN EXCHANGE FOR 50 DESTROYERS
1940-09	SEP	17	"CITY OF BENARES" SUNK WITH 191 CHILDREN EVACUEES NORTH ATLANTIC,
1940-10	OCT	24	SS EMPRESS OF BRITAIN SUNK SO. ATLANTIC U-32
1940-11	NOV	5	"JERVIS BAY" ENGAGED "ADMIRAL SCHEER" TO DIVERT FROM CONVOY HX84
1940-11	NOV	6	SWEDISH SHIP "STUREHOLM" RESCUED 65 SURVIVORS FROM "JERVIS BAY"
1941-01	JAN	11	HMS SOUTHAMPTON SUNK OFF SICILY - AIR
1941-02	FEB	9	HMS JURA (Brit) SUNK CONVOY HG-53 AIR
1941-02	FEB	9	BRITANNIC SUNK CONVOY HG-53
1941-02	FEB	9	DAGMAR I SUNK CONVOY HG-53 AIR
1941-02	FEB	9	SS TEJO (Nor) SUNK CONVOY HG-53 AIR
1941-02	FEB	9	SS VARNA SUNK CONVOY HG-53 AIR
1941-02	FEB	20	COURLAND SUNK CONVOY HG-53 U-37
1941-05	MAY	5	HMS GREYHOUND SUNK MALTA AIR
1941-05	MAY	5	HMS GRIFFIN WITH GREYHOUND OFF MALTA/CRETE
1941-05	MAY	9	USS EAGLE LANDED SPITFIRES ON MALTA
1941-05	MAY	21	HMS AJAX SPENT AMMO IN AIR ATTACK OFF CRETE
1941-05	MAY	21	HMS DIDO SPENT AMMO IN AIR ATTACK OFF CRETE
1941-05	MAY	22	HMS JUNO SUNK CRETE AIR
1941-05	MAY	22	HMS KANDAHAR PICKING UP SURVIVORS OFF MALTA/CRETE
1941-05	MAY	22	HMS KINGSTON PICKING UP SURVIVORS OFF MALTA/CRETE
1941-05	MAY	22	HMS NAIAD DAMAGED OFF MALTA/CRETE AIR
1941-05	MAY	22	HMS CARLISLE DAMAGED OFF MALTA/CRETE
1941-05	MAY	22	HMS FIJI SUNK
1941-05	MAY	22	HMS GLOUCESTER SUNK MALTA AIR
1941-05	MAY	22	HMS WARSPITE DAMAGED OFF MALTA CRETE AIR
1941-05	MAY	23	HMS KASHMIR SUNK OFF CRETE AIR
1941-05	MAY	23	HMS KELLY SUNK OFF CRETE AIR (MOUNTBATTEN ABD)
1941-05	MAY	26	HMS FORMIDABLE DAMAGED OFF MALTA
1941-05	MAY	23	GERMAN RAIDER "BISMARCK" SIGHTED BY HMS SUFFOLK
1941-05	MAY	24	BRITISH "HOOD" SUNK BY "BISMARCK"; THREE SURVIVORS
1941-05	MAY	24	BRITISH "PRINCE OF WALES" DAMAGED BY BISMARCK & "PRINCE EUGEN"
1941-05	MAY	24	HMS KING GEORGE V JOINS IN ON "BISMARCK" ATTACK
1941-05	MAY	26	"BISMARCK" FOUND AGAIN, DAMAGED BY AIRCRAFT FROM "ARK ROYAL"
1941-05	MAY	28	"BISMARCK" ATTACKED BY "RODNEY," "NORFOLK," "KING GEORGE V" AND "DORSETSHIRE"
1941-05	MAY	28	"BISMARCK" SUNK BY TORPEDOES FROM "DORSETSHIRE"
1941-05	MAY	29	HMS MASHOMA SANK AFTER BISMARCK BATTLE AIR
1941-05	MAY	29	HMS PERTH ATTACKED OFF MALTA/CRETE
1941-05	MAY	29	HMS ORION ATTACKED OFF MALTA/CRETE
1941-06	JUN	1	HMS CALCUTTA SUNK OFF MALTA/CRETE
1941-09	SEP	18	HMS UPHOLDER SANK ITALIAN TRANSPORTS NEPTUNIA & OCEANIA
1941-09	SEP	18	NEPTUNIA (It) SUNK OFF BENGHAZI BY HMS UPHOLDER
1941-09	SEP	18	OCEANIA (It) SUNK OFF BENGHAZI BY HMS UPHOLDER
1941-09	SEP	18	ORIANI (It) SUNK OFF BENGHAZI BY AIR
1941-09	SEP	23	MARAT (USSR) SUNK OFF LENINGRAD AIR
1941-09	SEP	23	KIROV (USSR) SUNK OFF LENINGRAD AIR

1941-11	NOV	14	ARK ROYAL SUNK MEDITERRANEAN U-81
1941-12	DEC	7	PEARL HARBOR BOMBED BY JAPANESE PLANES
1941-12	DEC		EIGHT U.S. SHIPS SUNK IN PACIFIC BY JAPANESE
1941-12	DEC	8	MANILA ATTACKED BY JAPANESE PLANES
1942-01	JAN		JAPANESE LANDED ON NEW GUINEA
1942-01	JAN		EIGHT U.S. SHIPS SUNK EAST COAST OF U.S. BY U-BOATS
1942-01	JAN		JAPANESE LAND ON NEW BRITAIN
1942-01	JAN		JAPANESE LAND ON NEW GUNIEA
1942-01	JAN		JAPANESE LANDED ON NEW BRITAIN
1942-01	JAN		SINGAPORE FALLS TO JAPANESE
1942-01	JAN		THREE U.S. SHIPS SUNK IN PACIFIC BY JAPANESE
1942-02	FEB		FIVE U.S. SHIPS SUNK IN PACIFIC BY JAPANESE
1942-02	FEB		EIGHTEEN U.S. SHIPS SUNK EAST COAST US - U-BOATS
1942-02	FEB	12	G. PRINZ EUGEN ENTERED N. ATLANTIC
1942-02	FEB	12	G. SCHARNHORST ENTERED N. ATLANTIC
1942-03	MAR		TWENTY-EIGHT U.S. SHIPS SUNK EAST COAST U.S.
1942-03	MAR	17	AMERICANS LAND NOUMEA, NEW CALEDONIA
1942-03	MAR	27	BRECONSHIRE SUNK MALTA
1942-03	MAR	27	CLAN CAMPBELL SUNK MALTA
1942-04	APR		FOUR SHIPS SUNK IN PACIFIC AND INDIAN OCEAN
1942-04	APR		TWENTY-SIX SHIPS SUNK EAST COAST U.S
1942-04	APR		THREE SHIPS SUNK IN SO. ATLANTIC RAIDER & ITALIAN SUB
1942-05	MAY	7	HMS EDINBURGH TORPEDOED CONVOY QP-11
1942-05	MAY	9	HMS WELSHMAN SUPPLIED AMMO TO MALTA
1942-05	MAY	9	USS WASP FERRIED AIRCRAFT TO MALTA
1942-05	MAY	10	HMS JACKAL SUNK CRETE AIR
1942-05	MAY	10	HMS JERVIS RETURNED TO ALEXANDRIA W SURVIVORS
1942-05	MAY	10	HMS KIPLING SUNK OFF MALTA/CRETE
1942-05	MAY	10	HMS LIVELY SUNK OFF MALTA/CRETE AIR
1942-05	MAY		FORTY-TWO SHIPS SUNK IN GULF AND E. COAST U.S.
1942-05	MAY		ONE SHIP SUNK IN INDIAN OCEAN BY JAPANESE SUB
1942-05	MAY		FOUR U.S. SHIPS SUNK IN CONVOY PQ-16 TO MURMANSK
1942-06	JUN		BATTLE OF MIDWAY ISLAND JAP CARRIERS SUNK
1942-06	JUN		FIFTY TWO SHIPS SUNK GULF AND E. COAST U.S.
1942-06	JUN		THREE SUNK BY JAPANDSE IN PACIFIC AND INDIAN OCEAN
1942-06	JUN		GERMAN RAIDERS STIER, TANNENBAUM AND MICHEL IN S. ATLANTIC AND INDIAN OCEAN
1942-06	JUN	27	HMS LONDON, HMS VICTORIOUS AN ESCORT TO CONVOY PQ-17 TO MURMANSK
1942-07	JUL	3	SS CHRISTOFER NEWPORT SUNK CONVOY PQ-17 U-457
1942-07	JUL	3	SS PAN KRAFT SUNK CONVOY PQ-17 AIR ATTACK
1942-07	JUL	3	SS FAIRFIELD CITY SUNK CONVOY PQ-17 AIR ATTACK
1942-07	JUL	3	SS BOLTOR CASTLE SUNK CONVOY PQ-17 U-255
1942-07	JUL	3-10	LUFTWAFFE AND U-BOATS SANK 23 SHIPS CONVOY PQ-17
1942-07	JUL	4	GERMAN BATTLESHIPS: LUTZOW, TIRPITZ, ADMIRAL HIPPER, ADMIRAL SCHEER RUMORED IN BARENTS SEA, EXPOSING CONVOY PQ-17

1942-07	JUL	21	JAPANESE LAND IN PAPUA-NEW GUINEA
1942-07	JUL		FORTY-ONE U.S. SHIPS SUNK INCLUDING CONVOY PQ-17
1942-08	AUG	7	AMERICANS LAND AT GUALDALCANAL
1942-08	AUG	8	AUSTRALIANS ATTACK JAPANESE AT DENIKI/KOKODA AREA
1942-08	AUG	9	BATTLE OF SAVO ISLAND OFF GUALDALCANAL
1942-08	AUG	9	BRITISH RAID ON DIEPPE
1942-08	AUG		SIXTEEN U.S. SHIPS LOST ATLANTIC TO U-BOATS
1942-08	AUG	13	ALMERIA LYKES LOST IN MEDITERRANEAN TO E-BOAT
1942-08	AUG	13	SANTA ELISA LOST IN MEDITERRANEAN TO E-BOAT
1942-09	SEP	13	HMS AVENGER ESCORT CARRIER WITH CONVOY PQ-18
1942-09	SEP	28	AMERICAN 32nd DIV AT PORT MORESBY
1942-09	SEP		THREE SHIPS LOST IN INDIAN OCEAN TO JAPANESE 7 GERMANSUBS
1942-09	SEP		MS AMERICAN LEADER SUNK IN SO. ATLANTIC BY RAIDER MICHEL
1942-09	SEP		NINETEEN U.S. SHIPS SUNK IN ATLANTIC BY AIR AND U-BOATS
1942-09	SEP		TWENTY-SEVEN LIBERTY SHIP STEPHEN HOPKINS SANK RAIDER "STIER" BEFORE SINKING HERSELF IN THREE-WAY BATTLE WITH G RAIDER TANNENFELS.
1942-10	OCT		TWENTY-TWO SHIPS SUNK ATLANTIC & MEDITERRANEAN
1942-10	OCT	26	SS PRESIDENT COOLIDGE STRUCK MINE AT ESPRITU SANTO
1942-11	NOV	2	DUTCH SHIP ZAANDAM DISAPPEARED WHILE REPATRIATING SEAMEN AND CIVILIANS IN SO. ATLANTIC
1942-11	NOV	3	BRITISH DEFEAT ROMMEL AT EL ALAMEIN
1942-11	NOV		TOBRUK RETAKEN BY ALLIES
1942-11	NOV		AMERICAN INVASION OF NORTH AFRICA
1942-11	NOV		FREE FRENCH FLEET TURNED OVER TO ALLIES AT ALGIERS
1942-11	NOV	19	AMERICAN 32d DIV ATTACKED JAPANESE AT BUNA
1942-11	NOV	23	AUSTRALIANS TOOK OVER KOKODA
1942-12	DEC	14	BUNA OCCUPIED BY AMERICANS
1942-12	DEC	20	JAPANESE BUILDING AIRFIELD AT MUNDA POINT, NEW GEORGIA
1943-01	JAN	3	ENTIRE BUNA AREA IN ALLIED HANDS
1943-01	JAN	7	JAPANESE LANDED AT LAE, NEW GUINEA
1943-01	JAN	22	PAPUAN CAMPAIGN OVER. ALLIED LOS 3095 K, 5451 W
1943-01	JAN	28	JAPANESE FROM LAE ATTACKED AUSTRALIANS AT WAU
1943-01	JAN	30	JAPANESE RETREATED FROM WAU TO LAE
1943-02	FEB	3	GERMAN SIEGE OF STALINGRAD BROKEN
1943-02	FEB		GENERAL PATTON BATTLE ROMMEL FORCES AT KASSERINE PASS
1942-02	FEB	8	GUALDALCANAL CAMPAIGN OVER
1943-02	FEB	13	SIEGE OF LENINGRAD LIFTED 20% OF POPULATION LEFT
1943-03	MAR		JAPANESE LANDED AT SALAMAUA, NEW GUINEA
1943-05	MAY	5	NORTH AFRICAN FIGHTING OVER, TUNIS OCCUPIED
1943-06	JUN	30	AMERICANS LANDINGS AT NASSAU BAY
1943-06	JUN	30	AMERICANS LANDED ON NEW GEORGIA AND RUSSELL ISLANDS
1943-06	JUN	30	AMERICANS LANDED ON RENDOVA ISLAND, OPPOSITE MUNDA
1943-06	JUN	30	AMERICANS LANDING AT WOODLARK AND KIRWANA ISLANDS

1943-07	JUL	4	DESTROYER USS STRONG SUNK OFF MUNDA
1943-07	JUL	5	BATTLE OF KULA GULF. "HELENA" SUNK
1943-07	JUL	5	GERMANS COUNTERATTACK RUSSIA IN OPERATION CITADEL
1943-07	JUL	9	AMERICAN ATTACK ON MUNDA COMMENCED
1943-07	JUL	10	DESTROYER "GWIN" SUNK, CRUISERS HONOLULU, ST LOUIS HIT
1943-07	JUL	15	GERMAN OPERATION "CITADEL" DEFEATED, AGAIN IN RETREAT
1943-07	JUL	17	JAPANESE ATTACK AT ZANANA REPELLED
1943-07	JUL	24	ALLIED 750 PLANE RAID OVER HAMBURG, GERMANY
1943-08	AUG	5	MUNDA AIRFIELD OCCUPIED BY AMERICAN FORCES
1943-08	AUG	15	AMERICANS LAND ON VELLA LAVELLA ISLAND
1943-09	SEP	1	AMERICAN AIR RAID ON MARCUS ISLAND
1943-09	SEP	18	AMERICAN AIR RAID ON TARAWA & MAKIN ISLANDS
1943-09	SEP	4	AUSTRALIANS LAND AT WOOTTEN, NEW GUINEA NEAR LAE
1943-09	SEP	23	MUSSOLINI OUSTED, PUPPET GOVERNMENT DECLARED IN ITALY
1943-10	OCT	5	AMERICAN AIR RAIDS ON WAKE ISLAND
1943-11	NOV		AMERICAN AIR RAIDS ON TRUK ISLAND
1943-11	NOV		MAKIN & TARAWA ISLANDS LANDINGS
1944-02	FEB	1	KWAJALIN ISLAND LANDINGS (SECURED FEB 7)
1944-02	FEB	17	ENIWETOK ISLAND LANDING (SECURED FEB 22)
1944-02	FEB	17	MASSIVE AIR AND SEA ATTACK ON TRUK ISLAND
1944-02	FEB	17	USS LEXINGTON, INDEPENDENCE TORPEDOED
1944-02	FEB	17	USS LISCOMBE BAY SUNK
1944-02	FEB	29	ADMIRALTY ISLAND, & LOS NEGROS LANDINGS
1944-03	MAR	30	AMERICAN AIR ATTACKS ON PALAU, YAP & WOLEI ISLANDS
1944-04	APR	22	HOLLANDIA, NEW GUINEA LANDINGS (TANAHAMERAH & AITAPE
1944-04	APR	29	AMERICAN AIR ATTACKS ON PONAPE
1944-05	MAY	17	TOEM, NEW GUINEA LANDING
1944-05	MAY	27	BIAK ISLAND CAMPAIGN STARTED (UNTIL AUGUST)
1944-06	JUN	6	ALLIED LANDINGS IN NORMANDY, FRANCE
1944-06	JUN	15	SAIPAN ISLAND LANDINGS
1944-06	JUN	19	BATTLE OF PHILIPPINE SEA
1944-07	JUL	2	NOEMFOOR ISLAND (NEW GUINEA) LANDING
1944-07	JUL	18	TOJO RESIGNED AS JAPAN WAR MINISTER
1944-07	JUL	21	GUAM LANDING
1944-07	JUL	24	TINIAN ISLAND LANDING
1944-07	JUL	26	MacARTHUR, NIMITZ & ROOSEVELT CONFERENCE AT HAWAII
1944-07	JUL	30	SANSAPOOR (NEW GUINEA) LANDING
1944-08	AUG	15	ALLIED LANDINGS AT ST TROPEZ, SO FRANCE
1944-09	SEP	12	MINDANAO LANDINGS
1944-09	SEP	13	LEYTE LANDINGS
1944-09	SEP	15	PELELIU, PALAU ISLAND LANDINGS

1944-12	DEC	14	GERMANS COUNTERATTACK AMERICANS IN BATTLE OF THE BULGE
1944-12	DEC	15	AMERICANS ADVANCE TO MANILA
1945-02	FEB	29	AMERICANS INVADE IWO JIMA
1945-04	APR	1	AMERICANS INVADE OKINAWA
1945-04	APR	12	PRESIDENT ROOSEVELT DIES
1945-05	MAY	7	GERMANY SURRENDER, WAR IN EUROPE OVER
1945-08	AUG	6	ATOMIC BOMB ON HIROSHIMA
1945-08	AUG	8	ATOMIC BOMB ON NAGASAKI
1945-08	AUG	14	JAPANESE SURRENDER OFFER RECEIVED
1945-09	SEP	1	MacARTHUR SIGNS SURRENDER DOCUMENT AT TOKIO BAY

Confirmation of these appendices has been compiled from the following references:

The Lonely Sea, Alistair Maclean

The Luftwaffe War Diaries, Claus Bekker (Ballantine LC 68-19007)

The Battle of the Atlantic, Donald Macintyre (Pan Books USBN 330-02371-3)

Sunk, Mochitsura Hashimoto (Avon - Henry Holt 1954)

U-Boats, The War in the Atlantic, Island Fighting (Time-Life Books)

Historical Atlas of the World (Rand McNally LC 81-51409)

A Careless Word, A Needless Sinking, Captain Arthur Moore

Also from the recollections of myself and many acquaintances in the maritime world.

You may order additional copies of *Peter: The Odyssey of a Merchant Mariner* by writing to:

> Peter Chelemedos
> P.O. Box 15617
> Seattle, WA 98115-0617

Enclose a check or money order for $22.95 per book, plus $3.00 shipping and handling.

Washington State residents add $2.13 sales tax.